Cognitive Behavioural Therapy

FOR

DUMMIES®

2ND EDITION

Cognitive Behavioural Therapy

FOR

DUMMIES®

2ND EDITION

by Rhena Branch and Rob Willson

A John Wiley and Sons, Ltd, Publication

Cognitive Behavioural Therapy For Dummies,® 2nd Edition

Published by
John Wiley & Sons, Ltd
The Atrium
Southern Gate
Chichester
West Sussex
PO19 8SQ
England

E-mail (for orders and customer service enquires): cs-books@wiley.co.uk

Visit our Home Page on www.wiley.com

For general information on our other products and services, please contact our Customer Care Department within the U.S. at 877-762-2974, outside the U.S. at 317-572-3993, or fax 317-572-4002.

For technical support, please visit www.wiley.com/techsupport.

Wiley also publishes its books in a variety of electronic formats. Some content that appears in print may not be available in electronic books.

British Library Cataloguing in Publication Data: A catalogue record for this book is available from the British Library

ISBN-13: 978-0-470-66541-1 (pbk) 978-0-470-97254-0 (ebk) 978-0-470-66612-8 (ebk) 978-0-470-66611-1 (ebk)

Printed and bound in Great Britain by TJ International Ltd, Padstow, Cornwall

10 9 8 7 6 5 4 3 2 1

WILEY

About the Authors

Rhena Branch, MSc, Dip CBT, is an accredited CBT therapist and holds a post-graduate clinical supervision qualification. Rhena runs a private practice with offices in North and Central London. She also teaches and supervises on the MSc course in CBT/REBT at Goldsmith's College, University of London. Rhena treats general psychiatric disorders and has a special interest in eating disorders. CBT for Dummies (second edition) is Rhena's fifth publication and she currently has two further books in press.

Rob Willson, BSc, MSc, Dip SBHS, currently divides the majority of his work time between private practice and conducting research on Body Dysmorphic Disorder at the Institute of Psychiatry, London. Previously he spent twelve years working at the Priory Hospital, North London where he was a therapist and therapy services manager. He also trained numerous CBT therapists over a seven-year period at Goldsmith's College, University of London. Rob's main clinical interests are anxiety and obsessional problems, and disseminating CBT principles through self-help. He has made several TV appearances including in the BBC documentary 'Too Ugly for Love'.

Dedication

For Felix and Atticus (from Rhena)

For Emma and Lucy (from Rob)

Authors' Acknowledgments

From Rhena: It's great to have the opportunity to produce a second edition of this book. My thanks to everyone involved at Wiley for your support and expert guidance throughout.

Thanks to Rob for your input into this and other projects.

Immense gratitude as always to my boys, for everything.

From Rob: I am grateful to Wiley for approaching (and eventually persuading) me to take on the first edition of CBT for Dummies, I know it has made CBT more accessible for many people. I would like to thank huge number of clients, clinicians, trainees, people interested in CBT, and people courageous enough to embark upon a course of self-help, not only for purchasing the first edition but also for giving so much positive feedback about the book.

Thanks to Rhena for her revisions and driving this second edition forward.

From both of us: Many researchers, fellow therapists and authors have influenced our understanding and practice of CBT over the years and therefore the content in this book. Founding fathers, Albert Ellis and Aaron T. Beck, of course merit special mention. Others include (in no specific order): Ray DiGiuseppe, Mary-Anne Layden, Jacqueline Persons, David A. Clarke, Adrian Wells, Stanley Rachman, Paul Salkovskis, Christine Padesky, Michael Neenan, David Veale, David M. Clark, David Burns, Kevin Gournay and many more. Special thanks goes to Windy Dryden for his extensive writings and for teaching us both so much.

Finally, a genuine thank you to all our clients (past and present) for allowing us to get to know you and learn from you.

Publisher's Acknowledgments

We're proud of this book; please send us your comments through our Dummies online registration form located at www.dummies.com/register/.

Some of the people who helped bring this book to market include the following:

Commissioning, Editorial, and Media Development

Project Editor: Simon Bell
(Previous Edition: Rachael Chilvers)

Commissioning Editor: Nicole Hermitage
(Previous Edition: Jason Dunne)

Assistant Editor: Ben Kemble

Developer/Copy Editor: Kate O'Leary
(Previous Edition: Brian Kramer, Colette Holden)

Technical Editor: David Kingdon

Publisher: David Palmer

Production Manager: Daniel Mersey

Cover Photos: ©Rphotos / Alamy

Cartoons: Rich Tennant (www.the5thwave.com)

Composition Services

Project Coordinator: Lynsey Stanford

Layout and Graphics: Joyce Haughey, Kelly Kijovsky

Proofreader: Lindsay Littrell

Indexer: Ty Koontz

Special Help

Brand Reviewer: Zoë Wykes

Publishing and Editorial for Consumer Dummies

Diane Graves Steele, Vice President and Publisher, Consumer Dummies

Joyce Pepple, Acquisitions Director, Consumer Dummies

Kristin A. Cocks, Product Development Director, Consumer Dummies

Michael Spring, Vice President and Publisher, Travel

Kelly Regan, Editorial Director, Travel

Publishing for Technology Dummies

Andy Cummings, Vice President and Publisher, Dummies Technology/General User

Composition Services

Gerry Fahey, Vice President of Production Services

Debbie Stailey, Director of Composition Services

Contents at a Glance

Table of Contents

Introduction

・・・

*C*ognitive behavioural therapy, or CBT, is growing in popularity as an efficient and long lasting treatment for many different types of psychological problem. If the word 'psychological' sends you running from the room screaming, try to consider the term referring to problems that affect your emotional rather than your physical sense of wellbeing. At some point in your life, something's going to go a bit wrong with your body. So why on earth do humans assume that their minds and emotions should be above the odd hiccup, upset, or even more serious difficulty?

This book gives you a comprehensive introduction to the theory and application of CBT techniques. Although we don't have the space to go into nitty-gritty specifics about how to use CBT to overcome every type of emotional or psychological problem, we do try to lead you in a helpful direction. We believe all the CBT principles and strategies outlined in this book can improve your life and help you to stay healthy, regardless of whether you've worked with or are currently working with a psychiatrist or other psychological professional.

In addition, whether you think your problems are minimal, you're living the life of Riley, you feel mildly depressed, or you've had years of uncomfortable psychological symptoms, CBT can help you. We ask you to be open-minded and to use the stuff in this book to make your life better and fuller.

About This Book

If you're embarking on a journey of self-help or self-improvement, we hope that this book provides a useful introduction to CBT techniques and will be of benefit to you. Depending on the degree of disruption and distress that your personal difficulties are causing you, this book may or may not be enough treatment to help you recover. The book may spur you on to get further help (Chapter 19 has more on seeking professional help) to really knock your emotional demons on the head. This book covers the following:

  ✔ The basics of using CBT as a scientifically tested and verified psychotherapeutic method of overcoming common emotional problems.

  ✔ Ways in which you can identify your problems and set specific goals for how you would rather be living your life.

- Techniques to identify errors in the way you may be thinking and to adopt more helpful thoughts, attitudes, philosophies, and beliefs.

- Behavioural experiments and strategies you can incorporate into your life to improve your day-to-day functioning.

- Information that can help you to understand, normalise, and address some common human problems. You may think that you're the only person in the world who feels and thinks the way you do. This book shows you that many of the problems you may be experiencing such as depression, anxiety, anger, and obsessions are in fact very common. You are not alone.

We hope that the whole experience will be at least a little entertaining in the process. So read on, welcome new concepts, and consider trying some of the ideas we offer in the book.

Conventions Used in This Book

To make your reading experience easier and to alert you to key words or points, we use certain conventions.

- *Italics* introduce new terms, underscore key differences in meaning between words, and highlight the most important aspects of a sentence or example.

- We use the terms 'him' in even-numbered chapters and 'her' in odd-numbered chapters when writing, with a view to incorporate gender equality.

- The case studies in the book are illustrative of actual clients we have treated and are not direct representations of any particular clients.

- **Bold** text is used to show the action part of numbered lists.

What You're Not to Read

This book is written in a rough order to help you progress from the basics of CBT on to more complex techniques and ideas. However, you can read the chapters in any order you like or just hit on the ones that cover subjects you think you want to know more about.

To make your reading experience even easier, we identify 'skippable' material:

- ✔ **Sidebars:** Within most chapters, we include sidebars of shaded text. These sidebars contain interesting titbits of information or occasionally expand on a topic within the chapter. Read them if they sound interesting to you and skip them if they don't.

- ✔ **Our acknowledgements:** Probably pretty boring to the average reader.

Foolish Assumptions

In writing this little tome, we make the following assumptions about you, dear reader:

- ✔ You're human.

- ✔ As a human, you're likely at some stage in your life to experience some sort of emotional problem that you'd like to surmount.

- ✔ You've heard about CBT, or are intrigued by CBT, or have had CBT suggested to you by a doctor, friend, or mental health professional as a possible treatment for your specific difficulties.

- ✔ Even if you don't think you're particularly in need of CBT right now, you want to discover more about some of the principles outlined in this book.

- ✔ You think that your life is absolutely fine right now, but you want to find interesting and useful information in the book that will enhance your life further.

- ✔ You're keen to find out whether CBT may be helpful to someone close to you.

- ✔ You're studying CBT and want to use this book as a 'hands on' adjunct to your training.

How This Book Is Organised

This book is divided into five parts and 25 chapters. The table of contents lists subheadings with more information about every chapter, but the following describes the major sections of the book.

Part I: Introducing CBT Basics

This part gives you a pretty good idea about what CBT consists of and how the techniques differs from other forms of psychotherapy. 'You think how you feel' is a good way of summing up CBT, and the chapters in this part expand on this simple idea. We explain common thinking errors as well as ways to counteract skewed thinking. You discover the basic CBT model of emotional disturbance and find out more about how you can make positive changes, even when your circumstances and other people in your life are unlikely to change for the better.

Part II: Charting the Course: Defining Problems and Setting Goals

This part helps you to define your emotional problems more accurately, see where your problems are springing from, and develop solid goals for your emotional future. Some of your valiant attempts to deal with your worries, terrors, and ideas about yourself are frequently counterproductive in the long term. These chapters explore this notion and give you ideas about more productive alternative strategies to produce long-term benefits.

Part III: Putting CBT into Action

Actions speak louder than words, and believe us when we say that actions also produce better results than words alone. Correcting your thinking is an important endeavour, but all your efforts to think healthily can fall apart at the seams unless you translate new beliefs into new action. The chapters in this part set out some good ways to test your new ways of thinking, strengthen healthy new beliefs, and promote helpful emotional responses to life, the universe, and everything else. If you don't believe us, try out the ideas for yourself! We also explore some common human difficulties such as anxiety and obsessional problems, addictions and poor body image.

Part IV: Looking Backwards and Moving Forwards

'But CBT ignores my past!' is an oft-heard complaint by individuals new to CBT. So we're here to tell you that CBT does not ignore your past. Yes, CBT concentrates on how your *current* thinking and behaviour cause your *current* difficulties. This part aids you in recognising experiences from your past that may have led you to form certain types of beliefs about yourself, other people, and the world around you. Assigning updated, helpful, and more accurate meanings to past events really can make a difference to the way you experience life today. So read on!

Part V: The Part of Tens

This section of the book is part fun and part solid CBT stuff. Looking here first can help you connect to other parts of the book and provide quick and easy tips for healthier living, boosting your self-esteem the right way, and lightening up your attitudes towards yourself and life in general.

Appendixes

Appendix A gives you a list of useful organisations and Web sites that you may wish to investigate.

Throughout the book, we refer to and explain various forms and CBT tools that may be helpful to you. Appendix B provides you with blank forms to photocopy at will and use to your heart's delight.

Icons Used in This Book

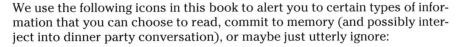

We use the following icons in this book to alert you to certain types of information that you can choose to read, commit to memory (and possibly interject into dinner party conversation), or maybe just utterly ignore:

This icon highlights practical advice for putting CBT into practice.

This icon is a cheerful, if sometimes urgent, reminder of important points to take notice of.

This icon marks out specific things to avoid or possible traps to keep your eye open for in your quest for better emotional health.

This icon highlights CBT terminology that may sound a bit like psychobabble but is commonly used by CBT practitioners.

This icon alerts you to stuff that has a bit of a philosophical basis and may need some mulling over in your spare time.

This icon indicates a CBT technique that you can try out in real life to see what results you get.

Where to Go From Here

We'd really like you to read everything in this book and then recommend it to all your friends and random people you meet on the street. Failing that, just use this book as your reference guide to CBT, dipping in and out of it as and when you need to.

Have a browse through the table of contents and turn to the chapters that look as if they may offer something helpful to you and your current difficulties.

When you've used the book in one way or another, you may decide that you want to get stuck into CBT treatment with a therapist. If so, consult Chapter 19 for more advice on getting treatment.

Part I
Introducing CBT Basics

The 5th Wave   By Rich Tennant

"Let's see if we can identify some of the stress triggers in your life. You mentioned something about a large wolf that periodically shows up and attempts to blow your house down..."

In this part . . .

You'll get to grips with what CBT stand for and why it's such a hot topic among mental health professionals. You'll get a good idea of how your thinking about events leads to how you feel. We'll get you started on recognising and tackling your negative thought patterns, and give you some tips about exerting control over your attention.

Chapter 1

You Feel the Way You Think

In This Chapter

▶ Defining CBT

▶ Exploring the power of meanings

▶ Understanding how your thoughts lead to emotions and behaviours

▶ Getting acquainted with the ABC formula

*C*ognitive behavioural therapy – more commonly referred to as *CBT* – focuses on the way people think and act to help them with their emotional and behavioural problems.

Many of the effective CBT practices we discuss in this book should seem like everyday good sense. In our opinion, CBT does have some very straightforward and clear principles and is a largely sensible and practical approach to helping people overcome problems. However, human beings don't always act according to sensible principles, and most people find that simple solutions can be very difficult to put into practice sometimes. CBT can maximise on your common sense and help you to do the healthy things that you may sometimes do naturally and unthinkingly in a deliberate and self-enhancing way on a regular basis.

In this chapter we take you through the basic principles of CBT and show you how to use these principles to better understand yourself and your problems.

Using Scientifically Tested Methods

The effectiveness of CBT for various psychological problems has been researched more extensively than any other psychotherapeutic approach. CBT's reputation as a highly effective treatment is growing. Several studies reveal that CBT is more effective than medication alone for the treatment of anxiety and depression. As a result of this research, briefer and more intense treatment methods have been developed for particular anxiety disorders such as panic, anxiety in social settings or feeling worried all the time.

Scientific research of CBT continues. As a result, more is being discovered about which aspects of the treatment are most useful for different types of people and which therapeutic interventions work best with different types of problems.

Research shows that people who have CBT for various types of problems – in particular, for anxiety and depression – stay well for longer. This means that people who have CBT relapse less often than those who have other forms of psychotherapy or take medication only. This positive result is likely due in part to the *educational aspects* of CBT – people who have CBT receive a lot of information that they can use to become their own therapists.

CBT is growing in popularity. More and more physicians and psychiatrists refer their patients for CBT to help them overcome a wide range of problems with good results. These problems include:

- ✔ Addiction
- ✔ Anger problems
- ✔ Anxiety
- ✔ Body dysmorphic disorder
- ✔ Chronic fatigue syndrome
- ✔ Chronic pain
- ✔ Depression
- ✔ Eating disorders
- ✔ Obsessive-compulsive disorder
- ✔ Panic disorder
- ✔ Personality disorders
- ✔ Phobias
- ✔ Post-traumatic stress disorder
- ✔ Psychotic disorders
- ✔ Relationship problems
- ✔ Social phobia

We discuss many of the disorders in the preceding list in more depth throughout this book but it is very difficult to cover them all. Fortunately, the CBT skills and techniques in this book can be applied to most types of psychological difficulties, so give them a try whether or not your particular problem is specifically discussed.

Understanding CBT

Cognitive behavioural therapy is a school of *psychotherapy* that aims to help people overcome their emotional problems.

- **Cognitive** means mental processes like thinking. The word 'cognitive' refers to everything that goes on in your mind including dreams, memories, images, thoughts and attention.

- **Behaviour** refers to everything that you do. This includes what you say, how you try to solve problems, how you act and avoidance. Behaviour refers to both action and inaction, for example biting your tongue instead of speaking your mind is still a behaviour even though you are trying *not* to do something.

- **Therapy** is a word used to describe a systematic approach to combating a problem, illness or irregular condition.

A central concept in CBT is that *you feel the way you think*. Therefore, CBT works on the principle that you can live more happily and productively if you're thinking in healthy ways. This principle is a very simple way of summing up CBT, and we have many more details to share with you later in the book.

Combining science, philosophy and behaviour

CBT is a powerful treatment because it combines scientific, philosophical and behavioural aspects into one comprehensive approach to understanding and overcoming common psychological problems.

- **Getting scientific.** CBT is scientific not only in the sense that it has been tested and developed through numerous scientific studies, but also in the sense that it encourages clients to become more like scientists. For example, during CBT, you may develop the ability to treat your thoughts as theories and hunches about reality to be tested (what scientists call *hypotheses*), rather than as facts.

- **Getting philosophical.** CBT recognises that people hold values and beliefs about themselves, the world and other people. One of the aims of CBT is to help people develop flexible, non-extreme and self-helping beliefs that help them adapt to reality and pursue their goals.

Your problems are not all just in your mind. Although CBT places great emphasis on thoughts and behaviour as powerful areas to target for change and development, it also places your thoughts and behaviours within a *context*. CBT recognises that you're influenced by what's going on around you and that your *environment* makes a contribution towards the way you think, feel and act. However, CBT maintains that you can make a difference to the way you feel by changing unhelpful ways of thinking and behaving – even if you can't change your environment. Incidentally, your environment in the context of CBT includes other people and the way they behave towards you. Your living situation, workplace dynamics or financial concerns are also features of your larger environment.

✔ **Getting active.** As the name suggests, CBT also strongly emphasises behaviour. Many CBT techniques involve changing the way you think and feel by modifying the way you behave. Examples include gradually becoming more active if you're depressed and lethargic, or facing your fears step by step if you're anxious. CBT also places emphasis on *mental behaviours*, such as worrying and where you focus your attention.

Progressing from problems to goals

A defining characteristic of CBT is that it gives you the tools to develop a *focused* approach. CBT aims to help you move from defined emotional and behavioural problems towards your goals of how you'd like to feel and behave. Thus, CBT is a goal-directed, systematic, problem-solving approach to emotional problems.

Making the Thought–Feeling Link

Like many people, you may assume that if something happens to you, the event *makes* you feel a certain way. For example, if your partner treats you inconsiderately, you may conclude that she *makes* you angry. You may further deduce that their inconsiderate behaviour *makes* you behave in a particular manner, such as sulking or refusing to speak to her for hours (possibly even days; people can sulk for a very long time!). We illustrate this common (but incorrect) causal relationship with the following formula. In this equation, the 'A' stands for a real or *actual* event – such as being rejected or losing your job. It also stands for an *activating* event that may or may not have happened. It could be a prediction about the future, such as 'I'm going to get the sack', or a memory of a past rejection, such as 'Hilary will dump me just like Judith did ten years ago!'. 'C' stands for *consequence*, which means the way you feel and behave in response to an actual or activating event.

A (*actual* or *activating* event) = C (emotional and behavioural *consequence*)

CBT encourages you to understand that your thinking or *beliefs* lie between the event and your ultimate feelings and actions. Your thoughts, beliefs and the meanings that you give to an event, produce your emotional and behavioural responses.

So in CBT terms, your partner does not *make* you angry and sulky. Rather, your partner behaves inconsiderately, and you assign a meaning to her behaviour such as 'she's doing this deliberately to upset me and she absolutely should not do this!' thus *making yourself* angry and sulky. In the next formula, 'B' stands for your *beliefs* about the event and the *meanings* you give to it.

> A (*actual* or *activating* event) + B (*beliefs* and *meanings* about the event) = C (emotional and behavioural *consequence*)

This is the formula or equation that CBT uses to make sense of your emotional problems.

Emphasising the meanings you attach to events

The *meaning* you attach to any sort of event influences the emotional responses you have to that event. Positive events normally lead to positive feelings of happiness or excitement, whereas negative events typically lead to negative feelings like sadness or anxiety.

However, the meanings you attach to certain types of negative events may not be wholly accurate, realistic, or helpful. Sometimes, your thinking may lead you to assign extreme meanings to events, leaving you feeling disturbed

Tilda meets up with a nice man that she's contacted via an online dating agency. She quite likes him on their first date and hopes he'll contact her for a second meeting. Unfortunately, he doesn't. After two weeks of waiting eagerly by the computer, Tilda gives up and becomes depressed. The fact that the chap failed to ask Tilda out again *contributes* to her feeling bad. But what really *leads* to her acute depressed feelings is the meaning she's derived from his apparent rejection, namely: 'This proves I'm old, unattractive, past it and unwanted. I'll be a sad singleton for the rest of my life.'

As Tilda's example shows, drawing extreme conclusions about yourself (and others and the world at large) based on singular experiences can turn a bad *distressing* situation into a deeply *disturbing* one.

Psychologists use the word 'disturbed' to describe emotional responses that are unhelpful and cause significant discomfort to you. In CBT terminology, 'disturbed' means that an emotional or behavioural response is hindering rather than helping you to adapt and cope with a negative event.

Consider the reactions of ten people

Different people can attach different meanings to a specific situation, resulting in the potential for a vast array of emotional reactions to one situation. For example, consider ten basically similar people who experience the same event, which is having their partner treat them inconsiderately. Potentially, they can have ten (or maybe more) different emotional responses to precisely the same event, depending on how they *think* about the event:

Person 1 attaches the meaning, 'That idiot has no right to treat me badly – who the hell do they think they are?' and feels angry.

Person 2 thinks, 'This lack of consideration means that my partner doesn't love me' and feels depressed.

Person 3 believes that 'This inconsideration must mean that my partner is about to leave me for someone else' and feels jealous.

Person 4 thinks, 'I don't deserve to be treated poorly because I always do my best to be considerate to my partner' and feels hurt.

Person 5 reckons the event means that 'I must have done something serious to upset my partner for them to treat me like this' and feels guilty.

Person 6 believes that 'This inconsideration is a sign that my partner is losing interest in me' and feels anxious.

Person 7 thinks, 'Aha! Now I have a good enough reason to break up with my partner, which I've been wanting to do for ages!' and feels happy.

Person 8 decides the event means that 'My partner has done a bad thing by treating me in this way, and I'm not prepared to put up with it' and feels annoyed.

Person 9 thinks, 'I really wish my partner had been more considerate because we're usually highly considerate of each other' and feels disappointed.

Person 10 believes that 'My partner must have found out something despicable about me to treat me in this way' and feels ashamed.

You can see from this example that very different meanings can be assigned to the same event and in turn produce very different emotional responses. Some emotional responses are healthier than others; we discuss this matter in depth in Chapter 6.

For example, if a potential girlfriend rejects you after the first date (event), you may think 'This proves I'm unlikeable and undesirable' (meaning) and feel depressed (emotion).

CBT involves identifying thoughts, beliefs and meanings that are activated when you're feeling emotionally disturbed. If you assign less extreme, more helpful, more *accurate* meanings to negative events, you are likely to experience less extreme, less disturbing emotional and behavioural responses.

Thus, on being rejected after the first date (event), you could think 'I guess that person didn't like me that much; oh well – they're not the one for me' (meaning), and feel disappointment (emotion).

You can help yourself to figure out whether or not the meanings you're giving to a specific negative event are causing you disturbance by answering the following questions:

- ✔ **Is the meaning I'm giving to this event unduly extreme?** Am I taking a fairly simple event and deriving very harsh conclusions about myself (others and/or the future) from it?

- ✔ **Am I drawing global conclusions from this singular event?** Am I deciding that this one event defines me totally? Or that this specific situation indicates the course of my entire future?

- ✔ **Is the meaning I'm assigning to this event loaded against me?** Does this meaning lead me to feel better or worse about myself? Is it spurring me on to further goal-directed action or leading me to give in and curl up?

If your answer to these questions is largely 'yes', then you probably are disturbing yourself needlessly about a negative event. The situation may well be negative – but your thinking is making it even worse. In Chapters 2 and 3 we guide you toward correcting disturbance-creating thinking and help you to feel appropriate distress instead.

Acting out

The ways you think and feel also largely determine the way you *act*. If you feel depressed, you're likely to withdraw and isolate yourself. If you're anxious, you may avoid situations that you find threatening or dangerous. Your behaviours can be problematic for you in many ways, such as the following:

- ✔ **Self-destructive behaviours,** such as excessive drinking or using drugs to quell anxiety, can cause direct physical harm.

- ✔ **Isolating and mood-depressing behaviours,** such as staying in bed all day or not seeing your friends, increase your sense of isolation and maintain your low mood.

- ✔ **Avoidance behaviours,** such as avoiding situations you perceive as threatening (attending a social outing, using a lift, speaking in public), deprive you of the opportunity to confront and overcome your fears.

Learning Your ABCs

When you start to get an understanding of your emotional difficulties, CBT encourages you to break down a specific problem you have using the *ABC format*, in which:

✔ **A** is the *activating event*. An activating event means a real *external* event that has occurred, a future event that you anticipate occurring or an *internal* event in your mind, such as an image, memory or dream.

The 'A' is often referred to as your 'trigger'.

✔ **B** is your *beliefs*. Your beliefs include your thoughts, your personal rules, the demands you make (on yourself, the world and other people) and the meanings that you attach to external and internal events.

✔ **C** is the *consequences*. Consequences include your emotions, behaviours and physical sensations that accompany different emotions.

Figure 1-1 shows the ABC parts of a problem in picture form.

Figure 1-1:
A is the activating event, **B** is your beliefs and thoughts, and **C** is the consequences, such as the emotions you feel after the event, and your subsequent behaviour.

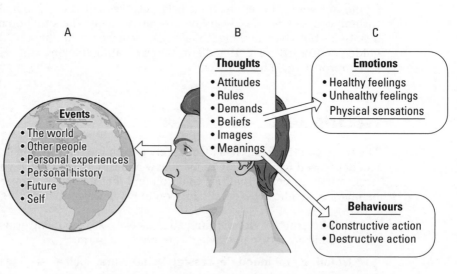

Writing down your problem in *ABC form* – a central CBT technique – helps you differentiate between your thoughts, feelings and behaviours, and the *trigger* event. We give more information about the ABC form in Chapter 3, and you can find a blank ABC form at the back of the book.

Consider the ABC formulations of two common emotional problems, anxiety and depression. The ABC of anxiety may look like this:

✔ **A:** You imagine failing a job interview.

✔ **B:** You believe: 'I've got to make sure that I don't mess up this interview, otherwise I'll prove that I'm a failure.'

✔ **C:** You experience anxiety (emotion), butterflies in your stomach (physical sensation), and drinking to calm your nerves (behaviour).

The ABC of depression may look like this:

✔ **A:** You fail a job interview.

✔ **B:** You believe: 'I should've done better. This means that I'm a failure!'

✔ **C:** You experience depression (emotion), loss of appetite (physical sensation), and staying in bed and avoiding the outside world (behaviour).

You can use these examples to guide you when you are filling in an ABC form on your own problems. Doing so will help ensure that you record the actual facts of the event under 'A', your thoughts about the event under 'B', and how you feel and act under 'C'. Developing a really clear ABC of your problem can make it much easier for you to realise how your thoughts at 'B' lead to your emotional/behavioural responses at 'C'. (Chapter 3 describes the ABC form more fully.)

Characterising CBT

We give a much fuller description of the principles and practical applications of CBT in the rest of this book. However, here's a quick reference list of key characteristics of CBT. CBT:

✔ Emphasises the role of the personal meanings that you give to events in determining your emotional responses.

✔ Was developed through extensive scientific evaluation.

✔ Focuses more on how your problems are being *maintained* rather than on searching for a single root cause of the problem.

✔ Offers practical advice and tools for overcoming common emotional problems (see Chapters 9, 12 and 13).

✔ Holds the view that you can change and develop by thinking things through and by trying out new ideas and strategies (head to Chapter 4).

✔ Can address material from your past if doing so can help you to understand and change the way you're thinking and acting now (Chapter 16 covers this in depth).

✔ Shows you that some of the strategies you're using to cope with your emotional problems are actually maintaining those problems (Chapter 7 is all about this).

✔ Strives to normalise your emotions, physical sensations, and thoughts rather than to persuade you that they're clues to 'hidden' problems.

✔ Recognises that you may develop emotional problems *about* your emotional problems, for example feeling ashamed about being depressed (see Chapter 6 for more on this concept).

✔ Highlights learning techniques and maximises self-help so that ultimately you can become your own therapist (head to Chapter 22).

Getting complicated

Sticking to the simple ABC formulation in which A+B=C can serve you well. But if that seems a little simplistic, you can consider the more complicated formulations shown here:

Effect on your personal world

This diagram shows the complex interaction between your thoughts, feelings and behaviours. Although your thoughts affect how you feel, your feelings also affect your thinking. So, if you're having depressed thoughts, your mood is likely to be low. The lower your mood, the more likely you are to act in a depressed manner and to think pessimistically. The combination of feeling depressed, thinking pessimistically and acting in a depressed manner can, ultimately, influence the way you see your personal world. You may focus on negative events in your life and the world in general and therefore accumulate more negative As. This interaction between A, B and C can become a vicious circle.

CBT pays a lot of attention to changing both unhealthy thinking patterns and unhealthy patterns of behaviour.

Chapter 2

Spotting Errors in Your Thinking

. . . .

In This Chapter

▶ Identifying classic pitfalls in human thought

▶ Correcting your thinking

▶ Getting to know the thinking errors you make most

. . . .

You probably don't spend a lot of time mulling over the pros and cons of the way you think. Most people don't – but to be frank, most people ideally ought to!

One of the central messages of CBT is that the thoughts, attitudes and beliefs you hold have a big effect on the way you interpret the world around you and on how you feel. So, if you're feeling excessively bad, chances are that you're thinking badly – or, at least, in an unhelpful way. Of course, you probably don't *intend* to think in an unhelpful way, and no doubt you're largely unaware that you do.

Thinking errors are slips in thinking that everyone makes from time to time. Just as a virus stops your computer from dealing with information effectively, so thinking errors prevent you from making accurate assessments of your experiences. Thinking errors lead you to get the wrong end of the stick, jump to conclusions and assume the worst. Thinking errors get in the way of, or cause you to distort, the facts. However, you do have the ability to step back and take another look at the way you're thinking and set yourself straight. In this chapter we show you how to do just that.

Months or years after the event, you've probably recalled a painful or embarrassing experience and been struck by how differently you feel about it at this later stage. Perhaps you can even laugh about the situation now. Why didn't you laugh back then? Because of the way you were thinking at the time.

To err is most definitely human. Or, as American psychotherapist Albert Ellis is quoted as saying, 'If the Martians ever find out how human beings think, they'll kill themselves laughing.' By understanding the thinking errors we outline in this chapter, you can spot your unhelpful thoughts and put them straight more quickly. Get ready to identify and respond in healthier ways to some of the most common 'faulty' and unhelpful ways of thinking identified by researchers and clinicians.

Catastrophising: Turning Mountains Back Into Molehills

Catastrophising is taking a relatively minor negative event and imagining all sorts of disasters resulting from that one small event, as we sum up in Figure 2-1.

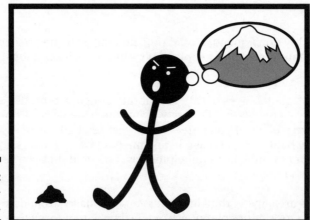

Figure 2-1:
Catastroph-
ising.

Consider these examples of catastrophising:

- You're at a party and you accidentally stumble headlong into a flower arrangement. After you extract yourself from the foliage, you scurry home and conclude that everyone at the party witnessed your little trip and laughed at you.

- You're waiting for your teenage daughter to return home after an evening at the cinema with friends. The clock strikes 10:00 p.m., and you hear no reassuring rattle of her key in the door. By 10:05 p.m., you start imagining her accepting a lift home from a friend who drives recklessly. At 10:10 p.m., you're convinced she's been involved in a head-on collision and paramedics are at the scene. By 10:15 p.m., you're weeping over her grave.

✔ Your new partner declines an invitation to have dinner with your parents. Before giving him a chance to explain his reasons, you put down the phone and decide that this is his way of telling you the relationship's over. Furthermore, you imagine that right now he's ringing friends and telling them what a mistake it was dating you. You decide you're never going to find another partner and will die old and lonely.

Catastrophising leads many an unfortunate soul to misinterpret a social faux pas as a social disaster, a late arrival as a car accident or a minor disagreement as total rejection.

Nip catastrophic thinking in the bud by recognising it for what it is – just thoughts. When you find yourself thinking of the worst possible scenario, try the following strategies:

✔ **Put your thoughts in perspective.** Even if everyone at the party did see your flower-arranging act, are you sure no one was sympathetic? Surely you aren't the only person in the world to have tripped over in public. Chances are, people are far less interested in your embarrassing moment than you think. Falling over at a party isn't great, but in the grand scheme of things it's hardly society-page news.

✔ **Consider less terrifying explanations.** What other reasons are there for your daughter being late? Isn't being late for curfew a common feature of adolescence? Perhaps the film ran over, or she got caught up chatting and forgot the time. Don't get so absorbed in extreme emotions that you're startled to find your daughter in the doorway apologising about missing the bus.

✔ **Weigh up the evidence.** Do you have enough information to conclude that your partner wants to leave you? Has he given you any reason to think this before? Look for evidence that contradicts your catastrophic assumption. For example, have you had more enjoyable times together than not?

✔ **Focus on what you can do to cope with the situation, and the people or resources that can come to your aid.** Engaging in a few more social encounters can help you put your party faux pas behind you. You can repair a damaged relationship – or find another. Even an injury following an accident can be fixed with medical care.

No matter how great a travesty you create in your mind, the world's unlikely to end because of it – even if the travesty comes to pass. You're probably far more capable of surviving embarrassing and painful events than you give yourself credit for – human beings can be very resilient.

All-or-Nothing Thinking: Finding Somewhere In-between

All-or-nothing or *black-or-white thinking* (see Figure 2-2) is extreme thinking that can lead to extreme emotions and behaviours. People either love you or hate you, right? Something's either perfect or a disaster. You're either responsibility-free or totally to blame? Sound sensible? We hope not!

Figure 2-2:
All-or-
nothing
thinking.

Unfortunately, humans fall into the all-or-nothing trap all too easily:

✔ Imagine you're trying to eat healthily in order to lose weight and you cave in to the temptation of a doughnut. All-or-nothing thinking may lead you to conclude that your plan is in ruins and then to go on to eat the other 11 doughnuts in the pack.

✔ You're studying a degree course and you fail one module. All-or-nothing thinking makes you decide that the whole endeavour is pointless. Either you get the course totally right or it's just a write-off.

Consider the humble thermometer as your guide to overcoming the tendency of all-or-nothing thinking. A thermometer reads degrees of temperature, not only 'hot' and 'cold'. Think like a thermometer – in degrees, not extremes. You can use the following pointers to help you change your thinking:

✔ **Be realistic.** You can't possibly get through life without making mistakes. One doughnut doesn't a diet ruin. Remind yourself of your goal, forgive yourself for the minor slip, and resume your diet.

✔ **Develop 'both–and' reasoning skills.** An alternative to all-or-nothing thinking is *both–and reasoning*. You need to mentally allow two seeming opposites to exist together. You can *both* succeed in your overall educational goals *and* fail a test or two. Life is not a case of being either a success or a failure. You can *both* assume that you're an okay person as you are *and* strive to change.

All-or-nothing thinking can sabotage goal-directed behaviour. You're far more likely to throw in the towel at the first sign of something blocking your goal when you refuse to allow a margin for error. Beware of 'either/or' statements and global labels such as 'good' and 'bad' or 'success' and 'failure'. Neither people nor life situations are often that cut and dry.

Fortune-Telling: Stepping Away From the Crystal Ball

Often, clients tell us after they've done something they were anxious about that the actual event wasn't half as bad as they'd predicted. Predictions are the problem here. You probably don't possess extrasensory perceptions that allow you to see into the future. You probably can't see into the future even with the aid of a crystal ball like the one in Figure 2-3. And yet, you may try to predict future events. Unfortunately, the predictions you make may be unduly negative:

Figure 2-3: Fortune-telling.

✔ You've been feeling a bit depressed lately and you aren't enjoying yourself like you used to. Someone from work invites you to a party, but you decide that if you go you won't have a good time. The food will unpalatable, the music will be irksome and the other guests are sure to find you boring. So, you opt to stay in and bemoan the state of your social life.

✔ You fancy the bloke who sells you coffee every morning on the way to the office, and you'd like to go out with him on a date. You predict that if you ask him, you'll be so anxious that you'll say something stupid. Anyway, he's bound to say no thanks – someone that attractive must surely be in a relationship.

✔ You always thought that hang-gliding would be fun, but you've got an anxious disposition. If you try the sport, you're sure to lose your nerve at the last minute and just end up wasting your time and money.

You're better off letting the future unfold without trying to guess how it may turn out. Put the dustcover back on the crystal ball, flog the ouija board on eBay, leave the tarot cards alone and try the following strategies instead:

✔ **Test out your predictions.** You really never know how much fun you might have at a party until you get there – and the food could be amazing. Maybe the chap at the coffee shop has got a partner, but you won't be sure until you ask. To find out more about testing out your predictions, have a read through Chapter 4.

✔ **Be prepared to take risks.** Isn't it worth possibly losing a bit of cash for the opportunity to try a sport you've always been interested in? And can't you bear the possibility of appearing a trifle nervous for the chance to get to know someone you really like? There's a saying 'a ship is safe in a harbour', but that's not what ships are built for. Learning to live experimentally and taking calculated risks is a recipe for keeping life interesting and rewarding.

✔ **Understand that your past experiences don't determine your future experiences.** Just because the last party you went to turned out to be a dreary homage to the seventies, the last person you asked out went a bit green, and that scuba-diving venture resulted in a severe case of the bends doesn't mean that you'll never have better luck again.

Typically, fortune-telling stops you from taking action. It can also become a bit of a self-fulfilling prophecy. If you keep telling yourself that you won't enjoy that party, you're liable to make that prediction come true. Same goes for meeting new people and trying new things. So, put on your party gear, ask him out for dinner and book yourself in for some hang-gliding.

Mind-Reading: Taking Your Guesses with a Pinch of Salt

So, you think you know what other people are thinking, do you? With *mind-reading* (see Figure 2-4), the tendency is often to assume that others are thinking negative things about you or have negative motives and intentions.

Figure 2-4:
Mind-
reading.

Here are some examples of mind-reading tendencies:

✔ You're chatting with someone and they look over your shoulder as you're speaking, break eye contact and (perish the thought) yawn. You conclude immediately that the other person thinks your conversation is mind-numbing and that he'd rather be talking to someone else.

✔ Your boss advises that you book some time off to use up your annual leave. You decide that he's saying this because he thinks your work is rubbish and wants the opportunity to interview for your replacement while you're on leave.

✔ You pass a neighbour on the street. He says a quick hello but doesn't look very friendly or pleased to see you. You think that he must be annoyed with you about your dog howling at the last full moon and is making plans to report you to environmental health.

You can never know for certain what another person is thinking, so you're wise to pour salt on your negative assumptions. Stand back and take a look at all the evidence to hand. Take control of your tendency to mind-read by trying the following:

- ✔ **Generate some alternative reasons for what you see.** The person you're chatting with may be tired, be preoccupied with his own thoughts or just have spotted someone he knows.

- ✔ **Consider that your guesses may be wrong.** Are your fears really about your boss's motives, or do they concern your own insecurity about your abilities at work? Do you have enough information or hard evidence to conclude that your boss thinks your work is substandard? Does it follow logically that 'consider booking time off' means 'you're getting the sack'?

- ✔ **Get more information (if appropriate).** Ask your neighbour whether your dog kept him up all night, and think of some ways to muffle your pet next time the moon waxes.

You tend to mind-read what you fear most. Mind-reading is a bit like putting a slide in a slide projector. What you *project* or imagine is going on in other people's minds is very much based on what's already in yours.

Emotional Reasoning: Reminding Yourself That Feelings Aren't Facts

Surely we're wrong about this one. Surely your feelings are real hard evidence of the way things are? Actually, no! Often, relying too heavily on your feelings as a guide leads you off the reality path. Here are some examples of emotional reasoning:

- ✔ Your partner has been spending long nights at the office with a co-worker for the past month. You feel jealous and suspicious of your partner. Based on these feelings, you conclude that your partner's having an affair with his co-worker.

- ✔ You feel guilty out of the blue. You conclude that you must have done something wrong otherwise you wouldn't be feeling guilty.

- ✔ You wake up feeling anxious, with a vague sense of dread. You assume that there must be something seriously wrong in your life and search your mind frantically for the source of your ill-feeling.

Often your feelings are simply due to a thought or memory that you may not even be totally aware of having had. Other times they can be symptoms of another disorder such as depression or anxiety problems (see Chapter 9 for information about anxiety disorders and Chapter 12 for more on depression). Some of the feelings you experience on waking are left over from dreams that you may or may not remember. As a rule of thumb, it pays to be somewhat sceptical about the validity of your feelings in the first instance. Your feelings can be misleading.

When you spot emotional reasoning taking over your thoughts, take a step back and try the following:

1. **Take notice of your thoughts.** Take notice of thoughts such as 'I'm feeling nervous, something must be wrong' and 'I'm so angry, and that really shows how badly you've behaved', and recognise that feelings are not always the best measure of reality, especially if you're not in the best emotional shape at the moment.

2. **Ask yourself how you'd view the situation if you were feeling calmer.** Look to see if there is any concrete evidence to support your interpretation of your feelings. For example, is there really any evidence that something bad is going to happen?

3. **Give yourself time to allow your feelings to subside.** When you're feeling calmer, review your conclusions and remember that it is quite possible that your feelings are the consequence of your present emotional state (or even just fatigue) rather than indicators of the state of reality.

4. **If you can't find any obvious and immediate source of your unpleasant feelings – overlook them.** Get into the shower despite your sense of dread, for example. If a concrete reason to be anxious does exist, it won't get dissolved in the shower. If your anxiety is all smoke and mirrors, you may well find it washes down the drain.

The problem with viewing your feelings as factual is that you stop looking for contradictory information – or for any additional information at all. Balance your emotional reasoning with a little more looking at the facts that support and contradict your views, as we show in Figure 2-5.

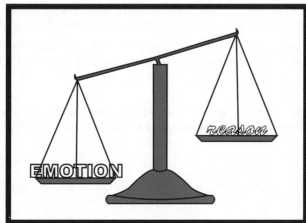

Figure 2-5: Emotional reasoning.

Overgeneralising: Avoiding the Part/Whole Error

Overgeneralising is the error of drawing global conclusions from one or more events. When you find yourself thinking 'always', 'never', 'people are . . .' or 'the world's . . .', you may well be overgeneralising. Take a look at Figure 2-6. Here, our stick man sees one sheep in a flock and instantly assumes the whole flock of sheep is black. However, his overgeneralisation is inaccurate because the rest of the flock are white sheep.

Figure 2-6: Overgeneralising.

You might recognise overgeneralising in the following examples:

✔ You feel down. When you get into your car to go to work, it doesn't start. You think to yourself, 'Things like this are always happening to me. Nothing ever goes right', which makes you feel even more gloomy.

✔ You become angry easily. Travelling to see a friend, you're delayed by a fellow passenger who cannot find the money to pay her train fare. You think, 'This is typical! Other people are just so stupid', and you become tense and angry.

✔ You tend to feel guilty easily. You yell at your child for not understanding his homework and then decide that you're a thoroughly rotten parent.

Situations are rarely so stark or extreme that they merit terms like 'always' and 'never'. Rather than overgeneralising, consider the following:

✔ **Get a little perspective.** How true is the thought that nothing *ever* goes right for you? How many other people in the world may be having car trouble at this precise moment?

✔ **Suspend judgement.** When you judge all people as stupid, including the poor creature waiting in line for the train, you make yourself more outraged and are less able to deal effectively with a relatively minor hiccup.

✔ **Be specific.** Would you be a *totally* rotten parent for losing patience with your child? Can you legitimately conclude that one incident of poor parenting cancels out all the good things you do for your little one? Perhaps your impatience is simply an area you need to target for improvement.

Shouting at your child in a moment of stress no more makes you a rotten parent than singing him a favourite lullaby makes you a perfect parent. Condemning yourself on the basis of making a mistake does nothing to solve the problem, so be specific and steer clear of global conclusions. Change what you think you *can* and *need* to but also forgive yourself (and others) for singular errors or misdeeds.

Labelling: Giving Up the Rating Game

Labels, and the process of labelling people and events, are everywhere. For example, people who have low self-esteem may label themselves as 'worthless', 'inferior' or 'inadequate' (see Figure 2-7).

Figure 2-7:
Labelling.

If you label other people as 'no good' or 'useless', you're likely to become angry with them. Or perhaps you label the world as 'unsafe' or 'totally unfair'? The error here is that you're globally rating things that are too complex for a definitive label. The following are examples of labelling:

- ✔ You read a distressing article in the newspaper about a rise in crime in your city. The article activates your belief that you live in a thoroughly dangerous place, which contributes to you feeling anxious about going out.

- ✔ You receive a poor mark for an essay. You start to feel low and label yourself as a failure.

- ✔ You become angry when someone cuts in front of you in a traffic queue. You label the other driver as a total loser for his bad driving.

Strive to avoid labelling yourself, other people and the world around you. Accept that they're complex and ever-changing (see Chapter 14 for more on this). Recognise evidence that doesn't fit your labels, in order to help you weaken your conviction in your global rating. For example:

- ✔ **Allow for varying degrees.** Think about it: The world isn't a dangerous place but rather a place that has many different aspects with varying degrees of safety and risk.

- ✔ **Celebrate complexities.** All human beings – yourself included – are unique, multifaceted and ever-changing. To label yourself as a failure on the strength of one failing is an extreme form of overgeneralising. Likewise, other people are just as complex and unique as you. One bad action doesn't equal a bad person.

When you label a person or aspect of the world in a global way, you exclude potential for change and improvement. Accepting yourself as you are is a powerful first step towards self-improvement.

Making Demands: Thinking Flexibly

Albert Ellis, founder of rational emotive behaviour therapy, one of the first cognitive-behavioural therapies, places demands at the very heart of emotional problems. Thoughts and beliefs that contain words like 'must', 'should', 'need', 'ought', 'got to' and 'have to' are often problematic because they're extreme and rigid (see Figure 2-8).

Figure 2-8:
Demands.

The inflexibility of the demands you place on yourself, the world around you and other people often means you don't adapt to reality as well as you could. Consider these possible examples:

- ✓ You believe that you *must* have the approval of your friends and colleagues. This leads you to feel anxious in many social situations and drives you to try to win everyone's approval – possibly at great personal cost.

- ✓ You think that because you try very hard to be kind and considerate to others, they really *ought* to be just as kind and considerate in return. Because your demand is not realistic – sadly, other people are governed by their own priorities – you often feel hurt about your friends (or even strangers) not acting the way you do yourself.

- ✓ You believe that you *absolutely should* never let people down. Therefore, you rarely put your own welfare first. At work, you do more than your fair share because you don't assert yourself, and so you often end up feeling stressed and depressed.

Holding *flexible preferences* about yourself, other people and the world in general is the healthy alternative to inflexible rules and demands. Rather than making demands on yourself, the world and others, try the following techniques:

- ✓ **Pay attention to language.** Replace words like 'must', 'need' and 'should' with 'prefer', 'wish' and 'want'.

- ✓ **Limit approval seeking.** Can you manage to have a satisfying life even if you don't get the approval of everyone you seek it from? Specifically, you'll feel more confident in social situations if you recognise your *preference* for approval rather than viewing approval as a dire need.

- ✔ **Understand that the world doesn't play to your rules.** In fact, other people tend to have their own rulebooks. So, no matter how much you value considerate behaviour, your friends may not give it the same value. If you can give others the right to not live up to your standards, you'll feel less hurt when they fail to do so.

- ✔ **Retain your standards, ideals and preferences, and ditch your rigid demands about how you, others and the world 'have to' be.** So keep acting consistently with how you *would like* things to be rather than becoming depressed or irate about things not being the way you believe they *must* be.

When you hold rigid demands about the way things 'have got to be', you have no margin for deviation or error. You leave yourself vulnerable to experiencing exaggerated emotional disturbance when things in life just don't go your way.

Mental Filtering: Keeping an Open Mind

Mental filtering is a bias in the way you process information, in which you acknowledge only information that fits with a belief you hold. The process is much like a filter on a camera lens that allows in only certain kinds of light. Information that doesn't fit tends to be ignored. If you think any of the following, you're making the 'mental filtering' thinking error:

- ✔ You believe you're a failure, so you tend to focus on your mistakes at work and overlook successes and achievements. At the end of the week, you often feel disappointed about your lack of achievement – but this is probably largely the result of you not paying attention to your successes.

- ✔ You believe you're unlikeable, and *really* notice each time your friend is late to call back or seems too busy to see you. You tend to disregard the ways in which people act warmly towards you, thus sustaining your view that you're unlikeable.

To combat mental filtering, look more closely at situations you feel down about. Deliberately collecting evidence that contradicts your negative thoughts can help you to correct your information-processing bias. Try the following:

- ✔ **Examine your filters closely.** For example, are you sifting your achievements through an 'I'm a failure' filter? If so, then only failure-related information gets through. If you look for a *friend's* achievements over the same week *without* a filter, you're likely to find him in far greater possession of success. So drop the filter when assessing yourself in the same way you do when looking at your friends' achievements.

✔ **Gather evidence.** Imagine you're collecting evidence for a court case to prove that your negative thought isn't true. What evidence do you cite? Would, for example, an assertion that you're unlikeable stand up in court against the proof of your friends behaving warmly towards you?

If you only ever take in information that fits with your negative thinking, you can very easily end up reinforcing undesirable thinking habits. The fact that you don't see the positive stuff about yourself, or your experiences, doesn't mean it isn't there (just bear in mind Figure 2-9!).

Figure 2-9:
Mental
filtering.

Disqualifying the Positive: Keeping the Baby When Throwing Out the Bathwater

Disqualifying the positive (see Figure 2-10) is related to the biased way that people can process information. Disqualifying the positive is a mental response to a positive event that transforms it into a neutral or negative event.

The following are examples of disqualifying the positive:

✔ You convince yourself that you're worthless and unlovable. You respond to a work promotion by thinking, 'This doesn't count, because anyone could get this sort of thing.' The result: Instead of feeling pleased, you feel quite disappointed.

✔ You think you're pathetic and feel low. A friend tells you you're a very good friend, but you disqualify this in your mind by thinking, 'She's only saying that because she feels sorry for me. I really am pathetic.'

Figure 2-10:
Disqual-
ifying
the positive.

Hone your skills for accepting compliments and acknowledging your good points. You can try the following strategies to improve your skills:

✔ **Become aware of your responses to positive 'data'.** Practise acknowledging and accepting positive feedback and acknowledging good points about yourself, others and the world. For example, you could override your workplace disappointment by recognising that *you're* the one who got the promotion. You can even consider that the promotion may well have been a result of your hard work.

✔ **Practise accepting a compliment graciously with a simple thank you.** Rejecting a sincerely delivered compliment is rather like turning down a gift. Steer your thinking towards taking in positive experiences. When others point out attributes you have, start deliberately making a note of those good points. Even if your current thinking bias leads you to doubt the validity of a compliment or good experience, try considering that you may well be wrong to do so. Trust what others say for a change!

If you frequently disqualify or distort your positive attributes or experiences, you can easily sustain a negative belief, even in the face of overwhelming positive evidence.

Low Frustration Tolerance: Realising You Can Bear the 'Unbearable'

Low frustration tolerance refers to the error of assuming that when something's difficult to tolerate, it's 'intolerable'. This thinking error means magnifying discomfort and not tolerating temporary discomfort when it's in your interest to do so for longer-term benefit, as we show in Figure 2-11.

Figure 2-11:
Low frustration tolerance.

The following are examples of low frustration tolerance:

✔ You often procrastinate on college assignments, thinking, 'It's just too much hassle. I'll do it later when I feel more in the mood.' You tend to wait until the assignment's nearly due and it becomes too uncomfortable to put off any longer. Unfortunately, waiting until the last moment means that you can rarely put as much time and effort into your coursework as you need to in order to reach your potential.

✔ You want to overcome your anxiety of travelling away from home by facing your fear directly. And yet, each time you try to travel farther on the train, you become anxious, and think 'This is so horrible, I can't stand it', and quickly return home, which reinforces your fear rather than helping you experience travel as less threatening.

The best way to overcome low frustration tolerance is to foster an alternative attitude of *high frustration tolerance*. You can achieve this way of thinking by trying the following:

✔ **Pushing yourself to do things that are uncomfortable or unpleasant.**
For example, you can train yourself to work on assignments even if you
aren't in a good mood, because the end result of finishing work in good
time, and to a good standard, outweighs the hassle of doing something
you find tedious.

✔ **Giving yourself messages that emphasise your ability to withstand
pain.** To combat a fear of travel, you can remind yourself that feeling
anxious is really unpleasant, but you *can* stand it. Ask yourself whether,
in the past, you've ever withstood the feelings you're saying you pres-
ently 'can't stand'.

Telling yourself you can't stand something has two effects. First, it leads you
to focus more on the discomfort you're experiencing. Second, it leads you to
underestimate your ability to cope with discomfort. Many things can be difficult to tolerate, but rating them as 'intolerable' often makes situations seem
more daunting than they really are.

Personalising: Removing Yourself from the Centre of the Universe

Personalising involves interpreting events as being related to you personally
and overlooking other factors. This can lead to emotional difficulties, such as
feeling hurt easily or feeling unnecessarily guilty (see Figure 2-12).

Figure 2-12:
Personal-
ising.

Here are some examples of personalising:

- ✔ You may tend to feel guilty if you know a friend is upset and you can't make him feel better. You think, 'If I was really a good friend, I'd be able to cheer him up. I'm obviously letting him down.'

- ✔ You feel hurt when a friend you meet in a shop leaves quickly after saying only a hurried 'hello'. You think, 'He was obviously trying to avoid talking to me. I must have offended him somehow.'

You can tackle personalising by considering alternative explanations that don't revolve around you. Think about the following examples:

- ✔ **Imagine what else may contribute to the outcome you're assuming personal responsibility for.** Your friend may have lost his job or be suffering from depression. Despite your best efforts to cheer him up, these factors are outside your control.

- ✔ **Consider why people may be responding to you in a certain way.** Don't jump to the conclusion that someone's response relates directly to you. For example, your friend may be having a difficult day or be in a big hurry – he may even feel sorry for not stopping to talk to you.

Because you really aren't the centre of the universe, look for explanations of events that have little or nothing to do with you.

Getting intimate with your thinking

Figuring out which thinking errors you tend to make the most can be a useful way of making your CBT self-help more efficient and effective. The simplest way of doing this is to jot down your thoughts whenever you feel upset and note what was happening at the time. Remember the maxim: When you feel bad, put your thoughts on the pad! See Chapter 3 for more on managing unhelpful thoughts by writing them down.

You can then review your thoughts against the list of thinking errors in this chapter. Write down beside each unhelpful thought the specific thinking error you're most probably making. With practice you can get better at spotting your thinking errors and challenging them. In all probability, you may notice that you're more prone to making some errors than others; therefore you know which alternative styles of thinking to develop.

You may also become aware of patterns or themes in the kinds of situations or events that trigger your negative thoughts. These can also help you to focus on the areas in which your thoughts, beliefs and attitudes need most work.

Chapter 3

Tackling Toxic Thoughts

In This Chapter

▶ Identifying the thoughts underpinning the way you feel

▶ Questioning your negative thoughts and generating alternatives

▶ Using the ABC self-help forms to manage your emotions

*I*n your endeavours to become your own CBT therapist, one of the key techniques you use is a tool known as an *ABC form*, which provides you with a structure for identifying, questioning and replacing unhelpful thoughts using pen and paper.

CBT therapists sometimes use similar tools to the ABC form which we offer in this chapter. All these tools can help patients to identify and replace negative thoughts. Different therapists may refer to these forms as *thought records, thought diaries, daily records of dysfunctional thoughts* or *dysfunctional thought records (DTRs)*. Fret not – in general, all of these forms are simply different ways of saying largely the same thing: Your thinking impacts your feelings and actions.

The way you think affects the way you feel. Therefore, changing your unhelpful thoughts is a key to feeling better.

In this chapter, we give you two versions of the ABC form: one to get you started with identifying your triggers, thoughts and feelings, and another that takes you right through to developing alternative thoughts so you can feel and act differently in the future.

Catching NATs

Getting the hang of the ABC form is often easier if you break down the process into two steps. The first step is to fill out the first three columns (*Activating* event, *Beliefs* and thoughts, *Consequences*) of the form, which you can find further on in this chapter (ABC Form I). This gives you a chance to focus on catching your *negative automatic thoughts* (NATs) on paper and to see the connection between your thoughts and emotions.

Using the ABC form is great, but if you don't have one to hand when you feel an upsetting emotion, grab anything you can write on to scribble down your thoughts and feelings. You can always transfer your thoughts to a form later. As has been said by many a CBT therapist: When you feel bad, stick it on the pad!

Making the thought–feeling link

A crucial step in CBT is to make the *thought–feeling link* or *B-to-C connection*; that is, seeing clearly for yourself the connection between what goes through your mind and your resulting emotions. When you see this connection, it can help you to make much more sense of why to challenge and change your thoughts.

Becoming more objective about your thoughts

One of the biggest advantages of writing down your thoughts is that the process can help you to regard these thoughts simply as hunches, theories and ideas – rather than as absolute facts.

The more negative the meaning you give to an event, the more negative you'll feel, and the more likely you'll act in a way that maintains that feeling. Crucially, when you feel negative, you're more likely to generate negative thoughts. See how easily you can get caught in a vicious circle? Just one of the reasons to take your negative thoughts with a bucket of salt!

Stepping Through the ABC Form 1

So, time to embark on this major CBT self-help technique using Figure 3-1. The basic process for completing the ABC form is as follows:

1. **In the 'Consequences' box, point 1, write down the emotion you're feeling.**

   Therapy's about becoming emotionally healthier and acting in a more self-helping or productive way. So, when you're filling out the ABC form, the most important place to start is with the emotion you're feeling.

Emotions and behaviour are *consequences* (C) of the interaction between the *activating event or trigger* (A) and the *beliefs or meanings* (B) in the ABC model of emotion.

Examples of emotions you may choose to list in the 'Consequences' box include:

- Anger
- Anxiety
- Depression
- Envy
- Guilt
- Hurt
- Jealousy
- Shame

Fill out an ABC form when you feel emotionally upset, when you've acted in a way that you want to change, or when you feel like acting in a way that you wish to change. We give you more information on how to help you understand and identify emotions in Chapter 6.

2. **In the 'Consequences' box, point 2, write down how you acted.**

   Write down how your behaviour changed when you felt your uncomfortable emotion. Examples of the behaviour that people often identify as their actions in this box include:

   - Avoiding something
   - Becoming withdrawn, isolated or inactive
   - Being aggressive
   - Binge-eating or restricting food intake
   - Escaping from a situation
   - Putting off something (procrastination)
   - Seeking reassurance
   - Taking alcohol or drugs
   - Using safety behaviours, such as holding on to something if you feel faint

3. **In the 'Activating Event' box, write down what triggered your feelings.**

As we discuss in Chapter 1, the A in ABC stands for *activating event or trigger*, which are the things that triggered your unhelpful thoughts and feelings. Activating events or triggers to put in this box can include:

- Something happening right now

- Something that occurred in the past

- Something that you're anticipating happening in the future

- Something in the external world (an object, place or person)

- Something in your mind (an image or memory)

- A physical sensation (increased heart rate, headache, feeling tired)

- Your own emotions or behaviour

An activating event can be pretty much anything. Use your feelings – rather than whether you think the event is important – as a guide to when you should fill out a form.

To keep your ABC form brief and accurate, focus on the specific aspect of the activating event that you're upset about. Use the table of emotions in Chapter 6 to help you detect the themes to look out for if you're unsure about what may have triggered your thoughts and feelings.

4. **In the 'Beliefs' box, write down your thoughts, attitudes and beliefs.**

Describe what the event (whatever you've put in the 'Activating Event' box) meant to you when you felt the emotion (what you've written under point 1 in the 'Consequences' box).

The thoughts, attitudes and beliefs you put in the 'Beliefs' box often pop up on reflex. They may be extreme, distorted and unhelpful – but they may *seem* like facts to you. Some examples of these NATs include:

- Here I go again, proving that I'm useless!

- I should've known better!

- Now everyone knows what an idiot I am!

- This proves that I can't cope like normal people do!

Thoughts are what count, so think of yourself as a detective and set out to capture suspect thoughts. If your thoughts are in the form of a picture, describe the image, or what the image means to you – then write them down in the 'Beliefs' box.

We think not only in words but also in pictures. People who are feeling anxious frequently describe that they see *catastrophic images* going through their mind. For example, if you fear fainting in a restaurant, you may get an image of yourself on the restaurant floor with staff fussing over you.

5. **In the 'Thinking Error' box, consider what your thinking errors may be.**

One of the key ways to become more objective about your thoughts is to identify the *thinking errors* that may be represented in the thoughts you list in this box. (Have a look at Chapter 2 for more details on common thinking errors.)

Questions that you might ask yourself in order to identify your thinking errors include:

- Am I jumping to the worst possible conclusion? (Catastrophising)

- Am I thinking in extreme – all-or-nothing – terms? (Black-and-white thinking)

- Am I using words like 'always' and 'never' to draw generalised conclusions from a specific event? (Overgeneralising)

- Am I predicting the future instead of waiting to see what happens? (Fortune-telling)

- Am I jumping to conclusions about what other people are thinking of me? (Mind-reading)

- Am I focusing on the negative and overlooking the positive? (Mental filtering)

- Am I discounting positive information or twisting a positive into a negative? (Disqualifying the positive)

- Am I globally putting myself down as a failure, worthless or useless? (Labelling)

- Am I listening too much to my negative gut feelings instead of looking at the objective facts? (Emotional reasoning)

- Am I taking an event or someone's behaviour too personally or blaming myself and overlooking other factors? (Personalising)

- Am I using words like 'should', 'must', 'ought' and 'have to' in order to make rigid rules about myself, the world or other people? (Demanding)

- Am I telling myself that something is too difficult or unbearable or that 'I can't stand it' when actually it's hard to bear but it *is* bearable and worth tolerating? (Having a low frustration tolerance)

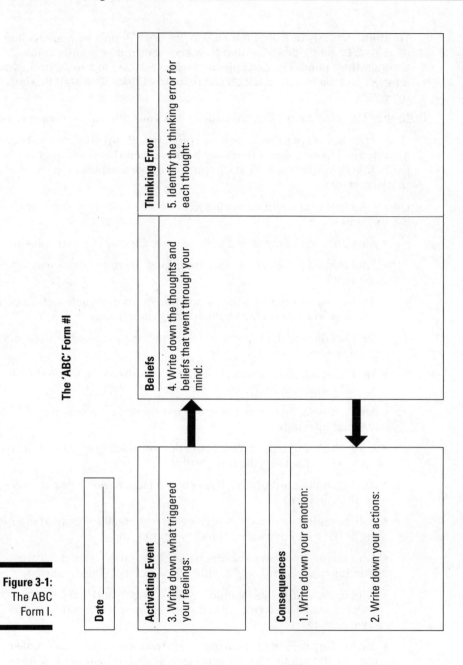

Figure 3-1:
The ABC
Form I.

The 'ABC' Form #I

Date _____

Activating Event	Beliefs	Thinking Error
3. Write down what triggered your feelings:	4. Write down the thoughts and beliefs that went through your mind:	5. Identify the thinking error for each thought:

Consequences
1. Write down your emotion:
2. Write down your actions:

Creating Constructive Alternatives: Completing the ABC Form II

When you feel more confident about identifying your As, Bs, Cs and thinking errors, you can move on to the ABC form II. This second form helps you question your unhelpful thoughts in order to reduce their intensity, generate and rate the effects of alternative thoughts and focus on acting differently.

The first five steps for completing the ABC form II (see Figure 3-2) are the same as those for the ABC form I. Then come five more steps. You can find a blank version of the ABC form II in Appendix B. In the ABC form II, column A is the Activating Event, column B is Beliefs, column C is Consequences, column D is Dispute and column E is Effect.

6. **Examine your negative thoughts more closely.**

   Ask yourself the following questions in order to examine and weaken your unhelpful thoughts:

   - Can I prove that my thought is 100 per cent true?

   - What are the effects of thinking this way?

   - Is my thought wholly logical or sensible?

   - Do people whose opinions I respect agree that this thought's realistic?

   - What evidence exists against this thought?

   - Is my thought balanced or extreme?

   - Is my thought rigid or flexible?

   - Am I thinking objectively and realistically or are my thoughts being biased by how I feel?

   Consider long and hard your negative or unhelpful thoughts in the light of the preceding questions. Don't simply give glib 'yes' or 'no' answers. Instead, think things through and perhaps write down your challenges to your unhelpful thoughts in column D. See the list of questions and prompters at the bottom of the ABC form II, which can help you further with this.

7. **Generate alternatives for each of your unhelpful thoughts, attitudes and beliefs.**

   This step is critical as it's your alternative thoughts that will help you to feel better! In column D, write down a flexible, non-extreme, realistic and helpful alternative for each thought, attitude or belief that appears in column B. The following questions may help you to generate some alternatives:

   - What's a more helpful way of looking at the situation?

   - Do I encourage friends to think in this way?

- When I'm feeling okay, how do I think differently?

- Have any past experiences shown me that another possible outcome exists?

- What's a more flexible or less extreme way of thinking?

- What's a more realistic or balanced way of thinking that takes into account the evidence that does *not* support my thought?

- What do I need to think in order to feel and act differently?

Some thoughts are more stubborn than others, and you won't turn your thinking around completely in one go. Wrestling with NATs for a while before they weaken is typical and appropriate. Think of yourself as *training* your mind to think more flexibly and constructively over a period of time.

Some intrusive thoughts, images and doubts can be made worse if you engage with them. If you have obsessive-compulsive disorder (OCD), health anxiety, body dysmorphic disorder (BDD), worry or a jealousy problem, be sure to develop the capability to live with doubt, and allow catastrophic thoughts to pass through your mind rather than challenging them. We explain this in more depth in Chapters 5, 9 and 13. So if you think you need to learn to live with doubt, or to tolerate upsetting, intrusive thoughts in general, we suggest steering clear of using ABC forms for these problems.

8. **In column E, rate the effects of your alternatives on your feelings.**

Rate your original feelings 0–100 per cent. Also note whether you experience any alternative healthier emotions such as:

- Concern

- Annoyance

- Sadness

- Remorse

- Disappointment

- Sorrow

You won't always notice a great deal of change in how you feel at first, so keep persevering! Changes in the way you behave and think tend to precede improved emotional responses. Keep thinking and acting in line with how you want to ultimately feel.

9. **Develop a plan to move forward.**

The final step on the ABC form II is to develop a plan to move forward. Your plan may be to conduct a behavioural experiment to help you gather more information about whether your thoughts are true or realistic, or to behave differently in a specific situation. Go to Chapters 4 and 5 for more ideas.

Figure 3-2:
An example of a filled-in ABC Form II.

The 'ABC' Form #II

Date March 18th

Activating Event (Trigger).	Beliefs, thoughts, and attitudes about A.	Consequences of A+B on your emotions and behaviours.	Dispute (question and examine) B and generate alternatives. The questions at the bottom of the form will help you with this.	Effect of alternative thoughts and beliefs (D).
2. Briefly write down what triggered your emotions. (e.g. event, situation, sensation, memory, image)	3. Write down what went through your mind, or what A meant to you. B's can be about you, others, the world, the past, or the future.	1. Write down what emotion you felt and how you acted when you felt this emotion.	4. Write an alternative for each B, using supporting arguments and evidence.	5. Write down how you feel and wish to act as consequence of your alternatives at D.
Returning to work for the first time after being off sick.	*Things will have changed and I won't know what to do* (Fortune Telling). *People will ask me awkward questions about why I've been off sick and I won't know what to say* (Catastrophising). *They'll think I'm crazy if they find out I've had depression* (Catastrophising, Mind Reading).	**Emotions** e.g. Depression, guilt, hurt, anger, shame, jealousy, envy, anxiety. Rate intensity 0–100. *Anxiety 70%* **Behaviour** e.g. Avoidance, withdrawing, escape, using alcohol or drugs, seeking reassurance, procrastination *Running over in my mind what I'll say to everyone.*	*I don't know whether things have changed. Even if they have I've coped with changes many times before. I'm sure my colleagues will help. Possibly one or two people will ask, and I can just keep my answers short. Mostly everyone will be glad to have me back. I've no reason to think they'll think I'm crazy. When Peter was off with stress people were mostly supportive and understanding. When Helen called last week she seemed to treat me just the same as normal.*	**Emotions** Re-rate 0–100. List any healthy alternative emotion e.g. Sadness, regret, concern. *Anxiety 40%* **Alternative Behaviour or Experiment** e.g. Facing situation, increased activity, assertion *Wait and deal with things when I get there, and stop trying to work it out in advance.*

Disputing (Questioning and Examining) and Generating Alternative Thoughts, Attitudes, and Beliefs: 1. Identify your 'thinking errors' at **B** (e.g. Mind Reading, Catastrophising, Labelling, Demands etc.). Write them next to the appropriate 'B'. 2. Examine whether the evidence at hand supports that your thought at **B** is 100% true. Consider whether someone whose opinions you respect would totally agree with your conclusions. 3. Evaluate the helpfulness of each **B**. Write down what you think might be a more helpful, balanced and flexible way of looking at **A**. Consider what you would advise a friend to think, what a role model of yours might think, or how you might look at **A** if you were feeling OK. 4. Add evidence and arguments that support your alternative thoughts, attitudes and beliefs. Write as if you were trying to persuade someone you cared about.

10. Set yourself some homework.

When you've completed several ABC forms, you may well begin to notice recurring themes, thoughts, attitudes or beliefs. Such repetitions may suggest that you need to add some other CBT techniques in order to overcome certain emotions or behaviours, for example:

- Facing a fear until it reduces (Chapter 9)

- Conducting a behavioural experiment to test out a thought (Chapter 4)

- Acting repeatedly 'as if' you believe an alternative thought, attitude or belief (Chapter 17)

- Completing a Zig-Zag form to strengthen an alternative thought, attitude or belief (Chapter 17)

Read on and set yourself some more therapy assignments using the CBT principles in this book.

Keeping your old ABC forms can be a rewarding record of your progress, and a useful reminder of how to fill them in if you need to use one again in the future. Many of our clients look back over their ABC forms after they feel better and tell us: 'I can't believe I used to feel and think like that!'

An ABC a day keeps the doctor at bay!

If you want to develop any skill, remember these three words: *Practice, practice, practice!* You may not need to fill out an ABC form everyday. Other days, you may need to complete more than one form. The point is that practising ABC forms regularly is worthwhile because:

- Practice helps change disturbing feelings and the thoughts that underpin them.

- Sinking a new thought into your head and heart takes repetition.

By completing forms on paper, you can become increasingly able to challenge unhelpful thoughts in your head – although you may still need to do it on paper sometimes.

As you progress in your ability to overcome difficulties and develop your CBT self-help skills, you may still find the ABC form useful when you're hit with a biggy. And remember: If you can't work out your unhelpful thinking on the hoof, do sit down and bash it out on paper.

Chapter 4

Behaving like a Scientist: Designing and Conducting Behavioural Experiments

....

In This Chapter

▶ Testing out your thoughts and assumptions as predictions

▶ Exploring theories and gathering information

▶ Designing and recording your experiments

....

*O*ften, CBT can seem like common sense. *Behavioural experiments* are particularly good examples of the common-sense side of CBT. If you want to know whether your hunch about reality is accurate, or your way of looking at something is helpful, put it to a test in reality.

This chapter is an introduction to behavioural experiments, a key CBT strategy. We include in this chapter an overview of several behavioural experiments that you can try out for yourself. We also give you examples of these experiments in action. As with the other examples we use in this book, try to look for *anything* useful you can draw from them. Try not to home in too much on how the examples differ from your specific problem. Instead, focus on what you have in common with the examples and work from there to apply the techniques to your own problems.

Even in a 'talking treatment' like CBT, actions speak louder than words. Aaron Beck, founder of cognitive therapy, encourages a therapeutic perspective where client and therapist work on 'being scientific together'. Beck emphasises that testing your thoughts in reality, rather than simply talking about them, underpins effective therapy.

Seeing for Yourself: Reasons for Doing Behavioural Experiments

The proof of the pudding's in the eating. The same can be said of your assumptions, behaviours, beliefs and predictions about yourself and the world around you. Use experiments to test out the *truth* about your beliefs and to assess the *usefulness* of your behaviours.

You can use behavioural experiments in the following ways:

- ✔ To test the validity of a thought or belief that you hold about yourself, other people or the world.

- ✔ To test the validity of an alternative thought or belief.

- ✔ To discover the effects that mental or behavioural activities have on your difficulties.

- ✔ To gather evidence in order to clarify the nature of your problem.

Living according to a set of beliefs because you think they're true and helpful is both easy and common. You can also easily stick to familiar ways of behaving because you *think* that they keep you safe from feared events, or that they help you to achieve certain goals. An example of this may be holding a belief that other people are out to find fault with you – with this thought in mind, you then work hard to hide your mistakes and shortcomings.

The beauty of a behavioural experiment is that you may well find that your worst imagined scenarios don't happen, or that you deal with such situations effectively when, or even if, they do occur.

We may be stating the obvious, but change can be less daunting if you keep in mind that you can always return to your old ways of thinking about things if the new ways don't seem any better. If your old ways seem to be the best option, nothing's stopping you from going back to them. The trick is to prepare yourself to try out new strategies and to give them a chance before returning to your former ways. Find out what works best for you and your particular situation.

Testing Out Predictions

When testing out your predictions, strive to get *unambiguous disconfirmation*, in so far as you can. Unambiguous disconfirmation means discovering *conclusively* that your fears *don't* come true, whether or not you actually do something to prevent them occurring. An example of unambiguous disconfirmation may be finding out that your dizziness is caused by anxiety, and that you won't collapse even if you don't sit down or hold on to something.

Go through the following four steps to devise a behavioural experiment:

1. **Describe your problem.**

   Write down the nature of your problem and include your *safety behaviours* (things you do to try to prevent your feared catastrophe – head to Chapter 7 for loads more on safety behaviour). Phrase the problem in your own words and make a note of how the problem negatively affects your life.

2. **Formulate your prediction.**

   Decide what you think will happen if you try out a new way of thinking or behaving in real life.

3. **Execute an experiment.**

   Think of a way of putting a new belief or behaviour to the test in a real-life situation. Try to devise more than one way to test out your prediction.

4. **Examine the results.**

   Look to see whether your prediction came true. If it didn't, check out what you've learned from the results of the experiment.

You can rate the degree to which you believe a prediction will come true on a percentage between 0 and 100 at the start of your experiment. After you've done the experiment and processed your results, re-rate your conviction in the original prediction.

Take care not to use subtle ways of keeping your feared catastrophe at bay, such as doing experiments only when you feel 'right', are with 'safe' people, have *safety signals* to hand (such as a mobile phone or a bottle of water), or are using safety behaviours (such as trying to control your anxiety with distraction or by gripping tightly to your steering wheel). Using these subtle safety measures during your exposure to a fear can leave you with the impression that you've had a narrow escape, rather than highlighting that your predicted fear didn't come true.

For example, consider the following experiment, which Nadine initiates to examine her fear of rejection and social anxiety:

✔ **Describe the problem.** Nadine's afraid of people thinking negatively of her and of being rejected by her friends. In social situations, Nadine monitors her body language and censors what she says, taking great care not to cause offence. She often plans in advance what she's going to say.

✔ **Formulate a prediction.** Nadine predicts 'If I express an opinion or disagree with my friends, they'll like me less.' She rates her conviction in this idea as 90 per cent.

✔ **Execute an experiment.** For the next six social gatherings Nadine attends, she decides that she'll speak up and try to offer an opinion. If at all possible, she'll find a point on which to disagree with someone.

✔ **Examine the results.** Nadine discovers that no one took exception to her saying more. In fact, two friends commented that it was nice to hear more about what she thought about things. Nadine re-rates her conviction in her original prediction as 40 per cent.

By conducting a behavioural experiment, Nadine observed that her feared prediction – 'Others will like me less if I express my opinions' – didn't happen. This result gives Nadine the opportunity to change her behaviour according to the results of her experiment; therefore, to speak up more often. It also helps to reduce how much she believes the original prediction. Nadine can now adjust her thinking based on evidence gathered through the experiment.

Nigel used a behavioural experiment to test out his prediction that he wouldn't enjoy engaging in social activities. Since self-isolating and disengaging from previously enjoyed activities promotes depression, Nigel really needs to understand the benefits of becoming more active. Nigel worked through an experiment as follows:

✔ **Describe the problem.** Nigel's depression typically leads to him having gloomy and pessimistic thoughts. He tends to avoid going out with his friends or doing any of his regular hobbies because he doesn't feel like it these days. He believes that he won't enjoy himself; therefore, there's no point in trying any of these activities. (As we note in Chapter 12, self-isolating behaviour is one of the key ways in which depression is maintained.)

✔ **Formulate a prediction.** Nigel chooses to experiment with the prediction 'Even if I do go out, I won't enjoy myself and I'll end up feeling even worse once I get home.' He rates his strength of conviction in this thought as 80 per cent.

✔ **Execute an experiment.** Nigel plans to structure his week and to schedule two occasions to see friends. He also plans to spend two half-hour sessions riding his bike, which he used to enjoy. He rates each day over the next seven days in terms of his mood and of how much he enjoys his activities.

✔ **Examine the results.** Nigel notices that he does get some enjoyment from seeing his friends, although less than he usually would. Although he doesn't particularly enjoy his cycling and feels more tired than usual, he notes that he at least felt glad he had done something. He re-rates his conviction in his original prediction as 40 per cent, and decides to conduct further experiments to see whether his mood and energy levels improve over the next two weeks if he continues to be more active.

This experiment helped Nigel to see that he felt better for doing *something*, even if he didn't enjoy cycling or socialising as much as he would when he wasn't depressed. Noting these results can help Nigel to stick to a schedule of activity and ultimately help him to overcome his depression.

Seeking Evidence to See Which Theory Best Fits the Facts

The scientific principle known as *Occam's razor* states that all things considered, the simplest theory is usually the best. Whichever theory explains a phenomenon most simply is the one a scientist adopts. When you want to test out a theory or idea you hold about yourself, others or the world, developing an *alternative theory* is a good idea. This gives you the chance to disprove your original theory and to endorse the healthier alternative.

Some emotional problems don't respond well to attempts to disprove a negative prediction. In such cases, you may be better off developing some *competing theories* about what the problem actually is. You then devise experiments to gather more evidence and see which theory reflects reality most accurately.

For example, imagine that your boss never says a cheerful 'good morning' to you. You develop the following two theories:

- ✔ Theory A: 'My boss doesn't like me at all.'
- ✔ Theory B: 'My boss isn't friendly in the mornings and is a bit rude, but he's like this to a lot of employees, not just me.'

You're now in a position to gather evidence for whether theory A or B best explains the phenomenon of your boss failing to be cheerful towards you in the mornings.

A *theory* is just an idea or assumption that you hold, which to your mind, explains why something happens – a seriously technical word for a simple concept.

Often, developing one additional theory to compete with your original theory is enough. However, you can develop more alternative theories if you think they may help you get to the bottom of what you're experiencing. Taking the above example, you may have a third theory, such as 'My boss is cheerful only with employees that he knows very well', or even a fourth theory, such as 'My boss is cheerful only with employees of the same rank or above him'.

Developing competing theories can be particularly helpful in the following situations:

✔ **Dealing with predictions that may be months or years away from being proven.** If you fear you'll go to hell for having an intrusive thought about causing harm to someone, then this outcome is likely to be sometime away. Similarly, if you have *health anxiety* and spend hours each day preoccupied with the idea that physical sensations in your body may be signs that you'll become ill and die, you're unlikely to know straightaway whether this will actually happen. With these kinds of catastrophic thought, you need to design experiments to help you gather evidence that supports the theory that you have a worry or anxiety problem, rather than a damnation or terminal illness.

✔ **Dealing with beliefs that are impossible to prove or disprove conclusively.** Perhaps you're anxious about others having negative opinions of you. You cannot know for sure what other people think, but even if someone tells you that your fears are unfounded, you can never know with absolute certainty what he's thinking. Similarly, if you have jealous thoughts that your partner desires someone else, but he reassures you otherwise, you may remain uncertain of his true feelings.

For both of these situations, you can employ the theory A or theory B strategy:

✔ Design an experiment to gather evidence to support the idea that your jealous feelings are based on your jealous *thoughts* (theory B), rather than on reality (theory A).

✔ Similarly, devise an experiment to test out whether your original theory A that, 'People don't like me', or alternative theory B that, 'I often think that people don't like me because I'm so worried about others' opinions of me that I end up seeing a lot of their behaviour as signs of dislike', best explains your experiences in social situations.

Here is an example of how Alex used the competing theories approach to get a better understanding of his physical sensations. Originally, Alex assumed his theory that uncomfortable bodily sensations signalled the onset of a heart attack was correct. By testing this in practice, Alex was able to consider that an alternative theory – uncomfortable bodily sensations are a by-product of anxiety – may be more accurate.

✔ **Describe the problem.** Alex suffers from panic attacks. He feels hot and his heart races, sometimes out of the blue. When he feels these sensations, he fears he's having a heart attack. Alex sits down to try to reduce the strain on his heart (an example of a safety behaviour). He goes out of his way to avoid situations in which he has experienced these symptoms.

✔ **Develop competing theories.** Alex devises two theories about his raised heart rate:

   • Theory A: 'My heart beating quickly means I'm vulnerable to having a heart attack.'

   • Theory B: 'My heart beating quickly is a consequence of anxiety.'

✓ **Execute an experiment.** Alex decides to deliberately confront situations that tend to trigger off his raised heart rate and to stay in them, *without sitting down*, until his anxiety reduces. He predicts that if theory B is correct, then his heart rate will reduce after his anxiety subsides and he can leave the situation without having come to any harm.

✓ **Examine the results.** Alex finds that his heart rate does indeed reduce when he stays with his anxiety. He's struck by what a difference this knowledge makes to his confidence, and that he's not going to come to any harm from his raised heart rate when he resists the urge to sit down. He concludes that he can reasonably have about 70 per cent confidence in his new theory that his raised heart rate is a benign consequence of anxiety.

You can't always prove conclusively that something isn't so. However, you can experiment to see whether certain emotional states, and mental or behavioural activities, have a beneficial or detrimental effect on the kinds of thoughts that play on your mind.

Conducting Surveys

You can use the clipboard and pen of the survey-taker in your endeavours to tackle your problems, by designing and conducting your own survey. Surveys can be especially helpful in terms of getting more information about what the average person thinks, feels or does.

We suggest you have more than one type of behavioural experiment in your repertoire. Surveys are very useful if you believe that your thoughts, physical sensations or behaviours are out of the ordinary. If you have upsetting, intrusive thoughts and images, or experience urges to say socially unacceptable things (symptoms typical of obsessive-compulsive disorder, OCD), feel pulled to the edge of high places (as in vertigo), or get a sense of impending doom when you're not in a familiar place (symptoms associated with agoraphobia), you may think that you're the only person who ever feels this way. Use surveys to see whether other people have the same thoughts and urges. You'll probably discover that other people experience the same things as you do. You may also discover that the symptoms you experience are actually less of a problem than the way you currently deal with them.

Henry suffers from OCD. His particular obsessional problem is related to frequent intrusive images of harm coming to his family. Henry's convinced that he's the only person in the world who gets such unpleasant and unwanted images entering his mind. Henry concludes that there's something very different and wrong about him because he has such images. He tests his theory about his abnormality by conducting the following survey:

- ✔ **Describe the problem.** Henry's convinced that his intrusive thoughts about his family being hurt in a car accident are unusual, and mean that he has to protect his family by changing the image in his mind to them being happy at a party.

- ✔ **Formulate a prediction.** Henry comes up with the prediction 'No one will admit to having the kind of thoughts I have'. He rates his strength of belief as 70 per cent.

- ✔ **Execute an experiment.** Henry tests his perception that his images are abnormal by devising a checklist of intrusive thoughts and asking his friends and family members to tick any that they experience.

- ✔ **Examine the results.** Henry's surprised at the variety of thoughts that people report entering their minds. Henry concludes that perhaps his images aren't so abnormal after all. He re-rates his conviction in his original prediction as 15 per cent. Henry also learns that other people simply discount their unpleasant images and don't worry that they mean anything sinister.

Charlotte worries a lot about her health and the possibility of developing a life-threatening illness. Sometimes, Charlotte notices funny sensations in her body and instantly interprets them as signs of an undiagnosed disease. Charlotte assumes that no one else gets unusual bodily sensations from time to time.

- ✔ **Describe the problem.** Charlotte worries that the bodily sensations she experiences are a sign of disease. She's unsatisfied by frequent reassurance from her family doctor and husband. Charlotte's problems are based partly on two ideas:

    - Physical sensations must have a clear medical explanation.

    - Any sensible person would seek an immediate explanation for the physical sensations she's currently experiencing.

- ✔ **Formulate a prediction.** Charlotte makes the following prediction: 'Most people won't have many physical sensations, and if they do they go immediately to see their doctor.' She rates her strength of conviction in this idea as 80 per cent.

- ✔ **Execute an experiment.** Charlotte devises a list of physical sensations, including many of those that she worries about herself. Her checklist requires people to tick whether they've ever experienced the sensation and to indicate how long they might leave it before consulting their doctor about such sensations. She asks ten people to fill out her questionnaire.

- ✔ **Examine the results.** Charlotte's shocked that many people reported experiencing some of the bodily sensations she described and stated that they'd leave going to their doctor for several days, or even weeks. Some people reported that they probably wouldn't bother seeing their doctor at all regarding some sensations. Charlotte concludes that perhaps she's worrying too much about her health, and plans to delay consulting her doctor when she next has unexplained physical sensations. Her strength of belief in her original prediction reduces to 30 per cent.

Making Observations

Observations can be an easier way of getting started with doing experiments to test out the validity of your thoughts. Observations usually involve collecting evidence related to a specific thought by watching other people in action.

You may assume, for example, that no one in their right mind would admit to not understanding an important point about a work procedure. If they did, they'd no doubt be ridiculed and promptly sacked on the basis of highlighting their incompetence.

Test this assumption by observing what other people actually *do*. Behave like a scientist and gather evidence of others admitting lack of understanding, asking for clarification or owning up to mistakes. Observe whether your prediction that they'll be ridiculed or fired is accurate. Making observations to gather evidence both for and against your assumptions is another way of behaving like a scientist.

Ensuring Successful Behavioural Experiments

To get the highest level of benefit when designing and carrying out behavioural experiments, keep the following in mind:

- Ensure that the type of experiment you choose is appropriate. Make your experiments challenging enough for you to gain a sense of accomplishment from conducting them. Equally, take care to devise experiments that won't overwhelm you.

- Have a clear plan about how, when and where (and with whom, if relevant) you plan to carry out your experiment.

- Be clear and specific about what you want to find out from your experiment – 'to see what happens' is too vague.

- Decide in advance how you'll know whether your prediction comes true. For example, what are the clues that someone's thinking critically of you?

- Plan what you'll do if your prediction comes true. For example, how do you respond assertively if someone is actually critical of you?

 ✔ Use the behavioural experiments record sheet in this chapter to plan and record your experiment.

 ✔ Consider what obstacles may interrupt your experiment and how you can overcome them.

 ✔ When evaluating the outcome of your experiment, check that you're not being biased (for example, discounting the positive or mind-reading, thinking errors we describe in Chapter 2) in the way you process your results.

 ✔ Consider whether you rely on any (including subtle) safety behaviours. Safety behaviours can affect the results of your experiment or determine how confident you feel about the outcome – for example, thinking that you avoided collapsing by concentrating hard, rather than discovering conclusively that your feelings of dizziness are a result of anxiety, not imminent fainting.

 ✔ Plan ways to consolidate what you discover from your experiment. For example, should you repeat the experiment, devise a new experiment, change your daily activities, or some other action?

Treating your negative and unhelpful thoughts with scepticism is a key to reducing their emotional impact. Experiments can help you to realise that many of your negative thoughts and predictions are not accurate in reality. Therefore, we suggest you take many of your negative thoughts with a pinch or more of salt.

Think about therapy as an experiment, rather than a lifelong commitment, especially at the beginning. By thinking in this manner, you can feel less under pressure and more able to approach therapy with an open mind.

Keeping Records of Your Experiments

All good scientists keep records of their experiments. If you do the same, you can look back over your results in order to:

 ✔ Draw conclusions.

 ✔ Decide what kind of experiment you may want to conduct next in order to gather more information.

 ✔ Remind yourself that many of your negative predictions won't come true.

To help you keep records of your experiments, photocopy Figure 4-1, and use it as often as you like, following the instructions in the figure.

Behavioural Experiment Record Sheet

Date: _____

Prediction or Theory	Experiment	Results	Conclusion/Comments
Outline the thought, belief, or theory you are testing. Rate your strength of conviction 1–100%	Plan what you will do (including where, when, how, with whom), being as specific as you can.	Record what actually happened including relevant thoughts, emotions, physical sensations, and other people's behaviour.	Write down what have you learned about your prediction or theory in light of the results. Re-rate your strength of conviction 0–100%.

Figure 4-1:
Photocopy
and fill in
your own
Behavioural
Experiment
Record
Sheet.

Guidance on carrying out a behavioural experiment: 1. Be clear and specific about the negative and alternative predictions you are testing. Rate your strength of conviction in the prediction or theory you are testing or evaluating. 2 Decide upon your experiment, and be as clear as you can be as to how you will measure your results. 3. Record the results of your experiment, emphasizing clear, observable outcomes. 4. Evaluate the results of your experiment. Write down what these results suggest in terms of the accuracy of your predictions, or which theory the evidence supports. 5. Consider whether a further behavioural experiment might be helpful.

Try to have a no-lose perspective on your experiments. If you do one experiment and it goes well, then great! However, if you plan an experiment but ultimately avoid doing it, you can at least identify the thoughts that blocked you. Even if your negative predictions turn out to be accurate, you have an opportunity to see how well you cope – and very probably that it isn't the end of the world – and then decide whether you need to take further action. The point is, you can always gather information that you can make into a useful experience.

Don't take our word for it . . .

This book's full of suggestions on how to reduce and overcome emotional problems. If you're sceptical about whether CBT can work for you, you're in very good company. However, loads of scientific evidence shows that CBT is more effective than all other psychotherapies.

So, CBT may well work for you, but how can you tell? The answer is to consider applying a specific tool or technique for a period of time as an experiment to see how the technique works for you. Depending on the outcome, you can then choose to do more, modify your approach or try something different.

Chapter 5

Pay Attention! Refocusing and Retraining Your Awareness

*T*raditionally, CBT has tended to concentrate many of its techniques on helping people change the *content* of their thinking – from a negative to a more realistic thought, for example. However, modern CBT has begun to tackle another area of human psychology – how we focus our attention.

This chapter does not discuss *what* you think, but does discuss *how* you manage your thoughts and attention. We introduce *task concentration training* and *mindfulness*, two techniques for managing problematic thoughts and exerting some power over your attention. This chapter has two main messages:

✔ For the most part, your thoughts, no matter how distressing and negative, are not the real problem. Rather, the importance or meaning you attach to those thoughts is what causes you the problem. If you view the notion, 'I'm a hopeless case', as a thought rather than a fact, you can greatly lessen its impact.

✔ When you have an emotional problem, your mind tends to attach unhelpful meanings to aspects of yourself, the world around you and other people. You can also tend to *overfocus* on particular aspects of these unhelpful meanings. Fortunately, you can develop the ability to steer your attention towards, and away from, any features of your experience you choose, which can help improve your mood and reduce anxiety.

Training in Task Concentration

Becoming adept at redirecting your attention away from yourself (this includes your bodily sensations, thoughts and mental images), in certain situations, is the essence of *task concentration*. Rather than thinking about yourself, you focus your attention towards your external environment and what you're doing.

Task concentration involves paying less attention to what's going on inside of you and more attention to what's happening outside of you.

Task concentration can be particularly useful in situations that trigger anxiety in you. Task concentration can help you to counterbalance your tendency to focus on threats and on yourself when you feel anxious.

As you begin to practise task concentration, break down the process into two rehearsal arenas – just as when learning to drive you begin on quiet roads and eventually advance on to busier roads.

The two rehearsal arenas are as follows:

✓ **Non-threatening situations:** Here, you typically experience little or no anxiety. For example, if you have social phobia, you may feel a little anxious walking through a park, travelling on a very quiet train or socialising with family members and close friends.

✓ **More challenging situations:** Here, you may experience moderate to severe anxiety. More challenging situations may include shopping in a busy grocery store, travelling on a train during rush hour or attending a party with many guests whom you may not know.

Typically, you gradually progress from non-threatening situations to more challenging situations as you practise and develop greater skill.

After you've practised redirecting your attention in situations you regard as relatively non-threatening, you can move on to using the techniques in increasingly challenging situations.

Choosing to concentrate

The point of task-concentration exercises is not to lessen your overall concentration, but to concentrate harder on different aspects of the external environment. Some tasks require you to focus your attention on certain behaviours – such as listening to what another person is saying during a conversation, or attempting to balance a tray of drinks as you walk through a crowded room.

In other situations, you may feel anxious but you don't have a specific task to attend to. In such a situation, for example while sitting in a crowded waiting room, you can direct your attention to your surroundings, noticing other people, the features of the room, sounds and smells.

With practice, you can be both task- and environment-focused rather than self-focused, even in situations that you regard as highly threatening.

The following exercises aim to increase your understanding of how paying attention to sensations and images limits your ability to process information around you. The exercises will also help you realise that you can attend to external task-related behaviours. In other words, you can master *choosing* what you pay attention to in situations when your anxiety is triggered.

Intentionally directing your attention away from yourself does not mean distracting yourself from your sensations or suppressing your thoughts. Sometimes, people try to use thought suppression as a means of alleviating uncomfortable sensations and anxiety. However, suppression usually works only briefly, if at all.

Concentration exercise: Listening

For this exercise, sit back-to-back with someone else, perhaps a friend or your therapist. Ask the person to tell you a story for about two minutes. Concentrate on the story. Then, summarise the story: note how much of your attention you direct towards the task of listening to the other person, towards yourself and towards your environment – try using percentages to do this. Your partner can give you feedback on your summary to give you some idea how you did.

Now do the exercise again, but this time round sit face-to-face with the storyteller and make eye contact. Ask the person to tell you a story, but on this occasion consciously distract yourself by focusing on your thoughts and sensations, and then redirect your attention towards the storyteller. Summarise the story, and note (using percentages again) how you divide your attention between yourself, listening to the other person and your environment.

Repeat the storytelling activities, sitting back-to-back and then face-to-face, several times until you become readily able to redirect your attention to the task of listening after deliberate distraction through self-focusing. Doing so helps you to develop your ability to control where you focus your attention.

Concentration exercise: Speaking

Follow the same steps for this speaking exercise as you do for the listening exercise, as we describe in the preceding section. Starting with your back to the back of the other person, tell a two-minute story, focusing your attention on making your story clear to the listener.

Next, position yourself face-to-face with the listener, making eye contact. Deliberately distract yourself from the task of storytelling by focusing on your feelings, sensations and thoughts. Then, refocus your attention towards what you're saying and towards the listener, being aware of her reactions and whether she understands you.

Again, using percentages, monitor how you divide your attention among yourself, the task and your environment.

Concentration exercise: Graded practice

For this exercise, prepare two lists of situations. For your first list, write down five or so examples of situations you find non-threatening. As you write down the situations, practise distracting yourself by focusing on your internal sensations and thoughts. Now read back through the list of these situations, but this time try refocusing your attention outwards. For your second list, write down ten or so examples of situations you find threatening. Arrange the situations in a hierarchy, starting from the least anxiety-provoking and graduating up to the most anxiety-provoking. Now you can work through your hierarchy by deliberately entering the situations while practising task concentration until you reach the top of your list. This means you can start to practise mastering your anxiety in real-life situations.

Concentration exercise: Taking a walk

For this exercise, walk through a park, paying attention to what you hear, see, feel and smell. Focus your attention for a few minutes on different aspects of the world around you. First, focus your attention mainly to what you can hear. Then shift your attention to focus on smells, and then on to the feel of your feet on the ground, and so on. You can move your attention around to different sensations, which can help you tune your attention onto the outside world. Switching between your five senses can also help you realise that you have the ability to direct your attention as you choose.

After you've practised directing most of your attention to individual senses, try to integrate your attention to include all aspects of the park. Try to do this for at least 20 minutes. Really let yourself drink in the detail of your surroundings. Discover what hooks your attention. You may be drawn to water or have a keen interest in birds, plants, or perhaps even woodland smells. Notice how you feel much more relaxed and less self-conscious as you train your attention on the world around you.

Tuning in to tasks and the world around you

If you're suffering from anxiety, you're probably self-focused in social situations and fail to notice the rest of the world. On top of feeling unnecessarily uncomfortable, your self-focus means that you're likely to miss out on a lot of interesting stuff. Luckily, you can change your attention bias and overcome much of your anxiety.

You can also use re-training your attention onto the outside world to help interrupt yourself from engaging with the stream of negative thoughts that accompanies depression, which will help you to lift your mood.

Here's an example of how you can use task-concentration techniques to overcome anxiety, specifically anxiety, worry and panic episodes (see Chapter 9 for more on these).

Harold was particularly worried that people would notice that he blushed and sweated in social situations. He believed that people would think he was odd or a nervous wreck. Harold constantly self-monitored for blushing and sweating and tried very hard to mask these symptoms of his anxiety.

Here's Harold's list of situations, with each one becoming gradually more challenging:

1. Having dinner with his parents and brother.
2. Socialising with his three closest mates at a local pub.
3. Using public transport during quiet periods.
4. Eating lunch with colleagues at work.
5. Going to the cinema with a friend.
6. Walking alone down a busy street.
7. Socialising with strangers at a party.
8. Going to the grocery shop alone.
9. Going to the gym alone.
10. Initiating conversation with strangers.
11. Using public transport during busy periods.
12. Eating alone in a restaurant.
13. Going for an interview.
14. Offering his opinion during work meetings.
15. Giving a presentation at work.

Harold used the principles of task concentration to increase his ability to focus deliberately on chosen external factors in non-threatening situations. When Harold was at the pub with his mates, he focused his attention on what his friends were saying, other people in the pub, the music and the general surroundings. Harold also deliberately distracted himself by focusing on whether he was blushing and sweating, and then he refocused his attention again.

Harold then used the same techniques in more-threatening situations. In the grocery store, Harold found that the more he focused on his blushing and sweating, the more anxious he felt and the less able he was to pack up his shopping. When he paid attention to the task of packing his groceries, made eye contact with the cashier and even made a bit of small talk, Harold's anxiety symptoms reduced, and he became more aware of what he was doing and what was going on around him.

Harold worked diligently through his hierarchy of feared situations and now feels much more confident and relaxed in social situations.

Imagine that you're going to be called on by the police to act as an eyewitness. For a few minutes, try to take in as much information as you can about the environment and the people around you. Notice how much more detail you can recount when you choose to focus outwards, compared with when you're concentrating on your thoughts and physical sensations.

Tackling the task concentration record sheet

You can keep an account of your task-concentration practice, and note the results, by using the task-concentration record sheet in Table 5-1. The brief instructions at the top of the sheet are there to remind you how to do your concentration exercises. You can find a blank copy of the form in Appendix B.

Table 5-1	Harold's Task-Concentration Record Sheet			
Who were you with? *Where were you?* *What were you doing?*	*Record your focus of attention. Note what you focused on most.* *1. Self %* *2. Task %* *3. Environment and other people %* *(Total = 100%)*	*Use task concentration to direct your attention outwards. Remember to focus on your task or environment. Note what you did.*	*Record how you felt.*	*Record anything you learned from the exercise. Note how the situation turned out, changes in your anxiety level, and your ability to complete the task.*
Eating by myself in restaurant. *Lunchtime.*	*1. Self 40%* *2. Task 35%* *3. Environment and other people 25%*	*Took my time to eat rather than rushing.* *Made eye contact with waiter.* *Tried to eat my meal mindfully and enjoy it.* *Observed other diners.* *Kept my head up and didn't hide away at a corner table.*	*Anxious.* *Scared at first.*	*My anxiety lessened as I ate.* *No one seemed to think I was odd for eating alone.* *I felt less awkward than I expected to feel.* *It took a lot of effort at first to keep my attention on the task of eating but it got easier.*

Becoming More Mindful

Mindfulness meditation, commonly associated with Zen Buddhism, has become popular in the past few years as a technique for dealing with depression, and managing stress and chronic pain. Evidence shows that mindfulness meditation can help reduce the chance of problems such as depression returning, and adds another weapon to your armoury against emotional problems.

Being present in the moment

Mindfulness is the art of being present in the moment, without passing judgement about your experience. The mindfulness process is so simple – and yet so challenging. Keep your attention focused on the moment that you're experiencing *right now*. Suspend your judgement about what you're feeling, thinking and absorbing through your senses. Simply observe what's going on around you, in your mind and in your body without doing anything. Just allow yourself to be aware of what's happening.

Mindfulness literature talks about the way your mind almost mechanically forms judgements about each of your experiences, labelling them as good, bad or neutral depending on how you value them. Things that generate good and bad feelings within you get most of your attention, but you may ignore neutral things or deem them to be boring. Mindfulness meditation encourages awareness of the present moment with an uncultured mind, observing even the seemingly mundane without judgement. The whole experience is a bit like looking at the world for the first time.

When you meet someone you know, try to see her through fresh eyes. Suspend your prior knowledge, thoughts, experiences and opinions. You can try this with acquaintances or people you know very well, such as family members and close friends.

Try mindfulness exercises when you're in the countryside or walking down the street. Whether the surroundings are familiar to you or not, try to see the details of the world around you through fresh eyes.

Letting your thoughts pass by

You can develop your mindfulness skills and use them to help you deal with unpleasant thoughts or physical symptoms. If you have social anxiety, for example, you can develop the ability to *focus away* from your anxious thoughts.

Watching the train pass by

Imagine a train passing through a station. The train represents your thoughts and sensations (your 'train of thought'). Each carriage may represent one or more specific thoughts or feelings. Visualise yourself watching the train pass by without hopping into any carriage. Accept your fears about what other people may be thinking about you without trying to suppress them or engaging with them. Simply watch them pass by like a train through a station.

Standing by the side of the road

Another version of the exercise is to imagine that you're standing on the side of a reasonably busy road. Each passing vehicle represents your thoughts and sensations. Just watch the cars go by. Observe and accept them passing. Don't try to hitch-hike, redirect the flow of traffic or influence the cars in any way.

Discerning when not to listen to yourself

One of the real benefits of understanding the way that your emotions influence the way you think, is to know when what you're thinking isn't likely to be helpful or very realistic. Being mindful means learning to experience your thoughts without passing judgement as to whether they're true or not.

Given that many of the negative thoughts you experience when you're emotionally distressed are distorted and unhelpful, you're much better off letting some thoughts pass you by, recognising them as *symptoms* or *output* of a given emotional state or psychological problem. Chapter 6 contains a table which covers the *cognitive consequences* of specific emotions, giving you an idea of the types of thoughts that can occur as a consequence of how you're feeling.

Becoming more familiar with the thoughts that tend to pop into your head when you feel down, anxious or guilty makes it easier for you to recognise them as thoughts and let them come and go, rather than treating them as facts. This familiarity gives you another skill to help manage your negative thoughts in addition to challenging or testing them out in reality.

Incorporating mindful daily tasks

Becoming more mindful about little everyday tasks can help you to strengthen your attention muscles. Essentially, everything you do throughout the day can be done with increased awareness. For example, think about the following:

✔ Washing-up mindfully can help you experience the process more fully. Notice the smell of the washing-up liquid, the temperature of the water and the movement of your hands.

✔ Eating mindfully can give you a more enjoyable eating experience. Slow down the speed at which you eat, and pay attention to the texture of the food, the subtlety of the flavours and the appearance of the dish.

Tolerating upsetting images and unpleasant ideas

Certain psychological problems such as depression and anxiety disorders like OCD are frequently accompanied by unwelcome, unsettling images or thoughts. Depressed people can have ideas about harming themselves or even get strong visual images of doing so – even when they've no real intention of taking suicidal action. These thoughts are understandably very distressing and people may worry that they indicate a real risk. Happily this is not often the case; most of these thoughts are merely an unpleasant bi-product of depressed mood. It's easy to misinterpret these images and thoughts as dangerous or portentous but learning to see them as what they really are – just unpleasant symptoms of depression or anxiety – can render them less frightening.

Not all suicidal ideas are to be ignored. If you find yourself becoming increasingly preoccupied with ideas of harming yourself or ending your life, seek help immediately. This advice is especially important if you've begun to develop a plan and find your suicidal thoughts comforting. Talk to your doctor, a family member or friend, or take yourself to the psychiatric emergency unit at your nearest hospital. Chapter 12 deals with depression. You can also read Chapter 21 for valuable information about seeking professional help.

People with OCD (more on this disorder in Chapter 13) often experience intrusive thoughts and images. The content of these thoughts and mental pictures can vary widely but they're frequently about harming people you love or acting in a way that dramatically violates your moral code. Other emotional or anxiety problems can also give rise to a host of nightmarish ideas and images. Some classics may include:

✔ Losing control of your bladder or bowels in public

✔ Blurting out something really offensive

✔ Behaving in a sexually inappropriate manner

✔ Jumping on to a train track

✔ Driving your car recklessly

✔ Harming an animal

✔ Harming yourself or another person (a child or loved one)

✔ Having a panic attack in a public place

✔ Making a bad decision which results in irreparable consequences

✔ Being harshly rejected or humiliated

✔ Experiencing thoughts and images about death or violence (to self and others)

When you have such unsolicited ghoulish mental activity, it's very understandable that you want to get rid of it. Typically however, the harder you try to rid yourself of such thoughts and images, the more they take hold. This is because your attempts to eliminate, avoid or neutralise unwelcome thoughts are driven by the fundamental rule:

> 'I must not have such thoughts; they're unacceptable and mean something dreadful.'

When you put effort into preventing or eliminating a certain thought, you're inadvertently focusing more attention on it. If you regard certain kinds of mental activity as taboo, then you increase your fears of it occurring. Paradoxically, you may end up increasing the frequency of intrusive images and thoughts plus elevating your disturbance in response to them. Everyone has intrusive thoughts and images from time to time. Even if you're not in any form of psychological or emotional distress, you're not immune to the occasional gruesome mental image. People without anxiety or depression, however, are more readily able to dismiss the thought or image as unpleasant (or even shocking) but of ultimately no real importance. You can begin to tolerate unpleasant thoughts by adopting the following attitude:

> 'I don't like these thoughts but they aren't abnormal or important. They don't mean something about me.'

Knowing a thought is just a thought

Because the content of these type of thoughts is so abhorrent to you, they can *feel terribly* important. You might assume that they mean you're more likely to do some horrendous deed or that something terrible is now going to happen to a loved one because you thought them. More accurately, these type of thoughts are merely a reflection of what you hold dear and value. Rather cruelly, you tend to get afflicted by the kind of thoughts that run counter to your true character and value system.

You can try to think of intrusive thoughts and images as 'waking nightmares'. When you have a nasty dream you probably shake it off pretty quickly because you just think 'Yuck; oh well, it was just a bad dream'. You probably don't usually give the content of your dreams much credence. Do the same with unpleasant images that come when you're awake. Just because you're awake doesn't make them any more valid or important.

Even though some thoughts and images are uncomfortable – you can tolerate them. As you increase your tolerance for unwelcome mental images, you simultaneously reduce your fear of them. Disliking specific kinds of thought is okay but remind yourself that thoughts are *all* they are.

Letting unwelcome thoughts extinguish by themselves

Worrying and upsetting thoughts and images won't last forever. If you do nothing, they'll eventually fade away. As we've already mentioned, trying to control unwelcome thoughts rarely works for long. The key is treating these thoughts as though they're of no importance. When something is of little or no importance, you tend to ignore it or give it little attention. Instead of fighting against these trivial (though tormenting) thoughts, do nothing. Take off the boxing gloves and just let your mind move onto other more neutral images and thoughts naturally. Doing so sounds pretty simple and straight-forward but just letting go can be hard to master. Your feelings of anxiety, disgust or horror about intrusive thoughts can compel you to action. Resist the pull of your feelings.

Try these tips:

- ✔ Let unwelcome thoughts play out in the background as though they were just noise. Think of these thoughts like static on the radio or street noise outside your office window. You can filter them out and refocus your attention onto a task.

- ✔ Get your mind busy doing something else more interesting or compel-ling. Pick up the phone and make some important calls, do a crossword puzzle or go for a walk.

- ✔ Raise your heart rate. Going for a run, playing a sport or vacuuming vig-orously can help relieve anxiety and clear your mind.

As you pay less attention to unwelcome thoughts, you'll probably find that your adverse feelings about them become less intense. Eventually just allow-ing your thoughts to extinguish will become much easier because you'll have reduced their emotional impact.

It may be tempting to ask for reassurance from friends (or even your CBT therapist) that your thoughts are not dangerous. This can be a slippery slope since you unwittingly reinforce fear and intolerance of unwanted thought con-tent. Instead of repeatedly seeking reassurance, remember to treat thoughts of this ilk as unimportant. You probably don't dwell on or talk incessantly about unimportant things – so practise the same policy in this instance.

Part II
Charting the Course: Defining Problems and Setting Goals

The 5th Wave   By Rich Tennant

"I've tried Ayurveda, meditation, and aromatherapy but nothing seems to work. I'm still feeling nauseous and disoriented all day."

In this part . . .

More than a feeling . . . we help you to clearly name your emotions and also help you to work out the difference between helpful and unhelpful emotions. In this part you discover what you want to change in your life, and realise how some of your current solutions to problems may not be benefiting you in the long run. We also offer alternatives to current solutions that may not actually be working for you!

Chapter 6

Exploring Emotions

*T*his chapter aims to introduce you to some of the key differences between the unhealthy negative emotions you may experience and their healthy counterparts. The information we offer also helps you to discover ways to identify whether you're experiencing a healthy or an unhealthy emotional response.

You may be wondering why we're focusing on *negative* emotions in this chapter and neglecting positive feelings such as happiness. You may be asking: 'What *is* it with these two? They're so bleak!' The reason for dealing with the negative is that few people pitch up for therapy because they're having problems with positive emotions. Not a lot of people come to us looking for a way to overcome their relentless feelings of contentment. The emotions that give people trouble typically include guilt, anger, depression and shame.

Although feeling bad when bad things happen is natural, you don't need to make things worse for yourself by giving yourself unhealthy negative emotions. Healthy negative emotions are generally less profoundly uncomfortable and less problematic than their unhealthy counterparts. For example, feeling intensely *sad* (a healthy negative emotion) is less uncomfortable than feeling intensely *depressed* (an unhealthy emotion). Likewise, feeling intense sadness can prompt you to do things to improve your situation, but depression's more likely to lead to your inaction and resignation.

Fortunately, you can *think* what to *feel*, to a greater or lesser extent, which can reduce your emotional discomfort. By choosing to think in healthy and helpful ways, you're more likely to experience healthy emotions.

Naming Your Feelings

If someone asks you how you feel, you may have difficulty describing exactly which emotion you're feeling. You may not be sure what name to give to your internal experience, or perhaps you're feeling more than one emotion at the same time.

Don't get caught up on words! When you start to make a distinction between healthy and unhealthy feelings, what you call them isn't terribly important. The main point is to be able to analyse your thoughts and behaviours, and to take notice of where your attention is focused (CBT refers to this as *attention focus*). These three areas are ultimately your most reliable guides as to which type of emotion you're experiencing.

For the sake of clarity, therapists can often encourage people to use different words for unhealthy and healthy alternatives to common feelings. For example, you could use the word 'anger' to describe an unhealthy emotion and 'annoyance' to describe the healthy counterpart.

Some people find it simpler to choose a descriptive word for their emotion and to add the term 'healthy' or 'unhealthy' to that word. Whatever way you prefer to describe your emotions is okay – the important bit's understanding the category each emotion falls into. Different people have different ways of describing things. Think about how you'd describe an oil painting compared with the way a friend or art critic may talk about it. Similarly, people describe emotional states in diverse ways. You, a friend and a psychotherapist (someone highly skilled in discussing emotions) may all use very different words to describe the same type of feeling.

If you're not used to talking about the way you feel, you may have a hard time finding the words to reflect your feelings.

The following is a reference list of common human emotions and their synonyms, which you can use to increase your vocabulary of *emotive* (relating to emotions) terminology. This list is not broken down into healthy and unhealthy emotions.

- ✔ **Angry:** aggressive, annoyed, bad-tempered, complaining, confounded, cross, displeased, enraged, fractious, fuming, furious, hostile, ill-tempered, incensed, irritated, livid, miffed, peevish, prickly, resentful, testy, touchy, truculent.

- ✔ **Anxious:** agitated, apprehensive, bothered, concerned, edgy, fearful, fretful, frightened, jumpy, nervous, nervy, panicky, restless, tense, troubled, uneasy, vexed, worried.

- **Ashamed:** belittled, debased, defamed, degraded, discredited, disgraced, dishonoured, humiliated, mortified, scorned, smeared, sullied, tarnished, undignified, vilified.

- **Disappointed:** crestfallen, deflated, dejected, discouraged, disenchanted, disheartened, disillusioned, dismayed, gutted, let down, thwarted.

- **Embarrassed:** awkward, diminished, discomfited, humiliated, ill at ease, insecure, self-conscious, small, timid, uncomfortable, unconfident, unsure of oneself.

- **Envious:** green with envy, malevolent, malicious, Schadenfreude, sour, spiteful.

- **Guilty:** answerable, at fault, blameworthy, condemned, culpable, deplorable, indefensible, inexcusable, in the wrong, liable, reprehensible, unforgivable, unpardonable.

- **Hurt:** aggrieved, broken-hearted, cut to the quick, cut up, damaged, devastated, gutted, hard done by, harmed, horrified, injured, marred, offended, pained, wounded.

- **Jealous:** bitter and twisted, distrustful, doubtful, green-eyed, sceptical, suspicious, wary.

- **LOVE:** (we threw this one in just to lighten the mood) admiring, adoring, affectionate, besotted, blissful, crazed, devoted, enamoured, esteemed, fond, head over heels, infatuated, keen, loved-up, love-struck, mad about, on cloud nine, smitten, struck by cupid's arrow, worshipping.

- **Sad:** bereft, blue, depressed, distraught, distressed, down, downcast, downhearted, grief-stricken, heartsick, inconsolable, melancholic, mournful, shattered, sorrowful, tearful.

Thinking What to Feel

One benefit of understanding the difference between healthy and unhealthy emotions is that you give yourself a better chance to check out what you're thinking. If you recognise that you're experiencing an unhealthy emotion, you're then in a position to challenge any faulty thinking that may be leading to your unhealthy emotional response. Disputing and correcting thinking errors can help you to experience a healthy, negative emotion instead of an unhealthy feeling (see Chapter 2 for more on thinking errors and how to correct them).

A common axiom is 'I think therefore I am'; a CBT version is 'I think; therefore I feel.'

Feelings aren't as one-dimensional as they may seem. How you feel is more than just the emotion itself, because feelings don't just come out of thin air – they have a context. When you begin to make a distinction between your healthy and unhealthy emotions, look at the *interaction* between your thinking, your actions, your attention focus, your memory, your themes or triggers, and the way you feel. Take a look at Table 6-1 in the section that covers comparing healthy and unhealthy emotions further on in this chapter, which gives a clear breakdown of the characteristics of healthy and unhealthy emotions.

Understanding the Anatomy of Emotions

Figure 6-1 shows the complex processes involved in human emotion. Whenever you feel a certain emotion, a whole system is activated. This system includes the thoughts and images that enter your mind, the memories you access, the aspects of yourself or the surrounding world that you focus on, the bodily and mental sensations you experience, physical changes such as appetite, your behaviour, and the things you *feel like* doing.

As the diagram shows, these different dimensions interact in complex ways. For example, training your attention on possible threats is likely to increase the chance of anxious thoughts popping into your mind, and vice versa. Not sleeping well may increase the chances of you being inactive; continued inactivity can further disrupt your usual sleeping pattern. The advantage of understanding this system of emotion as presented in Figure 6-1 is that it gives you plenty of opportunity to make changes. Changing even one aspect of the system can make changing other parts easier.

An example of change is becoming more active if you've been inactive, which may alleviate your feelings of depression and make it easier for you to challenge your depressive, pessimistic thinking. Being prescribed antidepressant medication, which works by affecting brain chemistry, can take the edge off your depression. Use of antidepressants can make it easier for you to train your attention *away* from your negative thoughts and uncomfortable symptoms and *towards* possible solutions to some of your practical problems. (See Chapter 12 for more about overcoming depression.)

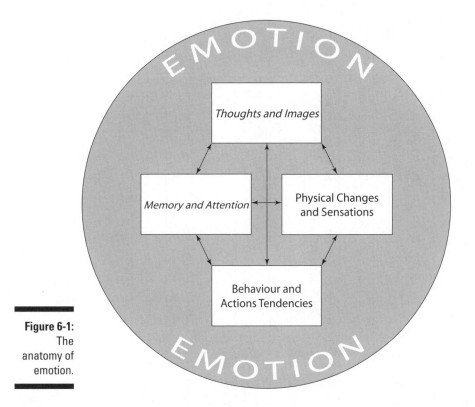

Figure 6-1:
The
anatomy of
emotion.

Comparing Healthy and Unhealthy Emotions

Deciphering between healthy and unhealthy versions of negative emotions can be challenging, especially when the process is new to you. Think of Table 6-1 as your emotional ready reckoner for the characteristics of both healthy and unhealthy emotions. Everything you may need to identify the emotion you're experiencing is in this table. Plus, if you do identify that an emotion you're experiencing is unhealthy, you can implement the thoughts, attention focuses and behaviours of the healthy version to aid you in feeling better.

Table 6-1 **Healthy and Unhealthy Emotions**

Emotion	Theme	Thoughts	Attention Focus	Behaviour/Action Tendencies
Anxiety (unhealthy)	Threat or danger	Has rigid or extreme attitudes	Monitors threat or danger excessively	Withdraws physically and mentally from threats
		Overestimates degree of threat		Uses superstitious behaviour to ward off threat
		Underestimates ability to cope with threat		Numbs anxiety with drugs or alcohol
		Increases threat-related thoughts		Seeks reassurance
Concern (healthy)	Threat or danger	Has flexible and preferential attitudes	Doesn't see threat where no threat exists	Faces up to threat
		Views threat realistically		Deals with threat constructively
		Realistically assesses ability to cope with threat		Doesn't seek unneeded reassurance
		Doesn't increase threat-related thoughts		
Depression (unhealthy)	Loss or failure	Has rigid and extreme attitudes	Dwells on past loss/failure	Withdraws from others
	Ruminates on unsolvable problems	Sees only negative aspects of loss/failure		
		Neglects self and living environment		
		Feels helpless	Focuses on personal flaws and failings	Attempts to end feelings of depression in self-destructive ways
		Thinks future is bleak and hopeless	Focuses on negative world events	

Emotion	Theme	Thoughts	Attention Focus	Behaviour/Action Tendencies
Sadness (healthy)	Loss or failure	Has flexible and preferential attitudes	Doesn't dwell on past loss/failure	Talks to significant others about feelings about loss/failure
		Sees both negative and positive aspects of loss/failure	Focuses on problems that one can change	Continues to care for self and living environment
		Is able to help self	Focuses on personal strengths and skills	Avoids self-destructive behaviours
		Is able to think about future with hope	Balances focus between positive and negative world events	
Anger (unhealthy)	Personal rule is broken or self-esteem is threatened	Has rigid and extreme attitudes	Looks for evidence of malicious intent in other person	Seeks revenge
		Assumes other person acted deliberately	Looks for evidence of offensive behaviour being repeated by other people	Attacks other person physically or verbally
		Thinks of self as right and other person as wrong		Takes anger out on innocent person, animal or object
		Cannot see other person's point of view		Withdraws aggressively/sulks
				Recruits allies against other person
Annoyance (healthy)	Personal rule broken or self-esteem is threatened	Has flexible and preferential attitudes	Looks for evidence that other person may not have malicious intent	Doesn't seek revenge

(continued)

Table 6-1 (continued)

Emotion	Theme	Thoughts	Attention Focus	Behaviour/Action Tendencies
		Considers other person may not have acted deliberately	Doesn't see further offence where it may not exist	Asserts self without physical/verbal violence
		Considers that both self and other person may be right to some degree		Doesn't take out feelings on innocent parties
		Is able to see other person's point of view		Remains in situation, striving for resolution (doesn't sulk)
				Requests other person to change their offensive behaviour
Shame (unhealthy)	Shameful personal information has been publicly revealed by self or others	Overestimates shamefulness of information revealed	Sees disapproval from others where it doesn't exist	Hides from others to avoid disapproval
		Overestimates degree of disapproval from others		May attack others who have shamed self, in attempt to save face
		Overestimates how long disapproval will last		May try to repair self-esteem in self-destructive ways
				Ignores attempts from social group to return to normal
Regret (healthy)	Shameful personal information has been publicly revealed by self or others	Is compassionately self-accepting about information revealed	Focuses on evidence that self is accepted by social group despite information revealed	Continues to participate in social interaction

Emotion	Theme	Thoughts	Attention Focus	Behaviour/Action Tendencies
		Is realistic about degree of disapproval from others		Responds to attempts from social group to return to normal
		Is realistic about how long disapproval will last		
Hurt (unhealthy)	Other person treats one badly (self is undeserving)	Has rigid and extreme attitudes	Looks for evidence of other person not caring or being indifferent	Stops communicating with other person/sulks
		Overestimates unfairness of other's behaviour		Punishes other person through silence or criticism, without stating what one feels hurt about
		Thinks other person doesn't care		
		Thinks of self as alone and uncared for		
		Dwells on past hurts		
		Thinks other person must make first move towards resolution		
Disappointment (healthy)	Other person treats one badly (self is undeserving)	Has flexible and preferential attitudes	Focuses on evidence that other person does care and isn't indifferent	Communicates with other person about feelings
		Is realistic about degree of unfairness of other's behaviour		Tries to influence other person to act in fairer manner
		Thinks other person acted badly but doesn't think that they don't care		

(continued)

Table 6-1 (continued)

Emotion	Theme	Thoughts	Attention Focus	Behaviour/Action Tendencies
		Doesn't think of self as alone or uncared for		
		Doesn't dwell on past hurts		
		Doesn't wait for other person to make first move		
Jealousy (unhealthy)	Threat to relationship with partner from another person	Has rigid and extreme attitudes	Looks for sexual/romantic connotations in partner's conversations with others	Seeks constant reassurance that partner is faithful and loving
		Overestimates threat to the relationship	Creates visual images of partner being unfaithful	Monitors and/or restricts partner's movements and actions
		Thinks partner is always on verge of leaving for another	Looks for evidence that partner is having an affair	Retaliates for partner's imagined infidelity
		Thinks partner will leave for another person who they have admitted to finding attractive		Sets tests/traps for partner
				Sulks
Concern for relationship (healthy)	Threat to relationship with partner from another person	Has flexible and preferential attitudes	Doesn't look for evidence that partner is having an affair	Allows partner to express love without needing excessive reassurance
		Is realistic about degree of threat to relationship	Doesn't create images of partner being unfaithful	Allows partner freedom without monitoring them

Emotion	Theme	Thoughts	Attention Focus	Behaviour/Action Tendencies
		Thinks partner finding others attractive is normal	Views partner's conversation with others as normal	Allows partner to express natural interest in opposite sex without imagining infidelity
Unhealthy envy (unhealthy)	Another person possesses something desirable (self lacks desired thing)	Has rigid and extreme attitudes	Focuses on how to get the desired possession without regard for any consequences	Criticises the person with desired possession
		Thinks about the desired possession in a negative way to try to reduce its desirability	Focuses on how to deprive other person of the desired possession	Criticises the desired possession
		Pretends to self that one is happy without desired possession even though this is untrue		Attempts to steal/destroy the desired possession in order to deprive others
Guilt (unhealthy)	Broken moral code (by failing to do something or by committing a sin), hurting or offending significant other	Has rigid and extreme attitudes	Looks for evidence of others blaming one for the sin	Desires to escape from guilt feelings in self-defeating ways
		Thinks one has definitely sinned	Looks for evidence of punishment or retribution	Begs for forgiveness

(continued)

Table 6-1 *(continued)*

Emotion	Theme	Thoughts	Attention Focus	Behaviour/Action Tendencies
		Thinks that one deserves punishment		Promises that a sin will never be committed again
		Ignores mitigating factors		Punishes self either physically or through deprivation
		Ignores other people's potential responsibility for sin		Attempts to disclaim any legitimate responsibility for the wrongdoing as an attempt to alleviate feelings of guilt
Remorse (healthy)	Broken moral code (by failing to do something or by committing a sin), hurting or offending significant other	Has flexible and preferential attitudes	Doesn't look for evidence of others blaming oneself for the sin	Faces up to healthy pain that comes with knowing that one has sinned
		Considers actions in context and with understanding before making a judgement about whether one has sinned	Doesn't look for evidence of punishment or retribution	Asks for forgiveness
		Takes appropriate level of responsibility for the sin		Atones for the sin by taking a penalty and/or making appropriate amends
		Considers mitigating factors		Doesn't have tendency to be defensive or to make excuses for the poor behaviour
		Doesn't believe that punishment is deserved and/or imminent		

Themes refer to situational aspects linked to emotion. Themes are the same for both healthy and unhealthy negative emotions. For example, when you feel *guilty* (an unhealthy negative emotion), the theme for that emotion is that you've 'sinned' by either *doing* or *failing to do* something. Another way of saying that you're guilty is that you've transgressed or failed to live up to your moral code. *Remorse*, the healthy alternative to guilt, results from the same theme as guilt. However, your thoughts, behaviours and focus of attention are different when you are remorseful and when you are guilty.

Themes can be useful in helping you to put your finger on the nature of the emotion you're experiencing. However, themes are not enough to help you decide whether your emotion is a healthy or unhealthy one. Consider the following situation:

> Imagine that you have an elderly aunt who needs your help to continue living independently. You usually visit her at the weekend and do jobs that she's too frail to do for herself, like changing light bulbs and cleaning windows. Last weekend you went skiing with friends instead of checking in on your aunt. She became impatient waiting for the light bulb in her hallway to be changed and tried to do it herself. Unfortunately, your aunt fell off the chair she was standing on and broke her hip.

Thematically, this situation is one in which you broke or failed to fulfil a personal moral code, resulting in hurting or offending someone else.

If you feel guilty (an unhealthy negative emotion), you're very likely to experience the following:

- ✔ **Type of thinking:** Your thinking becomes rigid and demand-based. You conclude that you've definitely done a bad thing (sinned). You assume more personal responsibility than may actually be legitimate, discounting or not considering mitigating factors. You may believe that some form of punishment is deserved and/or imminent.

- ✔ **Focus of attention:** You look for more evidence that you've sinned, or you look for evidence that others hold you responsible for the sin.

- ✔ **Behaviour (action tendency):** You may desire to escape from guilty feelings in self-defeating ways – for example, begging for forgiveness, promising that you'll never commit a sin again, punishing yourself, physically or through deprivation, or by attempting to disclaim any legitimate responsibility for the wrongdoing.

Action tendency refers to an urge for you to behave in a certain way that you may or may not actually act upon. Different emotions produce an urge within you to do certain things. In some cases, you may actually do or say something, and in others you may just be aware that you *want* to do or say something;

for example, *wanting* to run out of a room and hide when feeling ashamed, or feeling unhealthily angry and *wanting* to punch someone's lights out, without actually doing so. By contrast, you can think about the situation differently and feel remorse (a healthy negative emotion). Although the same theme (a broken or failed moral code, causing hurt or offence to a significant other) still applies, you experience the following:

- ✔ **Type of thinking:** Your thinking is more flexible and preference-based. You look at actions in context and with understanding before making a judgement about whether you sinned. You consider mitigating factors of the situation and do not believe that punishment is deserved and/or imminent.

- ✔ **Focus of attention:** You don't look for further evidence that you sinned. Neither do you look for evidence that others hold you responsible for the sin.

- ✔ **Behaviour (action tendency):** You face up to the healthy pain that comes with knowing that you've sinned. You may ask for, but not beg for, forgiveness. You understand the reasons for your wrongdoing and act on that understanding. You may atone for the sin by taking a penalty and/or making appropriate amends. You avoid defensiveness and excuse-making.

The theme involving both guilt and remorse is the same, but your thinking, action tendencies and focus of attention are very different.

Spotting the difference in thinking

As the example in the preceding section illustrates, unhealthy emotions can spring from rigid, *demand-based thinking*. Thoughts or beliefs like 'other people must behave respectfully towards me at all times' and 'I should always get what I want without hassle' can lead to unhealthy anger when other people and the world don't meet these demands.

Healthy emotions spring from flexible, *preference-based thinking*. So, thoughts and beliefs like 'I prefer others to treat me respectfully, but they're not bound to do so' and 'I prefer to get what I want without hassle, but no reason exists that this should always be the case' can lead to healthy annoyance when other people and the world don't meet your preferences.

Rigid thinking is a reliable indicator that you're having an unhealthy feeling. When you think rigidly, you're more likely to underestimate your ability to cope with and overcome the negative event in question. The more adept you become at identifying your thoughts, beliefs and attitudes as either rigid and demanding or flexible and preferential, the easier you can work out whether your feelings are healthy or unhealthy.

When you feel *guilty*, you think in an unhealthy, rigid, demand-based manner and may say things like the following:

- ✔ 'I absolutely shouldn't have left my aunt alone.'

- ✔ 'Leaving my aunt alone was a bad thing and means I'm a bad person.'

- ✔ 'I can't bear the pain of knowing that I've done this bad thing of leaving my aunt alone.'

You may then continue to think in the following guilt-enhancing ways:

- ✔ You fail to acknowledge that your aunt ultimately chose to try to change the light bulb herself. You fail to acknowledge that other members of your family can also check in on your aunt.

- ✔ You ignore the fact that you had no way of knowing that the light bulb needed changing, and that you had not foreseen your aunt taking such a risk.

- ✔ You expect that your aunt will blame your entirely. You think about the punishment that you believe you deserve.

By contrast, if you feel *remorseful*, you think in a healthy, flexible, preference-based manner and may say things such as:

- ✔ 'I wish I hadn't left my aunt alone, but regrettably I did.'

- ✔ 'Leaving my aunt alone may mean that I've done a bad thing but not that I'm a bad person.'

- ✔ 'I can bear the pain of knowing that I've done this bad thing of leaving my aunt alone.'

You can then continue to think in helpful ways:

- ✔ You can acknowledge your part in the accident occurring, but you can also consider that other members of the family failed to check in on your aunt.

- ✔ You can acknowledge that you didn't foresee your aunt taking the risk of changing a light bulb. Nor did you know that the bulb would burn out.

- ✔ You can expect that your aunt may be upset with you, but you believe that you don't deserve a severe punishment.

Taking legitimate responsibility for what happens in a situation enables you to think about the event in a holistic way. You don't need to prolong uncomfortable feelings of remorse beyond what is reasonable and appropriate to the situation. Your ability to solve problems isn't impeded by feelings of guilt.

Spotting the difference in behaving, and ways you want to behave

Another way of figuring out whether your emotion is in the healthy or unhealthy camp is to have a look at your actual behaviour or the way in which you feel inclined to behave.

Healthy negative emotions are accompanied by largely constructive behaviours, whereas unhealthy feelings usually go hand-in-hand with self-defeating behaviours. Problem-solving is still possible when you're healthily sad, annoyed, remorseful or regretful, but you have much greater difficulty planning clear ways to surmount your problems when you're unhealthily depressed, enraged, guilty or ashamed.

For example, if you respond to your aunt's falling over with *guilt-based action tendencies*, you may do one or more of the following:

- ✔ Go out and get quite drunk, trying to block out your guilty feelings.

- ✔ Visit your aunt in hospital and plead for her forgiveness.

- ✔ Promise that you'll never again let down your aunt, or anyone else dear to you, for as long as you live.

- ✔ Decide that you won't go on any other trips while your aunt is alive.

The preceding behaviours are problematic because they're extreme and unrealistic. These actions focus on self-punishment rather than look at the reality of the situation and how you can, in this example, best meet your aunt's needs.

On the other hand, if you're feeling healthy remorse your *action tendencies* may include some of the following:

- ✔ Endure the discomfort of knowing that your aunt has been hurt (rather than getting drunk to avoid it).

- ✔ Visit your aunt in hospital regularly and apologise for having left her alone.

- ✔ Understand that your aunt needs continuous support but that you have the right to go away with friends.

- ✔ Plan to stay with your aunt for a week or so after she's discharged from hospital.

- ✔ Resolve to plan your trips away more carefully and to arrange for nursing staff to be with your aunt when you're unavailable.

The preceding behaviours are geared towards making sure that your aunt doesn't hurt herself again during your absence. By taking an appropriate amount of responsibility for the accident, you can still look for ways to provide comfort for your aunt rather than concentrate on punishing yourself.

Spotting the difference in what you focus on

In addition to differences in types of thinking and behaving, you can distinguish healthy from unhealthy emotions by checking out the focus of your attention. If you're having an unhealthy emotion, your mind is likely to focus on catastrophic possibilities in the future based on the primary event.

If you're responding to the injured auntie situation from a place of *guilt*, you may focus your attention on the following:

- Blaming yourself for abandoning your aunt and for the accident happening.
- Feeling the pain of your guilt whilst neglecting to consider potential solutions to the problem of your aunt needing continuous care.
- Looking for evidence that your aunt blames you entirely for the accident.
- Looking for blame from other people, such as hospital staff and family members.

You continue to give yourself an unduly rough ride, thereby prolonging your distressing, guilt feelings by focusing on the bleakest possible aspects of your aunt's accident.

If you respond to the situation from a place of remorse, you are likely to focus your attention on the following:

- Accepting that leaving your aunt alone may have been a bad decision but that you had no intention of putting her at risk.
- Feeling the pain of remorse over the accident but also trying to find ways to improve the situation.
- Not seeking out evidence of blame from your aunt.
- Accepting evidence that hospital staff or family members do not blame you for the accident.

Thus, your attention focus when you respond from a place of remorse enables you to take some responsibility for your aunt's broken hip, but you don't dwell on the potential for blame and punishment.

Spotting Similarities in Your Physical Sensations

Butterflies in your stomach, blood racing through your veins, light-headedness, sweaty palms, heart pounding. Sound familiar? We expect so. If someone described these physical symptoms to you, you may try to guess what emotion they were experiencing. However, it would be difficult to confidently determine the specific emotion, because these sensations can accompany several different positive and negative emotional states. For example, you may get butterflies in your stomach when you're excited, angry, anxious or in love, as illustrated in Figure 6-2.

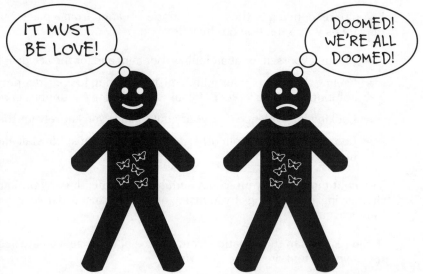

Figure 6-2:
Spot the similarities in your physical sensations.

The sensations that you feel in your body also tend to overlap in both healthy and unhealthy negative emotions. For example, you may get butterflies in your stomach when you're unhealthily anxious *and* when you're healthily concerned. Therefore, using your physical symptoms as a guide to judging the healthiness of your negative feelings isn't very reliable.

The main way in which your physical responses are likely to vary between the healthy and unhealthy categories is in their intensity. You probably find that sensations are more intense, uncomfortable and debilitating when you're having unhealthy emotions, such as anxiety and anger. You may also notice that uncomfortable physical sensations last longer when you're experiencing unhealthy negative emotions.

Incidentally, we believe that if you're experiencing butterflies, sweaty palms, racing blood, light-headedness and a pounding heart all at once, then you really *are* in love!

Identifying Feelings about Feelings

Getting two emotions for the price of one isn't such a great deal when two unhealthy negative emotions are on offer.

CBT professionals call feelings about feelings *meta-emotions*. The prefix *meta* comes from Greek and means 'beside' or 'after'.

Sometimes, you can give yourself a second helping of unhealthy emotion by holding rigid demands about which emotions you believe are acceptable for you to experience in the first place.

A common example of feelings about feelings is found in depression. Many people have guilty feelings about their depression. This guilt often comes from the demands people make of themselves, for example that they mustn't let other people down or put undue strain on loved ones. Here are some typical guilt-producing thoughts that are common in depressed people:

- ✔ 'I should be contributing more to the running of the home.'
- ✔ 'I must be able to demonstrate love and care to my children.'
- ✔ 'My partner and children are worried about me, and I'm making them suffer.'
- ✔ 'I shouldn't be neglecting my friends in this way.'

Recognising your meta-emotions is important, because meta-emotions can prevent you from dealing with your primary emotional problems. For example, you may be feeling guilty about having depression. If you can stop feeling guilty, you'll almost certainly find that you can work on overcoming your depression more effectively.

If you find that the concept of feeling guilty about being depressed really does strike a chord with you, go to Chapter 12, where we discuss it in more detail.

Handy emotional health checklist

The following is an abbreviated list of ways that can help you to find out the nature of a feeling and give it a name. The list can also help you assess whether an emotion is of the healthy or unhealthy negative variety.

✔ Have you identified a word to describe how you feel inside?

✔ Can you identify the theme of your emotion?

✔ How does your emotion lead you to behave? Are your actions or urges to act helpful or unhelpful?

✔ Are you thinking in a flexible way, or are you thinking in a rigid and demanding way?

✔ What are you paying attention to? Are you looking at the event from all angles?

✔ Is another emotion getting in the way of you being able to identify your first emotion? For example, are you feeling guilty or ashamed about your anger, depression or other emotion?

Defining Your Emotional Problems

The aim of CBT is to help you overcome your emotional problems and move you towards your goals. As with all kinds of problem-solving, *defining* your emotional problems is the first step in solving those problems.

Making a statement

Writing down a problem statement has three main components – the emotion, the theme or event (what you feel your emotion about), and what you do in response to that emotion. You can effectively describe an emotional problem by filling in the blanks of the following statement:

Feeling_____ (emotion) about _____ (theme or event), leading me to_____ (response).

For example:

Feeling *anxious* about *my face turning red in social situations*, leading me to *avoid going out to bars and clubs and to splash my face with water if I feel hot*.

Feeling *depressed* about *the end of my relationship with my girlfriend*, leading me to *spend too much time in bed, avoid seeing people and take less care of myself*.

When positives are negatives

Although this chapter deals with unhealthy negative emotions because these are the most common factors in emotional disturbance, you can't forget that negative positive emotions do also exist.

An example of a negative positive emotion is holding a *rigid demand*, such as 'I must get approval from my boss' and then feeling a surge of delight when the demand is met. You may feel good about the approval and your confidence may soar for a time, but you're still vulnerable to unhealthy negative feelings if you later fail to get your boss's approval. If you hold a *flexible preference* for your boss's approval, you can feel healthily pleased if you get approval and healthily disappointed if you don't.

Another example of unhealthy positive emotions is the feeling of euphoria associated with *hypomanic* (excessively happy or 'high') states. People who suffer from bipolar affective disorder (formerly known as manic depression) can experience alternating periods of extreme low-mood and extreme high-mood. During high periods, people with bipolar affective disorder are often prone to making rash decisions and behaving in erratic, sometimes risky ways. People with bipolar affective disorder may seem to be very happy when in fact they're hypomanic and suffering from a genuine psychiatric condition. Bipolar affective disorder can be treated effectively with medication and CBT. Many of the tips for overcoming *unipolar* (or general depression) that you can find in Chapter 12 are also very helpful for people with bipolar disorder. Appendix A lists organisations that you may find helpful.

If you think that you, or someone close to you, may have bipolar affective disorder, we strongly recommend seeing a psychiatrist to get a comprehensive assessment. Prescribed medication is an important part of managing the distressing conditions of this disorder. Psychiatrists generally have more specialised knowledge about the disorder and appropriate medications than general physicians.

One key CBT strategy for helping people to manage bipolar depression involves making an activity schedule (see Chapter 12). Write down a plan of your daily activities and stick to doing them regardless of your mood to help you achieve balance and consistency. The crucial point is to establish a *consistent* level of activity in your daily life. Sticking to a daily schedule of activities can help you avoid being under-stimulated during lows (thereby combating a downward spiral into depression) and help you avoid becoming over-stimulated during highs (thereby preventing an upward spiral into hypomania).

Rating your emotional problem

Human nature leads you to focus on how bad you feel, rather than how much better you feel. As you reduce the intensity of any emotional disturbance, you can find motivation in being able to see a difference. After you describe a problematic emotion, rate it on a scale of 0–10, based on how much distress the emotion causes you and how much it interferes with your life.

As you work on resolving your emotional problem by making changes to your thinking and behaviour, continue to rate the distress and interference it is causing you. Your ratings are likely to go down over time as you make efforts to overcome your unhealthy negative emotions. Review your ratings regularly, once a week or so. Doing this review helps remind you of your progress and replenishes your motivation to keep up the good work!

Share your ratings with your CBT therapist if you have one. Your therapist can haul out your rating records and show you the progress you've made if your motivation begins to flag.

Chapter 7

Identifying Solutions That Cause You Problems

In This Chapter

▶ Understanding how common coping strategies can maintain (and worsen) your problems

▶ Examining and eliminating safety behaviours

▶ Understanding why doing the opposite of your current strategies can help you

*T*he first step in any kind of problem-solving is to *define* the problem. This chapter is about assessing your problems and putting your finger on the way in which your current coping strategies are part of your specific problem.

Often, the problematic behaviours that maintain or worsen emotional problems are the very behaviours that people use to help themselves cope – hence the common CBT expression 'your solution is the problem'.

The reality is that you probably weren't taught how to best tackle emotional problems such as anxiety, depression and obsessions. We confess that even though we've been trained in the art of emotional problem-solving, when it comes to dealing with our own emotions, we can still manage to get it wrong.

In this chapter, we guide you towards identifying the fact that your coping strategies may make you feel better in the short term but that they're actually counterproductive – and that they can make things worse in the long term.

When Feeling Better Can Make Your Problems Worse

Aaron Beck, founder of CBT and Dennis Greenberger, a well-known CBT therapist, note that, if you can turn a counterproductive strategy on its head, you're well on the way to a real solution. This concept basically means that by doing the complete opposite of your established coping strategies you can recover from your problems. Exposing yourself to feared situations rather than avoiding them is a good example of turning a counterproductive strategy on its head. The more you avoid situations that you fear, the more afraid you become of ever encountering feared situations. Avoidance also undermines your sense of being able to cope with unpleasant or uncomfortable events. For example, never using a lift may temporarily stop your anxious feelings about being in an enclosed space, but avoiding lifts does not help you to overcome your fear of enclosed spaces once and for all.

Windy Dryden, who trained us in CBT, coined the phrase 'Feel better, get worse; feel worse, get better' when referring to people overcoming emotional problems. Many of the things that you may be doing – but in so doing maintaining your current problems – are driven by a highly understandable goal to reduce your distress. However, when you aim to get short-term relief, you may well be reinforcing the very beliefs and behaviours that underpin your problems.

One of the most powerful ways of changing your emotions in a lasting way, is to act against your unhelpful beliefs and to act on your alternative helpful beliefs (Chapters 3 and 16 contain more information about forming alternative healthy beliefs).

Here are some further examples of what we mean by *problem-maintaining solutions*:

- ✔ **Avoiding situations that you fear or that provoke anxiety.** Avoidance tends to erode rather than boost your confidence. You remain afraid of the situations you avoid, thus you don't give yourself a chance to confront and overcome your fears.

- ✔ **Drinking alcohol or taking drugs to block out uncomfortable feelings.** Often, those bad feelings persist in the long term, and you end up with the added problem of the effect of the alcohol or drugs (hangover, comedown). Also, you have the potential to develop a new problem – substance dependence (have a look at Chapter 10 for more information about addiction).

✔ **Concealing aspects of yourself that cause you shame.** Hiding things about yourself – such as imperfections in your appearance, childhood experiences, mistakes from the past or current psychological difficulties – can make you feel chronically insecure that someone may 'find you out'. Hiding shameful aspects of your experiences also denies you the opportunity to find out that other people have similar experiences, and that they won't think any less of you for revealing your secrets.

✔ **Putting off dealing with problems or tasks until you're in the mood.** If you wait to take action until 'the right time', until you 'feel like it' or when you feel sufficiently inspired, you may wait a very long time. Putting off essential tasks may save you some discomfort in the short term, but undone tasks also tend to weigh heavily on your mind.

The following sections deal with common counterproductive strategies for coping with common psychological problems. We explain that doing what makes you feel briefly better may be perpetuating your problem.

Getting Over Depression without Getting Yourself Down

If you're feeling depressed, you're likely to be less active and may withdraw from social contact. Inactivity and social withdrawal are often attempts to cope with depressed feelings, but they can reduce the positive reinforcement you get from life, increase isolation, increase fatigue, lead to the build-up of problems or chores, and leave you feeling guilty.

For example, if you've been feeling depressed for some time, you may use a number of ultimately negative strategies to relieve your depression:

✔ To avoid feeling ashamed about being depressed, you may avoid seeing friends. This coping strategy leaves you feeling more isolated and means you don't get the support you need.

✔ To avoid being irritable around your partner or children, you may try to minimise contact with them. Your children may become unruly, your relationship with your partner may suffer, and you may end up feeling guilty about not spending time with any of them.

✔ To avoid the embarrassment of making mistakes at work, you may stop going to work on a regular basis.

✔ To cope with feeling tired and to get some relief from your depression, you may take naps during the day. Unfortunately, napping can disrupt your sleeping pattern, leading to even more fatigue.

To see how your depression is affecting your activity levels, record a typical week on the *activity schedule* in Chapter 12 (and Appendix B). Then, as we explain in Chapter 12, combat depression by scheduling your activities and rest periods (but not naps because napping during the day can disrupt night time sleeping) for each day, and gradually build up your activity levels over time.

Loosening Your Grip on Control

Letting go of control is an especially relevant skill if you have any sort of anxiety problems, including obsessive-compulsive disorder (OCD), panic disorder and post-traumatic stress disorder (PTSD). But, it also applies to other types of emotional problems, such as anger and jealousy, and to eating disorders like anorexia and bulimia.

Here are some common examples of how you may be gripping the controls too hard:

- ✔ Trying to limit your body's physical sensations because you believe that certain bodily symptoms will result in harm to yourself. For example, 'If I don't stop feeling dizzy, I'll pass out.'

- ✔ Trying to control and monitor your thoughts because you think that if they get out of control, you'll go crazy.

- ✔ Being very controlling about the types of food you eat, when you eat and how much you eat.

- ✔ Trying to control your appetite and diminish your need for food.

- ✔ Suppressing upsetting thoughts, doubts or images because you believe that allowing them to enter your mind will cause harm to yourself or others. (This characteristic is very typical of OCD – check out Chapter 13 for more info.)

- ✔ Trying to control your body's physical reactions to anxiety, such as trembling hands, blushing or sweating, because you think that others will judge you harshly if they notice your symptoms.

Trying to control the uncontrollable is destined to leave you feeling powerless and ineffective. Instead of striving for control, look to change your attitude about needing control by accepting the discomfort of certain types of thoughts or bodily sensations (head to Chapter 9 for more information).

If you try too hard to gain immediate control, you often end up:

✔ Focusing more on feeling out of control, thus making yourself feel even more powerless than you did to start with.

✔ Trying to control things that go against biology, like the need for food, lead to preoccupation and a further diminished sense of control.

✔ Putting pressure on yourself to control symptoms and thoughts that aren't within your control, thus making yourself feel more anxious.

✔ Concluding that something must be deeply wrong with you because you can't keep symptoms under control, thus making yourself feel more anxious, and experiencing more racing thoughts and unpleasant physical sensations.

The next time you feel anxious in a public place or find yourself blushing, sweating or having disturbing thoughts, put the concepts in this section to the test by trying harder to stop yourself from having those thoughts, blushing or sweating. Chances are that you'll find your efforts produce even more of the thoughts and sensations you're trying so hard to control.

Feeling Secure in an Uncertain World

The need for certainty is a common contributing factor in anxiety, obsessional problems and jealousy.

Unfortunately, the only things you can be 100 per cent sure of, as the saying goes, are birth, death and taxes. Over and above that, humans live in a pretty uncertain universe. Of course, many things are predictable and pretty sure bets, like the sun rising in the morning and setting in the evening. However, other things in life are much more uncertain. 'Will I be pretty?' 'Will I be rich?' 'Will I live to a ripe old age surrounded by grandchildren and a few cats?' *Qué será, será*. Whatever will be, will be.

Trying to get rid of doubt by seeking unattainable certainty is like trying to put out a fire by throwing more wood on it. If you're intolerant of uncertainty, as soon as you quell one doubt another one's sure to pop up. The trick is to find ways to tolerate doubt and uncertainty – they exist whether you like it or not.

Here are some examples of how your demands for certainty may be reflected in your behaviour:

✔ **Frequent requests for reassurance.** Constantly asking yourself and other people questions, such as 'Is it safe to touch the door handle without washing my hands?', 'Do you find that person more attractive than me?', 'Are you sure I haven't gained weight?', 'Do you think I'll pass the exam?' or 'Are you sure I won't get mugged if I go out?' are all efforts to find some reassurance in an uncertain world. Unfortunately, excessive reassurance-seeking can reduce your confidence in your own judgement.

✔ **Repeated checking behaviours.** Checking behaviours are actions you perform in an effort to create more certainty in your world. Such actions include checking several times that your doors and windows are locked, frequently asking your partner where they've been, seeing lots of different doctors to ensure that a physical sensation isn't a sign of serious illness, checking that you can still feel your hip bones and not fat, and going over conversations in your mind to be sure that you haven't said anything offensive. The irony is that the more you check, the more uncertain you feel. You may feel temporarily better immediately following your checks, but it's not long before you feel compelled to carry them out again. Excessive checking can be very time-consuming and tiring, and it can lower your mood.

✔ **Superstitious rituals.** Superstitious rituals are things that you do to try to keep yourself safe or to prevent bad things from happening. Typically, superstitious rituals are not directly related to whatever it is that you fear most. Examples of rituals include touching wood, repeating phrases in your mind, wearing lucky clothes or jewellery, and avoiding unlucky numbers, out of a faulty belief that these rituals will stop unfortunate or tragic events befalling yourself or your loved ones. Engaging in superstitious behaviours can lead you to conclude that the ritual has prevented bad things from happening, rather than help you understand that many bad events are unlikely to occur regardless of whether you perform a ritual or not.

Superstitious thinking also involves making faulty links between your subtle behaviours or thoughts (and even *dreams*) and what happens in reality. If you think about a loved one coming to harm (due to acute anxiety about their safety), you may assume, falsely, that you caused a subsequent accident by imagining it. If you have a vivid image (or dream) of a young child being abducted, you may conclude 'If it happens, maybe I made it happen by imagining it!' Pretty disturbing stuff. What we point out to many of our clients is that we don't make superstitious links anywhere near as readily about good stuff. When was the last time you thought 'It's a beautiful day because I thought about the weather being fine this week' or 'My aunt's tumour is benign because I imagined it would be' or 'I've won the lottery because I willed it to happen'? If your superstitious thinking makes any real sense at all (and it really *doesn't*), then it has to hold true for both good and bad events.

✔ **Avoiding risk.** Risks – such as global tragedies, becoming ill, having an accident, making poor decisions or committing a social gaffe – are unavoidable and ever-present. You may be trying to eliminate risk by staying home or in 'safe' places, eating only certain foods, never deviating from set routines, over-planning for trips away, or over-preparing for unlikely events such as war, plague or famine. In fact, risk is a part of life and can only be avoided to a limited extent. The more you try to eliminate all risk from your life, the more you're likely to focus on all the possible things that could go wrong. You're fighting a losing battle and are likely to undermine your sense of security even further. Focusing too much on the risks inherent in every day life will leave you chronically worried and cause you to overestimate the probability of bad things happening to you.

✔ **Trying to influence others.** Examples of influencing others' behaviour include encouraging your partner to socialise only with members of the same sex, persuading your children to stay at home rather than go out with their friends, coercing family members into letting you eat very little, feeding others in lieu of eating yourself and asking your doctor to send you for yet another test. Demanding that other people act in ways to minimise your intolerance of uncertainty and risk can seriously damage your relationships. People close to you are likely to perceive you as controlling or suspicious.

Try to understand that uncertainty has always been a major feature of the world, and that people still manage to keep themselves safe and secure. You don't need to change the world to feel secure. You simply need to accept uncertainty and live with it. You *can* happily coexist with uncertainty – it's always been that way. Remind yourself that ordinary people cope with bad events every day and that you're likely to cope as well as others do if something wicked your way comes.

The next section deals with accepting uncertainty and letting go of unhelpful coping strategies.

Surmounting the Side Effects of Excessive Safety-Seeking

One of the main ways in which you maintain emotional problems is by rescuing yourself from your imagined catastrophes. Often, these anticipated disasters are products of your worried mind, rather than real or probable events. People with specific anxiety problems, such as the ones listed in this section, often take measures to reduce their anxiety and increase their sense of safety, but in effect make themselves even more intolerant of the inevitable uncertainty of everyday life.

The actions that people take to prevent their feared catastrophes from occurring are called *safety behaviours*.

Avoiding, escaping or trying too hard to stop a feared catastrophe prevents you from realising three key things:

- ✔ Your feared event may never happen.

- ✔ If your feared event *does* happen, most likely you'll find ways to cope. For example, other people or organisations may be available to help you out.

- ✔ The feared event may well be inconvenient, uncomfortable, upsetting and deeply unpleasant, but rarely is it terrible or unbearable.

Anxiety affects your thinking in two key ways: it leads you to overestimate the probability and gravity of danger, and to underestimate your ability to overcome adversity. Of course you want to keep yourself as safe as possible. But sometimes you may try to keep yourself safe from events that really aren't that dangerous.

Additionally, some of the things that you do to eliminate risk and safeguard yourself may actually result in more discomfort and disturbance than necessary – using ultimately unhelpful strategies to avoid feared outcomes is very prevalent in anxiety disorders. Here are some examples of counterproductive safety behaviours that you might be using to cope with specific anxiety problems:

- ✔ **Panic attacks:** Michael's panic attacks are maintained by his fear that feeling dizzy will make him collapse. Whenever he feels dizzy, he takes a sip of water, sits down or holds on to something. In this way, he prevents himself from finding out that he won't collapse simply because he feels dizzy.

- ✔ **Social anxiety:** Sally tends to over-prepare what she's going to say before she actually says it. She monitors her speech and body language and reviews in her mind what she did and said when she gets home. In this way, she maintains her excessive self-consciousness.

- ✔ **Post-traumatic stress:** Since she had a car accident, Nina avoids motorways, grips tightly on to the steering wheel when driving in her car, repeatedly checks the rear-view mirror, and avoids being a car passenger. Because she's being so careful, her anxiety about having another accident remains at the forefront of her mind.

- ✔ **Agoraphobia:** Georgina's afraid of travelling far from her home or familiar places for fear of losing control of her bowels and soiling herself. She has become almost housebound, and she relies heavily on her husband to drive her around. This means that she doesn't go out on her own and never discovers that her fears are unfounded.

✔ **Fear of heights:** James is afraid of heights because he believes that the 'pulling' sensation he experiences in high places means that he's at risk of unintentionally throwing himself to his death. To cope with this sensation, he digs his heels firmly into the ground and leans slightly backwards to resist his feelings. He also tries to avoid high places as much as he can. These behaviours fuel his fear and leave him believing that somehow he's more at risk than other people in high places.

After you've drawn up a list of your avoidance and safety behaviours, you can have a better understanding of what areas you need to target for change. In essence, the real solution to your problem lies in exposing yourself to feared situations without using any safety behaviours. You can then see that you are able to cope with anxiety-provoking events and that you need not rely on distractions or spurious attempts to keep yourself safe. Give yourself the chance to see that your anxiety is not harmful in itself and that anxious feelings diminish if you let them do so of their own accord. (Chapter 9 contains more information about dealing with safety behaviours and devising exposures.)

Wending Your Way Out of Worry

One of the dilemmas faced by people who worry too much is how to reduce that worry. Some degree of worry is entirely normal – of course problems and responsibilities will cross your mind from time to time. Yet, you may be someone who worries all of the time. Being a true worrywart is intensely uncomfortable. Understandably, you may want to stop worrying quite so much.

Two reasons may account for your excessive worrying:

✔ You may think that by worrying about unpleasant events, you can prevent those events from happening. Or, you may believe that your worry can give you clues as to how to prevent negative events from coming to fruition.

✔ You may think that worry protects you by preparing you for negative events. You may believe that if you worry about bad things enough, they won't catch you off guard and you'll be better fixed to deal with them.

If you can convince yourself that excessive worry really doesn't prevent feared events from happening or prepare you for dealing with bad things, you may be in a better position to interrupt your repetitive cycle of worries.

Ironically, many people worry about things in a vain attempt to get all possible worries out of the way so they can then relax. Of course, this never happens – worry's a moveable feast, and something else always comes along for you to worry about.

If you worry excessively about everyday events, you may try to solve every possible upcoming problem in advance of it happening. You may hope that your worry will solve potential problems, and thus you won't have to worry about them any more.

Unfortunately, trying too hard to put your mind at rest can lead to increased mental activity and yet more worry. All too often, people then worry that worrying so much is harmful, and they end up worrying about worrying!

Try to see your worrying as a bad habit. Instead of focusing on the content of your worries, try to interrupt the worry process by engaging your mind and body in activities outside of yourself. Chapter 5 has some helpful hints on refocusing your attention away from you actively worrying.

Preventing the Perpetuation of Your Problems

Sometimes, the things you do to cope with your problems can bring about the very things that you're trying to avoid. An example of this is when you try to push upsetting thoughts out of your mind. Pushing away unpleasant thoughts is called *thought suppression*, and can generally make unwanted thoughts intrude more often. Research shows that when people try to suppress an unwanted thought, it can intrude into their mind twice as often than if they accept the thought and let it pass.

Close your eyes and try really hard not to think of a pink elephant. Just for a minute, really push any images of pink elephants out of your mind. What happened? Most people notice that all they can think of are pink elephants. This demonstrates that trying to get rid of thoughts by pushing them out of your mind usually results in them hanging around more persistently.

Trying too hard not to do, feel or think specific things, and attempting to prevent certain events, can actually bring about what you most fear and wish to avoid. For example:

- Trying too hard not to make a fool of yourself in social situations can make you seem aloof and uninterested.

- Trying too hard to make sure a piece of work is perfect can lead you to miss a deadline, or become so nervous that you produce poor work.

- Insisting that you must succeed at a task, like passing an exam or learning a skill, makes you concentrate too much on *how well* you're doing and not enough on *what* you're doing. This misplaced attention focus can lead to poor results.

> ✔ Feeling jealous and repeatedly checking up on your partner, testing them or demanding reassurance that they're not about to leave you, can potentially drive your partner away.
>
> ✔ Lying in bed, trying to deal with fatigue when you're depressed, can lower your mood further and may lead to feelings of shame and guilt about your inactivity.

Helping Yourself: Putting the Petals on Your Vicious Flower

The *vicious flower exercise* is a way of putting together different elements of your problem to aid your understanding of how your problem is maintained. Look at the example in Figure 7-1, and turn to Appendix B for a blank flower to photocopy and fill in. Follow these steps to fill in your own vicious flower:

1. **In the Trigger box, write down the trigger that makes you feel anxious or upset.**

2. **In the central circle, write down the key thoughts and meanings you attach to the trigger.**

3. **In the flower petals, write down the emotions, behaviours and sensations you experience when your uncomfortable feeling is triggered. In the top petal, write down what you tend to focus on.**

Key negative thoughts, attitudes or beliefs are at the heart of your vicious flower. The petals are your attentional, emotional, physical and behavioural responses to the meaning you've attached to the trigger.

This chapter (and Chapter 6) suggests various emotions, behaviours, attention focus issues and thoughts to use to fill in your petals. If you suffer from anxiety, read Chapter 9; Chapter 12 for depression; Chapter 13 for obsessional problems; and Chapter 15 for an anger problem.

One of the most important aspects of building a vicious flower is to think through how the petals affect the thought or 'meaning' that underpins your emotional problem. For example, the effect of anxiety on your thinking is to make you more likely to interpret experiences as more dangerous than they really are. The effect of depression is to make your thinking more gloomy and negative (see Chapter 6 for more on these and other emotions).

Focusing your attention on a sensation usually makes that sensation feel more intense. Acting upon an unhelpful thought or meaning usually makes that meaning seem more real. Unpleasant physical sensations accompanying your reaction can make upsetting thoughts seem even more real. You can design behavioural experiments to test out the effect of increasing or reducing a behaviour on your problems (refer to Chapter 4).

When you understand the mechanisms that maintain your problems, it will seem far more practical and sensible to target your petals for change.

The 'physical sensations' petal is the aspect of your problem that you're least able to change directly because physical sensations are outside your immediate conscious control. However, you can minimise the impact of physical sensations by learning to tolerate them whilst you overcome your problem, and to interpret them as no more dangerous than they really are.

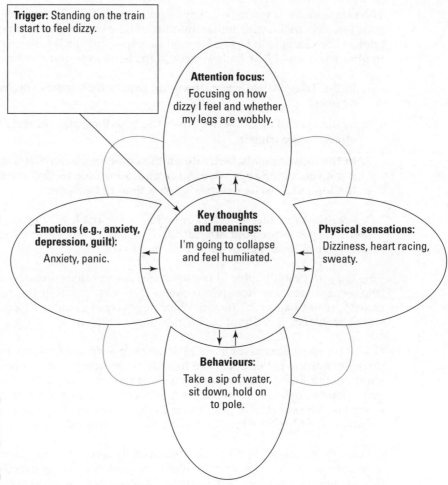

Figure 7-1:
A vicious
flower of
panic.

Put down that shovel and empty out your pockets!

One of the best metaphors for the kinds of behaviour we discuss in this chapter is the idea that some of your coping strategies may be like unwittingly trying to dig your way out of a hole. Naturally, the first step to overcoming your problems is to put down the shovel – to stop your self-defeating strategies, and gradually work out more productive ways of overcoming your emotional problems.

Over time, you may seek out bigger and better shovels in the guise of bigger and better avoidance and safety behaviours. We regularly invite those of our clients who suffer with agoraphobia, panic attacks, obsessive-compulsive disorder and body dysmorphic disorder, to share with us the contents of their pockets or handbags, which is often very illuminating. Examples of *safety props* that people carry 'just in case' include over-the-counter drugs, packets of tissues, antiseptic wipes, glucose sweets, handheld fans, make-up, plastic bags, paper bags, deodorant sprays, laxatives and alcohol.

To help clients eliminate safety behaviours, we often encourage them to throw out or hand over these seemingly innocent everyday items in the spirit of getting rid of problematic solutions. Go through your pockets and handbag and collect all of your safety props. Throw them in the bin or hand them over to someone who knows about your problems and has an interest in helping you (this person can be anyone in your life if you aren't currently seeing a CBT therapist). Be wary of purchasing or accumulating items to replace what you've already handed over or tossed away. Work on the basis that you only need essentials in your purse and pockets such as money, keys and travel cards.

Chapter 8

Setting Your Sights on Goals

In This Chapter

▶ Defining your goals for emotional and behavioural change

▶ Motivating yourself

▶ Recording your progress

*I*f we had to define the purpose of therapy, its purpose would *not* be to make you a straighter-thinking, more rational person. Rather, the purpose of therapy is to help you achieve your goals. Thinking differently is one way of achieving those goals. CBT can help you change the way you feel and behave. This chapter helps you define your goals and suggests some sources of inspiration for change.

Aaron Beck, founder of cognitive therapy, says that CBT is whatever helps you move from your problems to your goals. This definition emphasises the pragmatic and flexible nature of CBT, and encourages clients and therapists to select from a wide range of psychological techniques to help achieve goals in therapy. The crucial message, though, is that effective therapy is a constructive process, helping you to achieve your goals.

Putting SPORT into Your Goals

Many people struggle to overcome their problems because their goals are too vague. To help you develop goals that are clearer and easier to set your sights on, we developed the acronym SPORT, which stands for:

> ✔ **Specific:** Be precise about where, when and/or with whom you want to feel or behave differently. For example, you may want to feel concerned rather than anxious about making a presentation at work, and during the presentation you may want to concentrate on the audience rather than on yourself.

✔ **Positive:** State your goals in positive terms, encouraging yourself to develop more, rather than less, of something. For example, you may want to gain more confidence (rather than become less anxious) or to hone a skill (rather than make fewer mistakes).

Think of therapy as a journey. You're more likely to end up where you want to be if you focus on getting to your destination rather than on what you're trying to get away from.

✔ **Observable:** Try to include in your goal a description of a behavioural change that you can observe. Then, you can tell when you've achieved your goal because you can see a specific change.

If you're finding it hard to describe an observable change, think to yourself: 'How would the Martians, looking down from Mars, know I felt better simply by watching me?'

✔ **Realistic:** Make your goals clear, concrete, realistic and achievable. Focus on goals that are within your reach, and that depend on change from you rather than from other people. Try to visualise yourself achieving your goals. Realistic goals help you to stay motivated and focused.

✔ **Time:** Set a timeframe to keep you focused and efficient in your pursuit of a goal. For example, if you've been avoiding something for a while, decide when you plan to tackle it. Specify how long and how often you wish to carry out a new behaviour, such as going to the gym three times a week for an hour at a time.

Some goals, such as recovering from severe depression, can vary a lot in terms of how long they take to achieve. Setting schedules too rigidly can lead you to become depressed or angry at your lack of progress. So, set your deadlines firmly but flexibly, accept yourself if you don't achieve them on time, and persevere!

Homing In on How You Want to Be Different

Defining your goals and writing them down on paper forms the foundation of your CBT programme. This section helps you identify how you may want to feel and act differently.

Setting goals in relation to your current problems

To set a goal concerned with overcoming an emotional problem, you first need to define the problem, which we talk about in Chapter 6 (where we explore unhealthy emotions and behaviours and their healthy counterparts). Also refer to Chapter 7, in which we explore how attempts to make yourself feel better can sometimes make problems worse.

A *problem statement* contains the following components:

- ✔ Feelings/emotions
- ✔ A situation or theme that triggered your emotion
- ✔ The way you tend to act in the situation when you feel your problem emotion

Defining how you want to feel as an alternative

CBT can help you attain changes in the way you feel emotionally. For example, you may decide that you want to feel sad and disappointed, rather than depressed and hurt, about the end of your marriage.

Aiming to feel 'okay', 'fine' or 'relaxed' may not fit the bill if you're dealing with a tough situation. Feeling negative emotions about negative events is realistic and appropriate. Keep your goals realistic and helpful by aiming to have healthy emotions, and try to maintain an appropriate level of intensity of your emotions when faced with difficult events (take a look at Chapter 6 for more on healthy emotions).

Defining how you want to act

The second area of change that CBT can help you with is your behaviour. For example, after going through a divorce, you may decide that you want to begin seeing your friends and return to work, instead of staying in bed and watching TV all day.

You can also include changes to your mental activities within your goal, such as refocusing your attention on the outside world or allowing *catastrophic* (upsetting or worst-case scenario) thoughts to pass through your mind.

Making a statement

A *goal statement* is very similar to a problem statement – they have the same components, but the emotions and behaviours are different. A good goal statement involves the following:

To feel_____(emotion) about_____
_____(theme or situation) and to_____
____(behaviour).

So, for example, you may want to feel *concerned* (emotion) about *saying something foolish at a dinner party* (situation) and to *stay at the table in order to make further conversation* (behaviour).

Maximising Your Motivation

Motivation has a funny way of waxing and waning, just like the moon. Luckily, you don't necessarily have to feel motivated about changing before you can take steps forward. Motivation often follows rather than precedes positive action – often people find they 'get into' something once they've started. This section suggests some ways to generate motivation and encourages you to carry on working towards goals in the temporary absence of motivation.

Identifying inspiration for change

Lots of people find change difficult. Your motivation may flag sometimes, or you may not ever be able to imagine overcoming your difficulties. If either of these situations sounds familiar to you, you're in good company. Many people draw on sources of inspiration when starting with, and persevering through, the process of overcoming emotional problems. Sources of encouragement worth considering include the following:

- ✔ **Role models who have characteristics you aspire to adopt yourself.** For example, you may know someone who stays calm, expresses feelings to others, is open-minded to new experiences, or is assertive and determined. Whether real-life or fictional, alive or dead, known to you or someone you've never met, choose someone who inspires you and can give you a model for a new way of being.

- ✔ **Inspirational stories of people overcoming adversity.** Ordinary people regularly survive the most extraordinary experiences. Stories of their personal experiences can lead you to make powerful personal changes.

Focus on taking a leaf out of an inspirational individual's book, not on comparing yourself negatively with someone's 'superior' coping skills.

- ✔ **Images and metaphors.** Think of yourself as, for example, a sturdy tree withstanding a strong wind blowing against you, which can be an inspiring metaphor to represent you withstanding unreasonable criticism.

- ✔ **Proverbs, quotes and icons.** Use ideas you've heard expressed in novels, religious literature, films, songs or quotes from well-respected people to keep you reaching for your goals.

Focusing on the benefits of change

People often maintain apparently unhelpful patterns of behaviour (such as consistently arriving late for work) because they focus on the short-term benefit (in this case, avoiding the anxiety of being on a crowded bus or train) at the time of carrying out that behaviour. However, away from the immediate discomfort, these same people may focus on wishing they were free from the restrictions of their emotional problem (able to travel carefree on public transport).

Completing a cost–benefit analysis

Carrying out a *cost–benefit analysis* (CBA) to examine the pros and cons of something can help galvanise your commitment to change. You can use a CBA to examine the advantages and disadvantages of a number of things, such as:

- ✔ **Behaviours:** How helpful is this action to you? Does it bring short-term or long-term benefits?

- ✔ **Emotions:** How helpful is this feeling? For example, does feeling guilty or angry really help you?

- ✔ **Thoughts, attitudes or beliefs:** Where does thinking this way get you? How does this belief help you?

- ✔ **Options for solving a practical problem:** How can this solution work out? Is this really the best possible answer to the problem?

When using a CBA form similar to the one shown in Table 8-1, remember to evaluate the pros and cons:

- ✔ In the short term
- ✔ In the long term
- ✔ For yourself
- ✔ For other people

Table 8-1	The Cost–Benefit Analysis Form
Costs and Benefits of:	
Costs (Disadvantages)	**Benefits (Advantages)**

Try to write CBA statements in pairs, particularly when you're considering changing the way you feel, act or think. What are the *advantages* of feeling anxiety? And the *disadvantages*? Write down pairs of statements for what you feel, do or think *currently*, and for other, healthier alternatives. Tables 8-2 and 8-3 show a completed CBA form. You can find a larger, blank cost–benefit analysis form in Appendix B, which you can photocopy and fill in.

Table 8-2	Cost–Benefit Analysis: 'Costs and Benefits of Saying What Comes Into My Mind and Paying Attention to the Conversation'
Costs	**Benefits**
I may end up saying something stupid.	I won't have to think so much and I might be able to relax.
I may not come up with the best thing to say.	I can be more spontaneous.
I may end up running off at the mouth and people might not like me.	I'll be able to concentrate on what's being said and I won't seem so distracted.

Table 8-3	Second Cost–Benefit Analysis: 'Costs and Benefits of Preparing in My Head What I'm Going to Say Before Speaking'	
Costs	*Benefits*
I end up feeling very tired after going out.	I can make sure I don't say something foolish.
I can't relax into the conversation.	I may think of something funny or entertaining to say.
Sometimes I feel like the conversation moves on before I've had the chance to think of the right thing to say.	I can take more care not to offend people.

After you've done a CBA, review it with a critical eye on the 'benefits' of staying the same and the 'costs' of change. You may decide that these costs and benefits are not strictly accurate. The more you can boost your sense that change can benefit you, the more motivated you can feel in working towards your goals.

Write out a motivational flashcard that states the *benefits of change* and *costs of staying the same*, drawn from your cost–benefit analysis. You can then refer to this card to give yourself a motivational boost when you need it.

A large aspect of achieving a goal, whether learning to play the guitar or building up a business, is about accepting temporary discomfort in order to bring long-term benefit.

Recording your progress

Keeping records of your progress can help you stay motivated. If your motivation flags, spur yourself on towards your goal by reviewing how far you've come. Use a problem-and-goal sheet like that in Figure 8-1, to specify your problem and rate its intensity. Then define your goal, and rate your progress towards achieving it. Do this at regular intervals, such as every one or two weeks.

1. **Identify the problem you're tackling.** Include information about the emotions and behaviours related to a specific event. Remember, you're feeling an *emotion* about a *situation*, leading you to *behave* in a certain way.

2. **At regular intervals, evaluate the intensity of your emotional problem and how much it interferes with your life.** 0 equals no emotional distress, and no interference in your life, and 10 equals maximum possible emotional distress, at great frequency, with great interference in your life.

3. **Fill in the goal section, keeping the theme or situation the same, but specifying how you wish to feel and act differently.**

4. **Rate how close you are to achieving your goal.** 0 equals no progress whatsoever, at any time, and 10 means that the change in your emotion and behaviour is completely and consistently achieved.

Change doesn't happen overnight, so don't rate your progress any more frequently than weekly. Look for *overall* changes in the *frequency*, *intensity* and *duration* of your problematic feelings and behaviours.

Mercurial desires

People often find that they want to change their goals on a whim or a fancy. For example, you may have a goal of being more productive and advancing your position at work. Then, after going to a Summer Solstice rave, you decide that really your goal is to be free and to travel the world, communing with the essence of life. What you choose as your definitive goal is up to you. But be wary of being influenced too easily by whatever's foremost in your mind. Constantly abandoning former goals and adopting new ones can be a mask for avoidance and procrastination. Use the SPORT acronym, as described at the start of this chapter, to assess the durability and functionality of each of your chosen goals.

Using the form below, identify one of the main problems you wish to work on in therapy. A problem statement includes information about the emotions and behaviour related to a specific situation or event. For example: *'Feeling depressed about the end of my marriage leading me to become withdrawn and spend until around 6pm each day in bed'* or *'Feeling anxious about social situations leading me to avoid going to pubs, restaurants, and meetings, or to be extremely careful about what I say if I do socialise'*. Think of writing your problem statement as filling in blanks: *Feeling_____ (emotion) about_____ (situation), leading me to_____ (behaviour)*.

Use the same format to identify the goal you would like to achieve, but this time specify how you would like things to be different in terms of your emotions and behaviour.

PROBLEM No. ☐	DATE:	DATE:	DATE:	DATE:	DATE:
	RATING:	RATING:	RATING:	RATING:	RATING:
	DATE:	DATE:	DATE:	DATE:	DATE:
	RATING:	RATING:	RATING:	RATING:	RATING:

Rate the severity of your emotional problem 0 - 10. **0 = No distress/No impairment in ability to function 10 = Extreme distress/Virtuality unable to function in any area of life**

GOAL RELATED TO PROBLEM	DATE:	DATE:	DATE:	DATE:	DATE:
	RATING:	RATING:	RATING:	RATING:	RATING:
	DATE:	DATE:	DATE:	DATE:	DATE:
	RATING:	RATING:	RATING:	RATING:	RATING:

Rate how close you are to achieving your goal. **0 = No progress whatsoever 10 = Goal achieved and sustained consistently**

Figure 8-1:
The Problem-and-Goal Sheet.

Part III
Putting CBT into Action

The 5th Wave   By Rich Tennant

"I sense that you're becoming more defensive and unapproachable lately."

In this part . . .

Sometimes it can seem as if no one understands your problem, but we do! These chapters give you CBT ammunition to surmount depression, obsessions, addictions, poor body image, anxiety and even unbridled rage. Read on to gain more control over your problems and really begin to realise recovery.

Chapter 9

Standing Up to Anxiety and Facing Fear

In This Chapter

▶ Understanding the nature of anxiety

▶ Developing attitudes that help overcome anxiety

▶ Designing a programme to face your fears

A nxiety is a bully. And like most bullies, the more you let it shove you around, the pushier it gets. This chapter helps you get to know the nature of anxiety and to identify the ways in which it pushes you about. Fundamentally, you can beat anxiety, like any bully, by standing up to it.

Acquiring Anti-Anxiety Attitudes

Your thoughts are what count, because your feelings are influenced greatly by how you think. Feeling anxious increases the chance of you experiencing anxiety-provoking thoughts (refer to Chapter 6). Anxious thoughts can increase anxious feelings, and so a vicious cycle can develop. You can help yourself to face your fears by adopting the attitudes we outline in this section.

Thinking realistically about the probability of bad events

If you have any kind of anxiety problem, you probably spend a lot of time worrying about bad things that *may* happen to you or your loved ones. The more you focus your attention on negative events and worry about bad things being just around the corner, the more likely you are going to believe that they'll actually happen.

Proving for sure that bad events won't happen isn't that easy without a crystal ball or two, but you can acknowledge that you tend to *overestimate* the probability of bad things happening. Adjust your thinking appropriately to *counterbalance* for this tendency. Counterbalancing your attitude is a lot like riding a bike with the handlebars offset to the left – to steer straight, you need to turn the handlebars to the right, otherwise you keep veering off to the left. If you tend to always imagine the worst, straighten out your thinking by deliberately assuming that things are going to be okay.

Avoiding extreme thinking

Telling yourself that things are 'awful', 'horrible', 'terrible' or 'the end of the world' only turns up the anxiety heat. Remind yourself that few things are really that dreadful, and instead rate events more accurately as 'bad', 'unfortunate' or 'unpleasant but not 'the end of the world'.

Extreme thinking leads to extreme emotional reactions. When you mislabel a negative event as 'horrible', you make yourself overly anxious about unpleasant but relatively non-extreme events, such as minor public embarrassment.

Taking the fear out of fear

When people say things like 'Don't worry, it's *just* anxiety', the word 'just' implies – wrongly – that anxiety's a mild experience. Anxiety can, in fact, be a very profound experience, with strong bodily and mental sensations. Some anxious people misinterpret these intense physical symptoms as dangerous or as signs of impending peril. Common misreadings include assuming that a nauseous feeling means that you're about to be sick, or thinking that you're going crazy because your surroundings feel 'unreal'.

If you have concerns about your physical sensations you may consider seeing your family doctor prior to deliberately confronting your fears. Your doctor may then be able to advise you as to whether deliberately increasing your anxiety in the short term, in order to be free of it in the long term, is safe enough for you. It is rare for people to be advised against facing their fears.

Understanding and accepting common sensations of anxiety can help you stop adding to your anxiety by misinterpreting normal sensations as dangerous. Figure 9-1 outlines some of the more common physical aspects of anxiety.

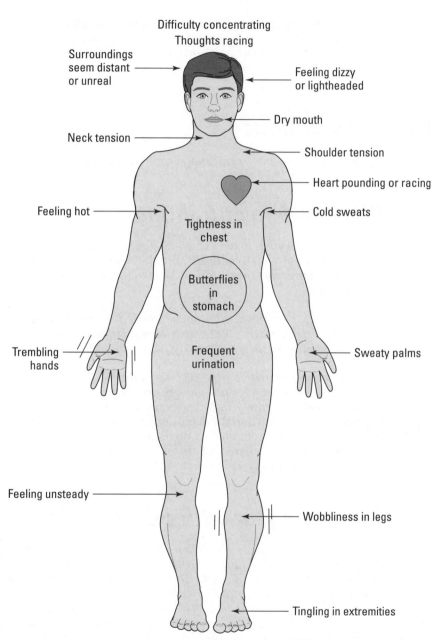

Figure 9-1:
Common
physical
sensations
of anxiety.

Undoubtedly, anxiety is an unpleasant, sometimes extremely disturbing experience. However, evaluating your anxiety as 'unbearable' or saying 'I can't stand it' only turns up the emotional heat. Remind yourself that anxiety is hard to bear but not unbearable.

Attacking Anxiety

The following are some key principles for targeting and destroying anxiety.

Winning by not fighting

Trying to control your anxiety can lead you to feeling more intensely anxious for longer (for more on this, read through Chapter 7). Many of our clients say to us: 'Facing my fears makes sense, but what am I supposed to do while I'm feeling anxious?'

The answer is . . . nothing. Well, sort of. Accepting and tolerating your anxiety when you're deliberately confronting your fears is usually the most effective way of making sure that your anxiety passes quickly.

If you're convinced that your anxiety won't diminish by itself, even when you do nothing, test it out. Pick one anxiety-provoking situation that you normally withdraw from – examples include using a lift, travelling on a busy bus, standing in a crowded room and drinking alone in a bar. Make yourself stay in the situation and just let your anxiety do its thing. Don't do anything to try to stop the anxiety. Just stay where you are and *do nothing* other than feel anxious. Eventually, your anxiety will begin to ebb away.

Defeating fear with FEAR

Perhaps the most reliable way of overcoming anxiety is the following maxim: FEAR – Face Everything And Recover. Supported by numerous clinical trials, and used daily all over the world, the principle of facing your fears until your anxiety reduces is one of the cornerstones of CBT.

The process of deliberately confronting your fear and staying within the feared situation until your anxiety subsides is known as *exposure* or *desensitisation*. The process of getting used to something, like cold water in a swimming pool, is called *habituation*. The principle is to wait until your anxiety reduces by at least half before ending your session of exposure – usually between twenty minutes and one hour, but sometimes more.

Repeatedly confronting your fears

As Figure 9-2 shows, if you deliberately confront your fears, your anxiety becomes less severe and reduces more quickly with each exposure. The more exposures you experience, the better. When you first confront your fears, aim to repeat your exposures at least daily.

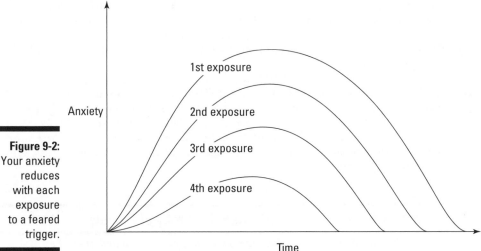

Figure 9-2:
Your anxiety
reduces
with each
exposure
to a feared
trigger.

Keeping your exposure challenging but not overwhelming

When confronting your fears, aim for *manageable exposure*, so that you can successfully experience facing your fears and mastering them. If your exposures are overwhelming, you may end up resorting to escape, avoidance or safety behaviours. The flipside of choosing overwhelming exposures is taking things too gently, which can make your progress slow and demoralising. Strive to strike a balance between the two extremes.

If you set yourself only easy, gentle exposures, you risk reinforcing the errone-ous idea that anxiety is unbearable and must be avoided. The point of expo-sure work is to prove to yourself that you *can* bear the discomfort associated with anxious feelings.

Taking it step by step

Avoid overwhelming or underchallenging yourself by using a *graded hierarchy* of feared or avoided situations. A graded hierarchy is a way of listing your fears from the mildest to the most severe.

If you want to kill your fear, let it die of its own accord.

You can use the following table to list people, places, situations, objects, animals, sensations or whatever triggers your fear. Be sure to include situa-tions that you tend to avoid. Rank these triggers in rough order of difficulty. Alongside each trigger, rate your anticipated level of anxiety on the good old 0–10 scale. *Voila!* You have a graded hierarchy. Table 9-1 shows you a blank form you can use.

After you have confronted your fear, rate the *actual* level of anxiety or discom-fort you experienced. Then, tailor your next exposure session accordingly. Most situations are not as bad as you expect them to be. In the unlikely event that the reality is worse than your expectations, you may need to devise more manageable exposures for the next few steps and work your way up the hier-archy more gradually.

Table 9-1	Graded Hierarchy of Anxiety	
Feared or Avoided Trigger	*Anticipated Anxiety or Discomfort 0–10*	*Actual Anxiety or Discomfort 0–10*

Jumping in at the deep end

Although we caution about striking a balance between under- and overchal-lenging yourself, jumping in with both feet does have its benefits. The sooner you can face your biggest fears, the sooner you can master them. Consider whether you can climb to the top of your hierarchy straight away.

Graded exposure is a means to an end. Going straight to your worst-feared situation without resorting to safety behaviours (which we talk about in the next section) can help you get rapid results, as long as you stick with the exposure long enough to discover that nothing terrible happens.

Shedding safety behaviours

You can overcome anxiety by turning your anxiety upside-down. The best way to make your anxiety go away is to invite it to do its own thing. As we explain in a bit more detail in Chapter 7, the things you do to reduce your fear in the short term are often the very things that start you feeling anxious in the first place. (Check out Chapter 7 for some common examples of safety behaviours.)

Recording your fear-fighting

Keep a record of your work against fear so you can check out your progress and make further plans. Your record can include:

- ✔ The length of your exposure session
- ✔ Ratings of your anxiety at the beginning, middle and end of your exposure session

A record helps you see whether you're sticking with your programme long enough for your fear to subside. If your fear doesn't seem to be reducing, make sure that you're still trying hard enough to reduce your fear by getting rid of those safety behaviours.

You can use the behavioural experiment record sheet in Chapter 4 to record your exposure and to compare your predicted outcome of confronting your fears with the actual outcome.

Overriding Common Anxieties

The following sections outline the application of CBT for some common anxiety problems. A full discussion of all of the specific types of anxiety problems lies outside the scope of this book. However, the CBT principles that we introduce you to here are the very best bet for overcoming most anxiety problems.

First, define what you're doing to keep your anxiety alive in your thinking (see Chapters 2 and 6), and alive in your behaviour (see Chapter 7). Then, start to catch your unhelpful thoughts and generate alternatives (Chapter 3), and test them out in reality (Chapter 4). Understanding where you focus your attention, and re-training your attention, can also be hugely helpful (see Chapter 5). We discuss anxiety about health and obsessions in Chapter 13, and fears of being ugly in Chapter 11.

Socking it to social anxiety

Attack *social anxiety* (excessive fear of negative evaluation by other people) by drawing up a list of your feared and avoided social situations and the safety behaviours you tend to carry out (check out Chapter 7 for more on safety behaviours).

Hang on to the idea that you can accept yourself even if other people don't like you. Be more flexible about how witty, novel and entertaining you 'have' to be. Systematically test out your predictions about people thinking negatively about you – how do people act when you don't try so hard to perform? Refocus your attention on the world around you and the people you interact with, rather than on yourself. For more help on retraining your attention, refer to Chapter 5. Once you've left the social situation, resist the tendency to play your social encounters back in your mind.

Waging war on worry

To wage war on your excessive worry, resist the temptation to try to solve every problem in advance of it happening. Try to live with doubt and realise that the most important thing is not what you specifically worry about but *how* you manage your worrying thoughts. Overcoming worry is the art of allowing thoughts to enter your mind without trying to 'sort them out' or push them away.

Pounding on panic

Panic attacks are intense bursts of anxiety in the absence of real danger, and can often seem to come out of the blue. Panic attacks often have very strong physical sensations such as nausea, heart palpitations, a feeling of shortness of breath, choking, dizziness and hot sweats. Panic sets in when people mistake these physical sensations as dangerous and get into a vicious cycle because these misinterpretations lead to more anxiety, leading to more physical sensations.

Put panic out of your life by deliberately triggering off panic sensations. Enter situations you've been avoiding and resist using safety behaviours. Realise, for example, that feeling dizzy doesn't cause you to collapse, so you don't need to sit down, and that other uncomfortable sensations of anxiety will pass without harming you. Carry out a behavioural experiment (see Chapter 4) to specifically test out whether your own feared catastrophes come true as a consequence of a panic attack.

Assaulting agoraphobia

Georgina was afraid to travel far from her home or from familiar places she felt safe in, which are common characteristics of *agoraphobia*. She feared losing control of her bowels and soiling herself. She had become virtually housebound and relied heavily on her husband to drive her around. She learned about the nature of anxiety and developed the theory that, although she may *feel* like she is going to soil herself, her sensations are due largely to anxiety and she will be able to 'hold on'.

To gain confidence and overcome agoraphobia, develop a hierarchy of your avoided situations and begin to face them, and stay in them until your anxiety reduces. This may include driving progressively longer distances alone, using public transport and walking around in unfamiliar places. At the same time, work hard to drop your safety behaviours so you can discover that nothing terrible happens if you do become anxious or panicky, and ride it out.

Dealing with post-traumatic stress disorder

Post-traumatic stress disorder (PTSD) can develop after being involved in (or witnessing) an accident, assault or other extremely threatening or distressing event. The symptoms of PTSD include being easily startled, feeling irritable and anxious, memories of the event intruding into your waking day, nightmares about the event or feeling emotionally numb. If you have PTSD you may be sustaining your distress by misunderstanding your normal feelings of distress in response to the event, trying to avoid triggers that activate memories of the event or trying too hard to keep yourself safe.

Fascinating phobias

One of the interesting things about anxiety problems is the wide variety of things that human beings fear. In our practice, we still encounter people with fears we've never heard of before. Crucially, what matters is not what you're afraid of but how negatively your fear is affecting your life.

Sometimes people are embarrassed by their phobias because they think others may find them silly or trivial. But extreme fear is never trivial – terror and fear can be very disabling, even if your fear is of something as simple as buttons. We suggest you seek out health professionals who take you seriously so you can get help for your phobia.

Common phobias include:

✔ **Acrophobia:** fear of heights or high levels

✔ **Agoraphobia:** fear of open spaces, crowded public places or being away from a place of safety

✔ **Aichmophobia:** fear of pins, needles and pointed objects

✔ **Arachnophobia:** fear of spiders

✔ **Claustrophobia:** fear of confined or small spaces

✔ **Emetophobia:** fear of vomiting

✔ **Haemophobia:** fear of blood and blood injury

✔ **Lockiophobia:** fear of childbirth

✔ **Noctiphobia:** fear of the night and the dark

✔ **Trypanophobia:** fear of injections

Less common phobias include:

✔ **Arachibutyrophobia:** fear of peanut butter sticking to the roof of one's mouth

✔ **Automatonophobia:** fear of ventriloquists' dummies, dolls, animatronic creatures or wax statues

✔ **Barophobia:** fear of gravity

✔ **Bibliophobia:** fear of books (if you've got this one, stick with us – you're doing well!)

✔ **Blennophobia:** fear of slime

✔ **Lutraphobia:** fear of otters

✔ **Lyssophobia:** fear of going insane

✔ **Necrophobia:** fear of death or dead things

✔ **Ombrophobia:** fear of rain or being rained on

✔ **Soceraphobia:** fear of parents-in-law

To combat PTSD, remind yourself that memories of a traumatic event intruding into your mind, and feelings of distress are normal reactions to trauma. Allowing memories to enter your mind and spending time thinking about them is part of processing traumatic events, and a crucial part of recovery. Many people find that deliberately confronting triggers or writing out a detailed first-person account can be helpful. At the same time it's important to reduce any excessive safety precautions you may have begun to take.

Hitting back at fear of heights

Begin to attack a fear of heights by carrying out a survey among your friends about the kind of feelings that they have when standing at the edge of a cliff or at the top of a tall building (see Chapter 4 for more on conducting surveys). You'll probably discover that your sensation of being unwillingly drawn over the edge is very common. Most people, however, just interpret this feeling as a normal reaction.

Put this new understanding into action to gain more confidence about being in high places. Work through a hierarchy of entering increasingly tall buildings, looking over bridges and climbing to the top of high cliffs.

Chapter 10

Abolishing Addictions

● ●

In This Chapter

▶ Recognising addiction

▶ Choosing to change

▶ Overcoming urges and cravings

▶ Making lifestyle changes to prevent relapse

● ●

*N*owadays, the term 'addiction' can be somewhat confusing. The word is bandied about to describe an unhealthy relationship with food, love, nicotine, adrenaline, pornography, gambling, and even relatively innocuous things like online gaming or pick'n'mix. For the sake of clarity, this chapter focuses mainly on dependency upon substances that aren't necessary, in any quantity, for survival – such as alcohol and illicit drugs. We also include gambling and pornography since these seem to be a growing problem with the advent of online gambling and pornographic websites. Even if your problem isn't with drugs, sex or poker, you'll still find information in this chapter that can help you to face up to and overcome any unhealthy compulsive behaviours you may have.

Putting a Name to Your Problem

Perhaps you're aware that your use of certain substances is causing problems in your everyday life and negatively impacting on your relationships. However, like many people, you may wish to deny the gravity of the problem.

Many people balk at the term 'addiction'. Unfortunately, there's no denying that stigma is attached to addiction of any kind. You may think that you're weak, morally decrepit or just plain bad for struggling with a dependency. However, although some people may judge you harshly for your problem, bear in mind that you don't *have* to accept their judgement wholly or without scepticism. As we discuss in Chapter 14, you can acknowledge your addiction *and* choose to accept yourself as a fundamentally worthwhile person with a specific problem. Shame about addiction frequently prevents people from accepting that they've got a problem in the first place and thus stops them from seeking appropriate help. Don't fall into this trap. Hold your head up and look your addiction squarely in the face. You really need to acknowledge your problem before you can move toward meaningful recovery.

Having more than one substance or behaviour that causes problems isn't unusual. For example, you might have an addiction to alcohol and also smoke marijuana occasionally. Frequently, dropping use of one substance leads to increased use of another. Be aware of substituting your primary addiction or 'drug of choice' for another one as you begin your journey to recovery. To truly overcome addiction you need to substitute your alcohol, drug or gambling use for harmless, healthy activities.

If you think you might have an addiction problem but aren't entirely sure, try answering the questions below. This short checklist can be used for both substance addiction and compulsive behaviours like gambling and pornography use. We use the term 'drug of choice' (or 'DOC' for short) in this checklist so that the questions make sense whatever your problem. Try to answer each question honestly; you don't need to share the information with anyone else at this point.

- ✔ Over the past week, have you lost time at work because of DOC use?

- ✔ Is your work performance suffering due to comedown, hangovers, lack of sleep or preoccupation with your DOC?

- ✔ Over the past week, have you used your DOC even though you may have promised yourself to resist?

- ✔ Are your finances suffering because of money spent on your DOC?

- ✔ Over the past week, have you used your DOC at times of day when others may consider it socially inappropriate or unacceptable?

- ✔ Do you find it very difficult to go for even one day (or a few days) without using your DOC?

- ✔ Do you get irritable and/or feel low when deprived of your DOC for any reason?

- ✔ Have activities that you once enjoyed been neglected in recent weeks due to DOC use?

- ✔ Have you had any accidents or injuries in recent weeks due to DOC use?

- ✔ Are your friends and/or family commenting about your DOC use or noticing changes in your behaviour?

✔ Do you make efforts to hide or minimise your DOC use in front of friends and family?

✔ Do you feel distinctly uncomfortable answering the questions in this checklist?

If you've answered 'yes' to even just one of these questions, chances are you have a dependency that may well develop into a full-blown addiction. Answering 'yes' to three or more items indicates that you do have an addiction. But don't despair! Recognising that you have the problem is an essential part of the ultimate solution.

To help you really acknowledge and accept that you have a problem, try writing it down. A single sentence is fine, such as 'I, Marcus, have a gambling addiction'. Seeing the truth in black and white can often help you resolve denial and shame.

Addiction is really not that different to mental health or physical problems. You're certainly not alone. The world's full of people dealing with addictions. Many recover, and so can you if you're willing to put in the blood, sweat and tears required to do so.

Familiarising Yourself with the Many Faces of Addiction

Anyone can develop an addiction whatever his current circumstances or background. Certain factors stemming from childhood, such as having alcoholic parents or experiencing social deprivation, may increase the chances of developing an addiction but this outcome is by no means inevitable. Many people with solid careers and families also fall prey to addiction; they're not exclusive to those living in more chaotic environmental situations.

Often people start 'self-medicating' an underlying mental health problem, such as anxiety or depression, with alcohol or drugs, or through behaviours like gambling. Substance use and engaging in compulsive behaviours (shopping, gambling, using pornography, sex, and so on) can take the edge off emotional pain in the immediate and short term. However, in the long term these strategies typically cause many more problems than they solve.

Consider the examples below illustrating three people with different addictions. These are merely snapshots; countless more types of people and possible scenarios exist, so don't worry if your situation doesn't fit neatly with any of them. Instead, focus on whatever does resonate with your particular experience.

Jack is 33 years old and works as a trader in the City. He enjoys his job but it can involve long hours and be very stressful. Though currently single, Jack hopes to settle down and start a family soon. Jack drank a lot and started experimenting with drugs while at university. At the time everyone seemed to be doing the same, so he didn't see his behaviour as a problem. Two years ago Jack started using cocaine at the weekends with his colleagues. Over the past year he's started using cocaine during the week and sometimes during his working day. Jack worries that, without cocaine, he'll have difficulty meeting the demanding pace of his job. Jack's last girlfriend ended the relationship because she disagreed with his drug use and grew tired of his mood swings. Jack is increasingly aware of his drug problem and the negative effects it has on his ability to form a relationship. However, he rationalises his addiction by telling himself that many of his colleagues use as much cocaine as he does, so it can't be that big a deal.

Kelly is a 45-year-old divorced mother of two, who works part time in a pharmacy. Kelly's ex-husband is often unemployed and is somewhat unreliable regarding childcare and maintenance payments. Kelly gets tired and overwhelmed looking after her two small children as well as trying to make ends meet. A few months ago she started taking strong codeine-based painkillers to ease migraine. She finds it easy to get the pills at work. Kelly now takes painkillers every day – whether she has a headache or not – because she finds that they calm her nerves. In the evening, she also often drinks a bottle of wine after putting the children to bed. Kelly worries that she's too dependent on codeine and alcohol but doesn't think she can cope without them.

Percy is a 28-year-old postgraduate student. He spends a lot of time in front of his computer and, when he needs a break from studying, he often surfs porn sites. Over the past few months Percy's porn use has increased and he finds it difficult to stop once he's started. Often he's up until the early hours of the morning with nothing to show for it in terms of academic work. His grades are suffering; he ends up sleeping late, misses lectures and sees less of his friends. Percy is deeply ashamed of his porn use and daren't talk about it with anyone. Some of his friends joke about porn surfing but Percy thinks that they'd consider him a 'pervert' if they knew about his problem.

Jack is in denial about the severity of his cocaine problem. Kelly knows she has a problem with alcohol and codeine but she underestimates her ability to cope without them. Percy is riddled with shame about his pornography addiction and can't imagine sharing it with anyone. Denial frequently prevents you from facing up to your problem and making the decision to quit. Chances are that if you spend time every day trying to convince yourself that you're in control of your substance use – you aren't.

Believing that you won't be able to cope with life stresses and problems without your addiction to rely on also prevents you from seeking help to quit. Most of life's problems are actually much easier to find solutions for when you're clean and sober. You probably will go through a rough time when you first give up, it's true, but with time and effort you'll rediscover healthy coping strategies and adopt some new ones.

Shame prevents you from admitting your problem fully to yourself and stops you from seeking much needed support. Remember that all humans are flawed in one way or another. The person most affected by your addiction is almost certainly you. Hard though it may be, take appropriate steps to get help (more on seeking professional support in the next section). Your addiction is a problem, a big one, but it isn't the sum total of who you are.

Accepting Yourself and Your Addiction

Addiction carries a massive stigma. Rather than making rash global and punitory conclusions about your fundamental character on the basis of your addiction, however, try a little compassion instead. We're not suggesting that you let yourself completely off the hook for whatever you may do to maintain your problem or for the effects it may have on those around you. But taking personal responsibility for your addictive behaviour while still maintaining your sense of basic self-worth is possible – though it may well require persistent effort.

No matter how extreme and all-consuming your particular problem may be, there's more to you than your addiction (see Chapter 14 for more on accepting yourself). Because moderate to severe addictions tend to affect all areas of your life, it can be easy to forget all that you were before your addiction took hold. You'll probably be pleasantly surprised by what you rediscover about your interests, values and personality once you kick the habit (see Chapter 18 on adhering to your values).

Securing Suitable Support

Chapter 21 goes into detail about how to get professional support for your mental and emotional problems. The same rules apply for seeking addiction treatment. Extra points to consider, however, include replacement drugs like methadone for heroin addiction, and other prescription drugs that may reduce cravings for alcohol in the early period of abstinence. You may also want to discuss an in-patient rehabilitation programme with your doctor if you don't feel confident that you can stay clean and sober in your normal environment. Most programmes last a minimum of 28 days and can set your feet firmly on the right path.

If you think your addiction is masking an underlying psychological problem like depression, be sure to talk to your doctor about it. You may benefit from antidepressant medication to help you stop self-medicating with harmful substances. Most medical professionals will be familiar with all sorts of addiction and won't be shocked by whatever you tell them. Be honest and accurate about the extent of your use so that professionals can properly assess your problem.

Support groups such as Alcoholics Anonymous (AA) and Narcotics Anonymous (NA) are available pretty much everywhere. Many people find them a tremendous help. Even if you don't agree with everything a support group purports, you may still gain something from attending. Try to keep an open mind about recovery from addiction and make use of whatever resources are on offer – the AA, for example, offers a twelve-step recovery programme.

Deciding to Desist

Deciding to give up using alcohol, drugs or a compulsive behaviour is a large and difficult step. After all, your DOC has probably been one of your biggest (if not *the* biggest) coping strategies for a long time. As with Kelly, Jack and Percy's examples earlier on, you may doubt your ability to cope with stress in your life without a little chemical help. Equally, pornography or gambling may be the only way you know to relax and distract yourself from your daily cares.

You may resolve to cut down on your use before deciding to give up entirely. This approach can work – but may actually be even harder than opting for an initial period of total abstinence. Many people report that 'stopping after one' is much more difficult than avoiding a substance like alcohol in the first place. The same holds true for gambling and related behaviours. It's hard to stop once you've got started.

Making a decision to stop involves really investigating the costs of your addiction and what you stand to gain by giving up. You need to clearly see that going through the discomfort of withdrawal in order to be addiction free will be worth it. The following sections help you to count the cost your addiction and reap the rewards of recovery.

Addiction is deceptive and powerful. You may find yourself thinking 'maybe my problem isn't *so* bad' after a period of abstinence and be tempted to chance your arm at moderate use. Doing so is rarely, *very rarely*, successful – particularly where drugs and alcohol are concerned. So when your addiction whispers sweet-nothings in your ear and gives you those 'come hither' eyes – remain strong.

Counting the costs

You may not be wholly aware of the price you're paying to maintain your addiction. The effects of drug and alcohol use can sneak up on you. Wittingly or unwittingly, you may have been denying, ignoring and minimising the negative impact of addiction on your life. Sometimes, not until you sit down and really think about it do you realise the full extent of the damage.

Figures 10-1 and 10-2 show how Jack and Percy worked out the costs of their addictions.

Use the Pricing-up Addiction form in Appendix B to work out the personal costs of your own addiction. List as many addiction costs as you can – however small. The better you understand the negative impact of your addiction on all aspects of your life, the greater your chance of sticking to your goal of giving it up. Review your list regularly to keep your motivation strong.

You can also use the Cost–Benefit Analysis (CBA) form found in Chapter 8 to help you weigh up what you stand to lose and gain from abstinence.

Highlighting health

Long-term health problems often result from excessive alcohol and drug use. Booking yourself in for a complete physical examination (including blood tests for liver function and so on) can be a very good idea in early recovery. As well as an overall check-up, your doctor may also be able to offer you additional support. In addition, a good old health scare can sometimes give you extra motivation to give up your addiction. Many of the health problems associated with excessive alcohol and drug consumption improve exponentially with length of abstinence. Thus regular health checks, as you continue with abstinence, may show positive physical changes and spur you on.

Even if you've been fortunate enough to escape any serious health implications, giving up drugs and alcohol is likely to make you feel much more physically fit and well. Sleep and appetite are likely to regulate and you'll probably feel generally more energetic and alert. You'll also look more healthy and vibrant. Your sex drive may improve too. So remember to keep the physical benefits of abstinence on your list of why gritting your teeth and carrying on is worth it.

Costs to relationships	My last girlfriend left me because she said I put cocaine before her. I want to settle down and start a family soon but my drug use prevents me from meeting a nice girl. Many of my friends say that I'm moody and difficult to be around. I see less of my old friends and now just hang out with people from work whot use drugs too. I haven't made time to see my sisters or my parents for months and I'm losing touch with them. I feel guilty about neglecting my family because I'm too busy getting high and drinking.
Costs to work/career/study	My concentration at work is suffering and I worry that one of the bosses will notice that my behaviour is a bit strange. A 'no tolerance' drug policy exists at work and I could be dismissed or at least formally reprimanded for doing cocaine on the job. I planned to do some further training courses this year but I've been too absorbed with cocaine to book them.
Costs to emotional and physical health	I feel really low in energy and quite depressed when coming down from cocaine. My moods are really erratic. My eating is irregular and I've lost a lot of weight. I no longer go to the gym or play tennis. I'm worried about what effect cocaine is having on my overall health and about damaging my nose
Financial costs:	This is costing me a small fortune. With the money I've spent on cocaine and alcohol I could have had two holidays this year.
Personal interest costs:	I don't do any of the things I used to enjoy. I don't see the friends that I have a lot in common with anymore. I don't look after my flat very well and I've lost interest in cooking. I'm just living from day to day and hit to hit, without any long-term planning.

Figure 10-1: Jack's Pricing-up Addiction Form.

Costs to relationships	I don't spend time socialising with my housemates because I'm holed up in my bedroom with the door locked. I feel so bad about my porn use that I can't imagine getting into a relationship with anyone right now.
Costs to work/career/study	My essay is late and I keep missing lectures because of being up all night surfing porn sites. I can't concentrate on studying and my interest in my course is waning
Costs to emotional and physical health	I feel so ashamed and depressed about my heavy pornography use. I'm always anxious about one of my housemates finding out and telling everyone. I couldn't ever live it down. My sleep pattern is really bad. I'm either up way too late in the night using porn or I'm lying awake feeling terrible about it and worrying about someone finding out.
Financial costs	I've given my credit card details to a few sites and I worry about spending more money on pornography that I can't afford
Personal interest costs	I used to be really into my studies and enjoyed spending time chatting with my housemates. Sometimes I'll spend a whole day in bed just avoiding everyone and feeling eaten up with shame about my addiction. I feel lonely and my self-esteem is really poor right now

Figure 10-2: Percy's Pricing-up Addiction Form.

Being honest about the benefits

Nothing's going to knock your negative feelings on the head like your DOC. That baby gives you much desired immediate relief and gratification. Unfortunately, it also gives you lots of longer-term generalised grief, hangovers, comedowns, mood swings, self-denigration, financial concerns and health risks. Lucky you. So yes, the benefits of your DOC are very potent but also very short-lived; the negative side effects of addiction typically hang around much longer. The trouble is that when you're trying to recover from addiction, the short-term benefits of using can seem very attractive and eclipse the negative effects in your mind. Being honest with yourself about the purpose your addictive behaviour serves is crucial; so too is investigating other ways of getting similar benefits without incurring the heavy costs. Over time you can develop a higher tolerance for negative emotions and everyday hassle without needing to turn to your addiction. Figure 10-3 shows how Kelly weighed up the benefits of using codeine and alcohol.

Benefits of using my drug of choice:	It certainly calms my nerves when I take codeine. I think less about my problems like money and parenting and I feel dulled to anxiety.
	Drinking wine helps me relax and unwind in the evenings. I don't think about how much I've got to do the next day or where the rent is going to come from.
	I'm less irritable with the kids when I've had a drink and a couple of codeine tablets.
	My anger toward my ex-husband goes away after I've had a few glasses of wine.
Healthy alternatives to my drug of choice	I could see my doctor and ask him if I should be on antidepressants or if he can refer me for counselling.
	Eating with the kids and then watching some television together relaxes me and it gives me time with them before bed.
	Facing up to my practical problems and investigating possible solutions would probably relieve much of my anxiety.
	Talking to mum on the phone often helps me to put things into perspective.
	Going for a bike ride with the kids usually guarantees me a good night's sleep and I feel happy about being active.
	Soaking in a candle-lit bath with the radio on in the background calms me down.

Figure 10-3: Kelly's 'What does my addiction do for me?' analysis.

Transforming Intention into Action

Intending to give up an addictive behaviour can go on for a very long time. You may find yourself putting it off until conditions are 'right' or when you feel 'inspired' to do so. For example, you may think 'once this work pressure is off I'll give up the cocaine' or 'when I meet someone and want to start a relationship I'll stop using pornography' or 'once I win back some money I'll knock gambling on the head'. If you wait for conditions to be perfect before you kick the habit, you may be waiting for a long time. Basically you're just giving yourself excuses to keep using.

If you know you ultimately need and want to give up an addiction, then you have little choice but to get on with it regardless of whatever else may be going on in your life.

Making a date

There's no time like the present. Try setting a firm date to quit. The earlier the better because you'll be less likely to go on a series of 'final blowouts' that you may well regret. Decide on a date to quit, ideally within the next one to five days, and plan to stick to it. You may even find yourself looking forward to the challenge!

Cruising through cravings

When you first give up any sort of addiction you'll get cravings. Sometimes you may find them annoying but easy to shrug off and other times they may feel like a monster devouring you. To increase your chances of remaining abstinent, you need to plan for and expect very intense cravings. Follow the tips below to help you ride them out:

- ✔ **Know your triggers.** Certain advertisements, environments and even people can trigger off your urge to use. Negative feelings and events can also make it hard to resist your DOC. Write down a list of triggers, when you know you're most at risk of relapsing, and plan what to do instead (see the next point).

- ✔ **Do something else.** One of the best ways to get through a period of craving is to take your mind off it. Although easier said than done, you *can* do it. Make a phone call, do a crossword puzzle, wash the dog, go for a run – do *anything* but use.

✔ **Get grateful.** Since most people engage in addictive behaviour to help forget woes and dissatisfactions, gratitude for what you have got can be a great relapse deterrent. Focus on the positive stuff in your life and think about how you can capitalise on it.

Get out that pen and paper again and make a list of at least 50 things you've got to be grateful for, however small they may be. (Yes, we said 50. You can find them if you look hard enough.) Review this list if and when you find yourself sinking into self-pity and hopelessness.

✔ **Gird your loins.** Yes, cravings truly do suck. But lots of things in life are painful and you probably cope with many of them every day. Be compassionate with yourself but also firm. You're big enough to take the pain without welching on your commitment to yourself.

The more often you experience cravings and yet resist using, the more your confidence in your ability to stay clean will grow. You can start to pride yourself on having a high threshold for discomfort and give yourself well-deserved credit for your successes.

Cravings are normal! Giving up an addiction without experiencing cravings would be decidedly odd. Accept your cravings and don't mistakenly decide that they mean that you're destined to lose the battle! Cravings are *not* a sign of weakness; rather, they show that you're struggling forward.

Extending the time between urge and action

An old, overcoming addiction adage says 'put at least half an hour between yourself and your money'. If your addiction requires cash to be realised, then make it harder for yourself to relapse by keeping yourself in self-imposed penury. If you need to go to the cash point before you can buy drink or drugs, you've got more time to talk yourself out of relapsing. Get rid of your credit cards so you can't gamble online. Treat yourself like a teenager who can't be trusted to spend your cash responsibly. In short, patronise yourself. You won't have to do this forever, but in early recovery making relapse as difficult as possible is sound sense.

Dealing with deprivation

When life deals you a particularly cruel hand and you're struggling with lots of uncomfortable emotions, being deprived of your DOC can seem a very hard loss indeed. You may find yourself hankering for the supposedly 'good old days' when you could lose yourself in a haze of alcohol, drugs, gambling or whatever. Getting used to dealing soberly and constructively with stress and negative emotions takes time. Be patient with yourself but also firm. If you give into addiction at the first sniff of discomfort, you're unlikely to successfully kick the habit. It would be great if life just cut you some slack and gave you an easy ride during your early recovery; but life doesn't play fair all the time. We use the acronym 'HARD LOSS' below to highlight some of the more common emotions and conditions that can pose a real challenge to recovery.

- ✔ **H: Hurt.** Feelings of hurt often lead to a sense of victimisation and a desire to use. You may also feel a thirst for revenge: 'I'll relapse and show them just what they've done to me!' The person you're really causing suffering to is yourself. No one likes feeling hurt but remind yourself that you've got personal responsibility for dealing with your feelings constructively.

- ✔ **A: Anger.** As with hurt, the desire to reach for the bottle, pills or computer mouse can be extreme when you're in a rage. Remember that your uncomfortable feelings will subside on their own. Instead of picking up your addictive substance, take some vigorous exercise or remove yourself from the situation until you feel calmer. See Chapter 15 for more on managing anger.

- ✔ **R: Reward.** 'I've been good all week and I deserve a reward'. Don't mislabel a relapse as a 'reward' drink or hit. Find other ways to treat yourself after a hard week at work or for completing a job. Plan ahead. Make yourself a nice meal or go out to the cinema.

- ✔ **D: Depression.** People often want to drink or use drugs to escape the pain of depression and perhaps to temporarily relieve sleep problems associated with depression. If you think that you're depressed look at the strategies we outline in chapter 10 and seek professional help.

- ✔ **L: Loneliness.** Feeling lonely can be a relapse risk. Especially during the early stages of recovery, scheduling in social activities and renewing friendships is important. Keep yourself in regular contact with friends and get out of the house at least a few evenings per week. Remind yourself that feeling lonely is uncomfortable and unpleasant but it won't kill you. So, you don't need to resort to your addiction as a means of escape.

- ✔ **O: Overwhelmed.** When you're trying to give up an addiction you need to be realistic and careful about how much stress you can manage. You'll increase your ability to cope with stress *without* risk of relapse with practice. In the initial stages of recovery, however, trying to reduce your everyday stresses is prudent. Again, forward planning can really help with keeping life demands under some degree of control.

- ✔ **S: Stagnant.** Oh, the curse of boredom. Letting yourself stagnate and get well and truly bored is a serious risk to your newfound sobriety. Keep your schedule varied and interesting to reduce your risk of turning to your addiction for entertainment.

✔ **S: Self-pity.** 'Poor little me; how I suffer!' Get a grip. We all suffer, struggle and feel the pain of this mortal coil. Ain't nothing special about you, sunshine. Don't allow your addictive urges to convince you that you need to use because you're so specially challenged in life. You're not. Recognise your personal difficulties and accept your problematic circumstances, both past and present. But saddle up and get back on the horse. Take courage and rise to meet your own personal challenges.

You can make recovery less onerous by reducing your propensity to experience unhealthy negative emotions in the first place. See Chapter 6 for information on helpful attitudes that promote healthy negative emotions and behaviours in response to bad events.

Putting positive obstacles in place

In early recovery you may need to avoid any opportunity or temptation to relapse like mice avoid cats – as if your life depended on it. Try to strike a balance between holding an 'I can do this' attitude and going out of your way to eliminate potential relapse triggers. Giving up an addiction is hard enough when conditions are wholly favourable let alone when someone's metaphorically cracking open a bottle of whisky in your face. Be realistic. Give yourself the best chance of success by putting obstacles in the path of relapse. Here's how Jack, Kelly and Percy put positive obstacles in place.

Jack decided to tell his colleagues that he was giving up cocaine so they'd tackle him if he gave in and used. He also stopped carrying any money with him beyond enough to buy a sandwich at lunch. Jack also stopped going out after work with his drug buddies and instead made a series of after-work commitments to his family and clean friends. He deleted his drug contacts from his phone and computer.

Kelly got rid of her corkscrew and wine glasses so that she'd be inconvenienced if she found herself wanting to drink wine in the evening. She also told her colleagues and boss that she had an allergy to codeine-based painkillers to make it virtually impossible for her to buy drugs from work. Kelly also made some promises to her kids to go bike riding on specific weekdays knowing that she'd be very unlikely to give in to drinking and let them down.

Percy cut up his credit cards and moved his computer into the living room of the shared house. He also put parental blocks on the Internet so that, even if he found himself alone in the house, he'd have to go through a series of settings to access pornography. Percy also made plans to cook for his housemates twice a week to take his mind off porn use and re-engage socially.

Get a pen and paper and write down all the possible positive obstacles that you can put between yourself and your addiction.

Leaving nothing to chance

Fingers crossed, God willing, touch wood, if the fates allow it . . . Overcoming an addiction isn't a matter of luck. You may find yourself thinking, 'Hopefully I won't feel like drinking when I go to that party tomorrow.' Fat chance. Either don't go to the party and do something else that you enjoy instead, or drive to it so that you can't drink. With addiction, forewarned is forearmed. Don't make the mistake of clutching a rabbit's foot or counting magpies. Take responsibility for your addictive behaviour and make the necessary arrangements to avoid caving in to temptation.

Creating constructive conditions for continued recovery

Overcoming addiction in a meaningful way (one that's going to last) involves lifestyle changes. Reinvesting in previously enjoyed activities and addressing neglected chores are part of overhauling your lifestyle to avoid relapse. You may also benefit from expanding your interests and increasing your involvement with groups and causes that have nothing to do with your old DOC. Keeping busy (but not overloading yourself) can really help close the gaps that your addiction previously filled. Consider pursuing some of the activities below:

- ✔ **Volunteering.** Doing voluntary work can give you a sense of satisfaction and help you meet new people.

- ✔ **Striving to improve your overall fitness.** Regular exercise increases your endorphin levels and has a real 'feel good' factor.

- ✔ **Joining or starting a film or book group.** Watching films and reading books are great solo past times but getting together with others once a month to discuss your opinions can be even better.

- ✔ **Pursuing further study or training courses.** Taking on new learning and skills can be very rewarding and absorbing. You may also further your career in the process. Studying also offers another great chance to meet new people.

- ✔ **Trying to meet that special someone.** Loads of reputable online dating sites and singles functions exist out there. Give it a whirl and see what happens.

Think hard about your interests. We all have things that really float our boat – classic cars, art, architecture, sport, animals, outdoor pursuits, history, crafts or carpentry. The possibilities are truly endless. Find out what pushes your personal interest buttons and make time to indulge yourself.

Sobriety or 'clean living' isn't a life sentence of boredom and deprivation. It's quite the opposite if you choose to make it so.

Cleaning house

Stop the rot by scourging your living space of all addiction-related stuff. You don't need reminders around the place when cravings descend. Throw out the ashtrays, needles, alcohol and old betting slips. Clean your home to reflect your new resolution to live life cleanly and positively.

A clean and tidy home can also help your mood remain stable. Part of looking after your physical and mental health is looking after your living environment. Even if you're not naturally tidy, make an extra effort to treat your home with the respect and attention you deserve to give yourself.

Taking up supportive socialising

When you first stop using your DOC you may need to reassess your existing friendships. Some people may turn out to be simply 'using mates' and have little else to offer you. You may need to be ruthless and sever ties with certain people.

The people in your life who've been worried about your addictive behaviour or stopped seeing you because of it, may well be the people you need most right now. Try re-engaging with them and let them know about your newfound abstinence so they can offer you much-needed support.

Addiction thrives on secrecy and recovery needs the public gaze. Tell appropriate people about your problem (and your plans to overcome it) in order to 'up the ante' and erode feelings of shame. Also bear in mind that people can't offer you support if they aren't aware that you may need it.

Planning to Prevent Relapse

If you follow the advice offered in the previous sections of this chapter, then you're well on your way to avoiding relapse. However, we also want to alert you to the following points that can slyly provoke relapse:

✔ **Making seemingly irrelevant decisions.** 'I'll just walk home via the pub to save the extra time of avoiding it because I'm running late' or 'I'll just pop into the casino to see my mate whose number I've lost' or 'Maybe I'll stay in this weekend as all my housemates are away and I can work in peace and quiet' or 'I've got a headache so I'll just take the one codeine tablet'. These kinds of thoughts and decisions may appear fairly innocent but they're not! Addiction is a slippery customer and it can lead you into thinking you're making a safe and sound decision when really you're setting yourself up to fall off the wagon. Beware of seemingly irrelevant decisions that are actually wolves in sheep's clothing. Double check your real motivation behind every decision you make in early recovery.

✔ **Finding the novelty wears off.** In the beginning everyone is so pleased and impressed by your abstinence. Maybe they make special allowances for you and check in on you regularly to tell you how well you're doing. Then one day you realise that your 'sobriety' is now being taken for granted. People are no longer especially interested in your recovery from addiction and actually neither are you. This situation's normal; it's what should happen. Once you're far enough away from your addiction people forget about it to a large extent; you're just you again. Rejoice in that rather than feeling neglected and hard done by. You don't need the constant pats on the back anymore. You're recovered, so enjoy.

✔ **Experiencing false bravado.** So you think you've been clean long enough that you can handle a little social drinking, drug use, moderate gambling or porn surfing. The fact that you have that thought and desire means you probably can't safely chance moderate use. Don't risk it. You've been okay without your DOC for this long – why put all your hard work at such risk?

✔ **Feeling everyone else can do it, so why can't I?** Because you have a history of addiction, and that's that. Yes, those fortunate addiction-free individuals can drink or have a smoke when they choose. You, however, have to be very careful indeed. This situation's not unfair or unjust – it's just the way it is for you.

Make a list of all the seemingly irrelevant decisions and addiction resurgence ideas you think you may fall prey to in future. Then challenge them with healthy, helpful and accurate recovery-reinforcing attitudes.

Chapter 11

Beating Body Image Blues

In This Chapter

▶ Living happily with your looks

▶ Making healthy improvements

▶ Appreciating your whole self

> *There's more to life than being really, really ridiculously good looking and I'm going to find out what it is.*
>
> Derek Zoolander (played by Ben Stiller in Zoolander)

*T*aking care of your physical health and appearance is both normal and natural. Looking after yourself through regular exercise, good eating and personal grooming is part and parcel of good mental health. However, many people place too much importance on being physically attractive. Looks can become an over-riding preoccupation and lead you into emotional disturbance and/or low self-esteem.

There's no denying that physical attractiveness has an impact on others. First impressions are often based on how you look *in combination* with how you behave. Psychologists define the term 'body image' as your internalised sense of what you look like. In many cases, the ideas people hold about their appearance are roughly accurate; in others, they can be quite divorced from reality.

In this chapter we touch on some of the more severe and debilitating types of body image disorder, help you to determine if you've got one and offer suggestions for treatment. The bulk of this chapter, however, deals with more commonly encountered body image problems. New ways of thinking about your physical self are introduced and strategies for building a better body image are explained.

First, let's define what we mean by 'healthy' and 'unhealthy' body image. Someone with a healthy body image may not necessarily love the way they look or even be above average in looks. Having a healthy body image is less about how attractive you are and more about *accepting* your looks as they stand. A healthy body image allows you to enjoy your life fully, whatever you look like, and be able to make the most of what nature gave you. People with unhealthy body images tend to desire looking radically different and imagine that they'd be far happier if only they were better looking.

You're certainly not the only person in the world who worries about physical appearance. Even people who are generally considered to be very attractive often are beset with body image problems. It just goes to show that your happiness with your appearance isn't inexorably linked to your objective attractiveness.

Making Friends with the Mirror

'Mirror, mirror on the wall, who's the fattest, ugliest, plainest, gawkiest, most freakish of them all?' (Delete as appropriate.) Does this refrain ring a familiar bell with you? Is your relationship with the mirror fraught with anxiety and horror? If so, join the club – it's a big one. Dissatisfaction with personal appearance is rife in the western world (and increasingly beyond). The severity of body image problems can vary from mild and irritating to severe and debilitating. At the mild end of the scale, you may just grumble about your looks but still be able to live an enjoyable life. If your body image problem is more extreme, however, it may lead to depression, poor self-esteem, social withdrawal and complicated disorders like body dysmorphic disorder (BDD), anorexia and/or bulimia.

BDD is a disorder that involves extreme preoccupation with one or more physical features. The features the BDD sufferer regards as unacceptable and abnormal are usually not that noticeable to other people. BDD sufferers often have compulsive behaviours such as masking physical areas of concern (through clothing and make-up) and checking in the mirror continually to ensure the perceived defect is still concealed (or hasn't worsened in some way). Both women and men can suffer from BDD.

Anorexia nervosa is an eating disorder characterised by severe fear of fatness, or indeed of being a normal healthy weight, coupled with intense efforts to lose weight. In the majority of cases, the sufferer believes she or he looks normal even though other people (including doctors and therapists) insist that they're underweight. Anorexia affects men and women alike, despite the misconception that it's a female illness. Typically, sufferers will have elaborate rules and rituals about food that enable them to restrict calorie intake. Efforts to lose weight include severe restriction of food intake, excessive use of laxatives, over-exercising and vomiting after eating.

Bulimia nervosa is another eating disorder but most sufferers are within a normal weight range. The disorder is characterised by periods of dieting punctuated by 'binges'. Typically, an individual will consume over the recommended daily intake of calories in one binge-eating episode. Following a binge, the sufferer purges either through self-induced vomiting, use of laxatives or both. Like anorexia, bulimia is also often considered a 'women only' problem; in reality, however, many boys and men develop bulimia too.

The following sections provide some questions to help you figure out whether body image is a problem for you.

Do I have a serious body image problem?

Do you think that you have a particular physical feature that's abnormal, defective or ugly? This feature may be anywhere on your body. Remember that your perception of this feature is what counts here, even if others disagree with you about it. Consider your responses to these questions:

1. Has a close friend, family member or health professional told you that your concerns about your feature are groundless and there's nothing noticeably different or wrong about the way you look?

2. Do you continue to be distressed about and preoccupied with your feature despite assurance from friends, family members and doctors?

3. If you add up all the time you think about, worry about or check your feature of concern in one day, does it amount to one hour (or more)?

4. Do your specific worries about your physical feature prevent you from socialising or stop you from forming intimate relationships?

If you answer 'yes' to any four out of the five questions listed above, you may have some degree of BDD. Disorder-specific CBT treatment can help you. A professional psychiatric assessment may also be useful; discuss the issue with your GP and ask for a referral. Even if you think your problems are at the mild end of the spectrum, we advise you to err on the side of caution and get a medical opinion anyway.

Do I have an eating disorder?

Extreme concerns about body image can result in eating disorders such as anorexia or bulimia. Answer these questions to ascertain your feelings in relation to food, weight gain or loss, and your self-image:

1. Are you very fearful of gaining weight, staying at the same weight or of others thinking that you're fat?

2. Do you try to strictly monitor how much you eat (portion size), what you eat (food groups) or calories consumed each day?

3. Do you become very distressed (depressed or agitated) if you eat more than you planned or consume a 'forbidden' food?

4. Despite having lost weight, do you feel dissatisfied with your size and convinced that you must lose more?

5. Do you try to hide the fact that you're trying to lose weight from friends and family because they've expressed concern that you're underweight?

6. Do you induce vomiting, drink lots of water or diet soft drinks to fill yourself up, use laxatives or exercise compulsively in order to lose more weight?

7. Are you preoccupied by food and your size? Do you find that they're almost always on your mind? (You may also have dreams about food and eating.)

8. Despite your best efforts, do you sometimes lose control and binge? A binge may be eating foods you typically avoid or larger portions than you normally allow yourself (you may feel intense guilt and regret afterward).

9. Do you have certain rituals about eating such as: chewing a certain number of times, cutting up food into small pieces, consuming less than others you're eating with, eating at specific times or wanting to eat in private?

10. Do you weigh yourself once a day or more? Check the prominence of your hip, joint and shoulder bones daily? Test out your size in relation to certain articles of clothing?

If you answer 'yes' to five or more of the above questions you may be either suffering from an eating disorder or be at risk of developing one. Talk to your GP and ask to be referred to a psychiatrist for an assessment. Medical units dedicated to treating eating disorders exist and many CBT therapists will have specialist knowledge of this problem.

If your perception of how you look is preventing you from going to work or school, socialising and generally pursuing your goals (see Chapter 8 for more about goals), don't hesitate to seek professional help. Conditions like BDD and eating disorders tend to worsen over time if untreated. We strongly advise that you get treatment as soon as possible. Chapter 21 provides lots of advice and information about getting professional help to deal with your problems.

Many people make a full recovery from the body image disorders we discuss in this chapter. Doing so involves a lot of determination and work – but it can be done. Be optimistic and stubbornly stick to a recognised and effective form of treatment (see Chapter 21 for pointers on where to seek help).

Considering hypothetical cases

You may not have found the questions in the sections relevant to you but still recognise that your relationship with your physical self is less than ideal. Many of us have bouts of self-loathing regarding our appearance; they may pass reasonably quickly or be indicative of more chronic dissatisfaction.

Have a gander at the following hypothetical examples:

> Jake is tall and slim. He got teased a lot during his school years and was called 'stretch' and 'bean pole'. Jake remains very self-conscious about his height and build. He constantly compares himself to his friends at the gym who are more compact, muscular and stocky. Jake has developed a habit of scrutinising himself when he gets undressed in front of the mirror. Generally, he's pretty uncomplimentary about what he sees: 'What puny little shoulders I have! My stomach muscles are non-existent. Why do I even bother working out? It clearly has no real effect'

> Jake's habitual harsh self-criticism in front of the mirror isn't doing his overall self-esteem or body image a lot of favours. But he's been doing so for so long that he doesn't realise how damaging this criticism actually is.

> Savannah hates her face; she thinks that her nose is too prominent and that her eyes are too far apart. She takes no notice of her glossy hair and even teeth. In fact, she's so dissatisfied with her facial appearance that looking in the mirror is painful. Since adolescence Savannah has avoided mirrors, spending as little time witnessing her own reflection as possible. She quickly does her hair and applies a modest amount of make-up each morning, then avoids looking in the mirror for the rest of the day.

> Savannah considers reflective surfaces to be her enemies. She completely discounts her best features and focuses instead on those she dislikes.

One of the key differences between people with a healthy body image and those with an unhealthy one is what they choose to focus on when they look at their reflection. People with poor body image typically home in on areas of dissatisfaction to the exclusion of other aspects of their looks. Those with a healthy body image are more likely to pay specific attention to areas and features that they consider to be their best points.

Both Jake and Savannah are continually reinforcing their negative body images through their use of mirrors. Jake uses the mirror too much in order to examine and berate his tall, slim shape. Savannah does the opposite; she hides away from the mirror because she fears confronting her 'imperfect' face. If either of these two examples reminds you of your own relationship with the mirror, you may benefit from following the three simple rules of healthy mirror use:

1. **Observe yourself in the mirror but suspend evaluation or judgement.** Try not to entertain thoughts about yourself as either attractive or ugly. Just use the mirror to do whatever it is you need it for, such as like fixing your hair or putting on make-up.

2. **Regulate how much time you spend on average before the looking glass.** If you stay in front of the mirror for too long you may end up criticising your appearance like Jake. If you avoid the mirror like Savannah, you may need to force yourself to observe your reflection more often. Avoiding mirrors can serve to reinforce the fictitious notion that your appearance will cause them to shatter!

3. **Resist selective scrutiny.** Instead of focusing your attention on individual aspects of your appearance, try to view yourself as a whole. Again, be vigilant about suspending judgement. Simply look and see your whole physical self without positive or negative evaluation.

These rules are indeed simple – but they're difficult to stick to if you've been using the mirror to find fault with your appearance for years. Learning to appreciate your physical self instead of perpetually pulling your looks to pieces takes determination and practice. Be stubborn and persist until you develop new healthy mirror habits.

Use the mirror as a tool to check if your hair is in place, shave, see whether you're suitably attired or if a bit of breakfast is lodged in your moustache. Don't use it as a weapon to beat yourself with.

Taking Advertising and Media Messages with a Pinch of Salt

The advertising industry is guilty of promoting the over-valuation of physical attractiveness. Preying on the average person's physical insecurities is obviously in the best interest of the fashion industry (including producers of cosmetics, clothing and personal hygiene products). Quite simply, it makes them money through product sales. Underlying many advertising messages is the sub-text: 'Buy our product and you too can look this hot!' Bikini-clad women grace the covers of car and technological gadget magazines, while Adonis-like men are a regular feature in soft drink and chocolate advertisements on television. Spotting an obvious link between wearing a bikini and listening to an iPod isn't easy, but the message is roughly consistent: 'These products are sexy; sexy people own them! Buy this and rub shoulders with the sexy people!' Or something along those lines.

Advertisements, magazines, films and television programmes frequently present a skewed representation of what the average person looks like or *ought* to look like. Models, for example, are typically unusually thin and tall. People on magazine covers and superstars of any ilk are photographed specifically to make them look their best. Photographs are often air brushed to remove any imperfections. No doubt many actors, models and celebrities are naturally very good-looking people, but photography can make them look flawless. Most of us average Joe types just don't look that special. Additionally, media coverage can make the most ordinary individual appear to be the height of physical perfection. Not all models, celebrities or actors are superlatively good looking. We're simply told to believe that they are. Many of the people in the centre of media attention may possess powers of attraction that aren't anchored in their physical characteristics. Instead of accepting everything that the media encourages you to accept as true, try using your own judgement more often. Most of the world's population are pretty average in looks.

Recognising your own body image issues

You can run into body image trouble if you aspire to look like someone exceptionally physically beautiful from the cover of *Vogue* or *GQ*. However, blaming poor body image on the media is much too simplistic. Much of your chronic dissatisfaction with your looks may well be down to your own thinking and behaviour. You may have unhealthy body image thinking and behavioural habits that you're only partially aware of.

Unhealthy thinking

Certain ways of thinking typically underpin an unhealthy body image:

- **Making rigid demands and rules about the way other people must (or must not) judge your appearance.** 'I couldn't stand it if someone thought I was plain or fat!' Fear of negative physical judgement isn't limited to members of the opposite sex (or the gender you're attracted to). Most people are also fearful of being judged as 'ugly' by peers or those they have no romantic or sexual interest in. It may seem hard to believe, but there are worse things in the world than being judged as physically unattractive. Lasting attraction is based on much more than conventional beauty. Try to think of yourself as a whole person and not just a set of physical attributes.

✔ **Linking your self-worth to your attractiveness.** If you have a poor body image you may automatically assume that beautiful people are superior to you, have more rights, deserve special treatment and lead charmed lives in general. You feel like the frog waiting for a kiss. We all have basic human worth regardless of how we look. Your worth isn't dictated by your attractiveness. You have a lot to contribute to this world besides being pleasing to the eye.

✔ **Placing too much importance on physical appearance and under-rating other characteristics that contribute to overall attractiveness such as personality, values and humour.** Beauty really is only skin deep. The people we find most attractive aren't necessarily supermodel material.

✔ **Overestimating the degree to which other people evaluate and even *notice* your looks.** If you suffer from severely poor body image you may assume that any person you catch glancing your way is thinking about how unfortunate looking you are. You may even assume that they won't want to know you on the basis of your looks. People are often far less interested in criticising your looks than you may assume. You may attract attention from others for any number of reasons or fall under their gaze simply because they're distracted and thinking about something else entirely. Try to bear in mind that your insecurity about your looks is unlikely to be terribly obvious (or interesting for that matter) to others.

✔ **Holding unrealistic expectations and standards for your own physical appearance.** There's a limit to the extent that you can improve and/or change your fundamental looks. If you constantly strive to look like a glamour model or a young film star, you may end up feeling chronically inadequate and dissatisfied in the looks department. Accepting your looks, and making the most of what you've got, is far more productive than striving for unrealistic and unattainable ideals.

Unhealthy behaviours

Common behavioural characteristics associated with an unhealthy body image include the following:

✔ **Comparing your physical appearance to others on a regular basis.** You may not be aware of how much time you spend comparing yourself with others in terms of attractiveness. Doing so can become a very insidious and pernicious habit. 'Is my backside bigger than hers?', 'Do I look younger than that person?', 'Am I as stylish as her?' and so on and so on. Regardless of whether or not you make a positive self-comparison against another poor, unsuspecting individual, you're not doing your overall body image any good. Instead, you're perpetuating the potentially damaging idea that looks are all important and feeding the fires of your preoccupation with external appearances.

Try doing the opposite for three weeks: observe others without judgement and resist the urge to make personal comparisons. Then check out any positive benefits to your overall satisfaction with your own looks (there'll probably be a slight increase) and your degree of preoccupation with physical appearance generally (chances are it will have reduced appreciably).

✔ **Over-preparing before going out in public.** Making sure that you look your best even to pop to the corner shop for a loaf of bread is a sure sign of poor body image (and/or over-emphasis on the importance of physical attractiveness).

You may truly believe that you look vastly different (better) when you're made-up, shaved or groomed than you do fresh out of bed or the shower – in the raw – but you're probably wrong about that. The difference has much more to do with your internal perception of how you look than the external reality. You may *feel* like you look much more appetising after completing your usual grooming regime, but if you did a survey of what others think you may well be surprised by how little difference they actually report.

✔ **Dieting or exercising constantly in order to improve your looks.** A bit later in this chapter we discuss making positive change to your lifestyle (and by association, your appearance) for positive reasons. The majority of us could probably reap health benefits from improved eating habits and more regular physical exertion. Many people, however, are perpetually dieting and waiting to gain some muscle tone or shed some weight before they can consider themselves 'worthwhile' or 'attractive' individuals. Accepting yourself as you are right now, *whilst* acknowledging areas that leave scope for improvement, allows you to make changes that promote health and happiness. Rather than striving to reach elusive physical ideals through fad diets, decide to make some long-term lifestyle changes.

✔ **Attempting to hide away from scrutiny, even from lovers**. If you really suffer from body shame you may avoid looking in the mirror (as discussed earlier in this chapter) and go to great lengths to prevent others from seeing your imperfections. You may be reluctant to wear a swimsuit or take off your shirt on a hot day at the beach. Perhaps you refuse to undress in front of your partner and insist on keeping the lights low when making love. Hiding away from the gaze of others (even those closest to you) may seem to make immediate sense – you feel less self-conscious. Ultimately, though, hiding away keeps you locked into a cycle of chronically poor body image.

If you really want to be more content with your physical appearance, you need to act in a way that reflects how you want to eventually feel. People who accept what they look like (flaws and all) generally don't wear cloaks to the beach or blindfold their lovers. The more you hide your body (or face) away, the more you perpetuate the belief that you've actually got something unacceptable to hide.

✔ **Seeking reassurance.** Asking people if they think you're fat, skinny, ugly, odd-looking and so on can become a habit. You may feel better for a short time but chances are your insecurities come to the fore again fairly quickly. You probably also dismiss reassurances and compliments because you think 'people are just being polite'. Reassurance seeking can also take other forms, such as comparing yourself to people who you think look worse than you. Doing so's a short-lived solution to poor body image because it keeps you focused on physical appearance.

If you recognise any of these behaviours, you may well have body image issues. With determination, however, you can accept what you look like and recognise that your physical appearance doesn't define everything about you.

Accepting yourself

Instead of increasing your dissatisfaction with your appearance through engaging in the thinking and behaving outlined in the previous section, try practising some self-acceptance. Accepting yourself as worthy *and* simultaneously striving to make improvements is entirely possible – whatever your natural physical appearance.

For example, consider Jake from earlier in the chapter. He can make a deliberate effort to improve his muscle tone but also consistently recognise that his natural shape is tall and slim – and that's okay. Rather than criticising his shape all the time, he can help his body image by developing new attitudes towards himself. Realistically, Jake is unlikely to suddenly fall in love with his physique. However, he can change his relationship with his body over time by resisting his mirror rituals and sending accepting messages to himself, such as 'I'd like to be more muscled but I accept my natural shape' or 'I'm not physically perfect but the way I look is good enough'. Jake can also help himself by dressing to suit his height and shape, working out but putting the emphasis on fitness and strength rather than on building visible muscles, and refusing to compare his body with other guys at the gym who are naturally more stocky.

Accepting other people is the flipside to the coin of accepting yourself. You can eventually accept yourself as imperfect, fallible, physically flawed and yet a worthy and valuable human being. Accepting yourself is easier to do (and maintain), however, if you also apply the same philosophy to everyone else. So don't allow yourself to be overly judgemental about other people's appearance. Accept others as they are and work on taking the emphasis off physical beauty generally.

Seeing yourself as a whole person

Hey, sweetheart, you're not just a pretty face! A whole person exists inside that physical container known as your body. Your external presentation is really just the conduit for all your internal attributes, feelings, ideas and musings; that is, all your human facets. Have a look at Figures 11-1 and 11-2. Figure 11-1 represents the amount of emphasis that many people with unhealthy body images assume others put on physical attractiveness in relation to other characteristics. You may also attach exaggerated importance to physical beauty yourself. Figure 11-2 represents a more accurate split between looks and other important components of interpersonal attraction. The items included in this figure are merely *some* of the *many* idiosyncratic aspects that people tend to pay specific attention to when choosing friends or romantic partners. Sure, physical attraction plays a part; but that can grow (or indeed, wane) over time as you get to know one another. Looks are only one small and instantly obvious part of lasting affiliation between people.

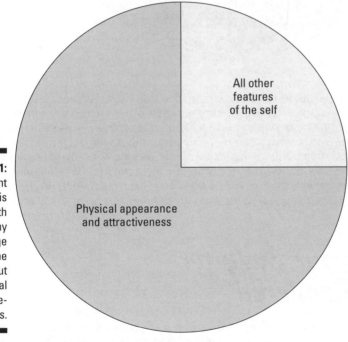

Figure 11-1:
The amount of emphasis people with unhealthy body image assume others put on physical attractiveness.

All other features of the self

Physical appearance and attractiveness

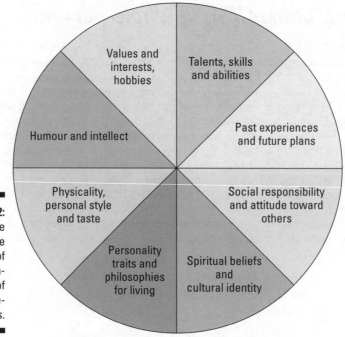

Figure 11-2:
A more
accurate
measure of
the com-
ponents of
attractive-
ness.

Values and interests, hobbies

Talents, skills and abilities

Past experiences and future plans

Humour and intellect

Social responsibility and attitude toward others

Physicality, personal style and taste

Personality traits and philosophies for living

Spiritual beliefs and cultural identity

Use this experiment to reinforce the idea that attractiveness isn't wholly dictated by actual physical beauty and that other virtues are of equal importance. On a piece of paper, make a list of at least five people who you really admire, find attractive or enjoy being around but who aren't particularly/ conventionally good looking. Draw on people you actually know personally and famous people. Next to their names write down the main characteristic you associate with that person. Review your list from time to time and especially when you catch yourself putting too much emphasis on physical appearance.

Saluting your Body for Services Rendered

Despite what society, the media and the advertising industry may invite you to believe (or what you may have spent years believing all on your own), there's more to you than meets the eye. Literally. Your face and body aren't merely for aesthetic purposes.

The eyes are described as windows to the soul. There's a reason for that. The look in your eyes, your facial expressions and body language convey countless messages. Whether we like it or not, other people can often read our feelings through our facial expression and what they see in our eyes.

Your face is a highly mobile feature, especially if you allow it to be. You might be inclined to try and control your facial expressions for fear of looking weird or unattractive. Part of having a healthy body image involves allowing yourself to fully use your face and body to express yourself. They can tell a myriad of stories even if you actually say little or nothing. The way you hold yourself, position your body and set your facial features conveys a plethora of messages to the casual or indeed studious observer. Your body and your face aren't simply features to be admired or rejected; they're vital and forceful means of communication. Communication is a hugely important and useful skill in all types of society. So whether or not you're a natural stunner, you're definitely (and inevitably) a natural communicator.

Spending so much time focusing on how you look that you neglect to fully recognise the other functions your face and body fulfil isn't uncommon.

We aren't here on earth just to look good and be sexually alluring. Male or female, we're active, vibrant, ever-changing beings. We all have skills, purposes, values and ideals that go far beyond physical appearance.

The following three sections highlight the other (frequently under-appreciated) purposes of your physical body and the activities it allows you to enact and enjoy.

Enjoying scintillating sensations

Your five senses – sight, sound, smell, taste and touch – allow you to take in the world and experience life.

Even when you lose one sense or are born without one, such as sight or hearing, your other senses typically compensate – which is pretty amazing. I (Rhena) spent a few years learning sign language and it made me understand just how interesting my senses are. The experiences of deaf people are just as rich as those of hearing people. The visual concentration needed to communicate via sign language is extraordinary (less so if you're deaf it turns out, since speaking and hearing are usually not options and hence not distractions). People who are deaf or blind are much more patient with the limitations of us sighted and hearing individuals than you may realise.

Your five senses are very much deserving of your appreciation and gratitude. Consider all they enable you to experience:

✔ **Pain:** Okay, pain isn't something you may usually pause to appreciate but it's a vital and inevitable part of human experience. Physical and emotional pain puts you in touch with your humanity and can give you many opportunities to learn and grow. Consider heartbreak, grief, disappointment, toothache, eating chillies, witnessing a traumatic event, hearing a loved one cry, seeing a really bad film, doing something regrettable, giving birth or falling off a skateboard – a wealth of experience is offered through pain.

✔ **Pleasure:** Oh, yes. All five of your senses provide you with a host of pleasures. Pleasant smells, tastes, sights, sounds and tactile sensations are associated with all manner of things, such as music, baking, making love, working hard, eating and drinking, creating art, being hugged, giving a hug; the list is endless.

Pain and pleasure often overlap to form a complete human experience. Some common examples include giving birth, running a marathon, completing a course of study, ending a relationship or beginning one, having an operation, doing physiotherapy, moving house, changing jobs, leaving home for the first time, and many, many more.

So, other than simply being a creature of physical beauty (or not,) you're also a creature of *experience*. In order to build a better understanding of yourself as a whole living person, you may need to think more about your senses and experiential existence and less about how hot you look in the buff.

Doing your daily duties

How often do you actually take time to consciously appreciate all that your body enables you to do? Like most of us, you may take your physical capabilities somewhat for granted. As we touched on in the last section and do so again in the nearby sidebar, people with physical disabilities or incapacities probably have a greater appreciation for all the human body can do than those of us who've never faced any significant physical ability challenges. We could all probably benefit from being more attentive to the fact that our bodies serve so many vital functions. Again, above and beyond appearance, your body does a great deal for you on a daily basis:

✔ **Job and career:** Your physical body allows you to pursue your career goals, earn a living, learn new skills and adopt new knowledge.

✔ **Housekeeping:** Being able to care for your environment, engage in DIY, drive a vehicle, keep on top of the laundry, do gardening, take out the bins, look after your children or other people in your family, do the shopping, cook meals, dust, hoover, iron and – everything else.

✔ **Personal care:** Just being able to look after your own physical needs is something to be grateful for every day.

✔ **Altruistic pursuits:** Taking care of others in need, helping out a friend, family member or neighbour are all selfless acts that can help you feel good inside. Without your physical abilities you'd be unable to behave in specific other-enhancing ways. People wouldn't benefit from your practical assistance and you wouldn't be as readily able to reap personal benefits from doing so.

You don't need to be an oil painting to be able to live a good and meaningful life. Your physical self (body and face) can bring you and others much joy and serve countless essential functions.

In the interest of improving your body image, and appreciating your whole self instead of simply focusing on your appearance, try the following experiment. Spend a little time each day appreciating and being grateful for your physical abilities. You can put pen to paper and make yourself a 'gratitude list' that can help you to appreciate your physical self more.

Valuing your vehicle for experience

You may spend so much time lamenting your appearance that you overlook the fact that without your physical shell (hypothetical warts and all) you'd be deprived of . . . *life*! We've already touched on this concept throughout this chapter but at the risk of repetition (and it bears repeating), you *need* your physical body to be able to live your life. That's the long and the short of it. So if you believe that you'd rather be dead than alive in an average looking or even less than average looking physical vehicle, get some professional help (see Chapter 21 for starters). And give your head a serious shake.

Instead of thinking solely about how attractive you may or may not think you *look*, try giving some headspace to how you *live*. Your body is the vehicle through which you get to:

✔ **Form relationships:** Being in contact with others, be it superficially, more profoundly or intimately, is part of your human experience – and is *not* exclusively dictated by your physical attractiveness.

✔ **Feel emotions:** Feelings are fantastic. Positive ones tend to be more rewarding than negative ones, sure, but both are part and parcel of living a full and enriched life (consult Chapter 6 for more about emotions).

✔ **Make life choices:** You get to overcome adversity, choose jobs and careers, build a family, live in line with your own personal standards and values (see Chapter 18), plus appreciate the world around you.

✔ **Pursue interests:** You can't go on safari without being physically here on the earth, but you *can* do it even if you're blessed with a face made for radio. Going on safari, by the way, is merely an example. Even visiting an art gallery or some other form of more commonplace interest-based activity is valid use of your fabulous, far from perfect form.

Really good-looking people have human rights too! If you're able to see that you're obviously good looking or are told you're beautiful all the time – you probably are. Yet you're still allowed to feel insecure physically and doubt your powers of attraction. Sometimes the pressure of being considered unusually attractive can be problematic. You may feel that unless you stay looking good your worth will evaporate. Or that you're only worthy, likable and significant because you look good or that looks are all you've got going for you.

None of these notions are true. Enjoy your good looks and use them to your advantage. But don't allow anyone to convince you that all you are is a good-looking person. You've got the right to experience life and pursue your interests as much as anyone else. Beautiful people fall prey to unhealthy body image just as average and below-average looking people do. So don't think you're excluded from the information offered in this chapter.

Choosing to Change for all the Right Reasons

Like many others battling with an unhealthy body image, you may make the following faulty conclusion about physical appearance:

Good looks = Worthwhile, lovable, successful person

Average/below average looks = Less worthwhile, unlovable, unsuccessful person Several adjectives can be applied to that kind of conclusion – but two of the most fitting are 'crazy' and 'damaging'. In short, it neither makes any real sense nor does you any good.

Here are some examples of what we consider the wrong reasons to make physical changes (to your body and/or face):

✔ Because you think that improving the way you look will make you a more worthwhile person

✔ Because you think that improving your looks will make you a more likable and lovable person

✔ To please a critical partner (who may be exacerbating your physical insecurity)

✔ In order to try to overcome sexual/romantic jealousy

✔ To win approval from people who you believe you're fundamentally inferior to (because of your looks)

Now here are some potentially sound reasons for changing one or more aspects of your appearance (body and/or face):

✔ To improve your health and fitness

✔ To increase enjoyment

✔ To improve your physical ability to perform specific activities and increase general mobility

✔ To reduce physical pain

✔ Out of a genuine desire to reduce self-consciousness and increase your social confidence

Note the distinction between 'confidence' and 'worth'! Worth is an overall value assigned to an object. For example, that diamond is worth £30,000. Because you're not an object, your human worth can't accurately be assessed like that of a jewel or car. Trying to judge your own (or another person's) overall worth is inappropriate, especially on the basis of external packaging!

Confidence is more about your belief in your abilities. For example, you may have a pretty solid sense of your own intrinsic worth but lack confidence as a cook, accountant or public speaker. Social confidence often corresponds with a healthy body image, it's true. However, this doesn't mean that you've got to either be super good looking or *believe that you are* to have a robust sense of your own worth *or* be socially confident. Having a realistic view of your looks *and* believing that you're a worthwhile, likable individual is perfectly possible. Believing in your ability to draw people toward you on the basis of your personality – and not just your appearance – usually amounts to social confidence.

Common targets for physical change and improvement often include:

✔ Hair styling and dying

✔ Makeovers and cosmetic advice

✔ Various detox treatments, for example colonic irrigation

✔ Weight loss or gain regimes

✔ Increased fitness and flexibility

✔ Facial and bodily hair removal

✔ Contact lenses to replace glasses and/or change eye colour

✔ Laser eye treatment

✔ Dental work, including braces and teeth whitening

✔ Skin treatments such as micro-derma abrasion, chemical peels, tattoo removals, scar and birthmark reduction

✔ Minor cosmetic operations like ear tucks, botox, collagen implants, mole removal

Less common and more complicated targets for physical change may include:

✔ Breast enlargement or reduction

✔ Harelip restructuring

✔ Nose reshaping and reconstruction

✔ Hair replacement treatments

✔ Major dental reconstruction

✔ Stomach bands or stapling for weight loss

✔ Major cosmetic surgery, including 'tummy tucks', 'face lifts' or skin grafting

These lists are by no means definitive and many other forms of physical cosmetic treatment and surgical intervention exist. There's no reason that you shouldn't seek one of these (or similar) treatments provided you truly believe that doing so will help you to accept yourself physically and build a healthy body image. But we strongly urge you to check and double-check your motivation before you embark on a treatment plan, however minor it may be.

Cosmetic surgery and other extreme ways of altering your appearance ought not be undertaken lightly. They can be risky and expensive. You need to accurately weigh up your current dissatisfaction with an aspect of your appearance against the risks inherent in cosmetic alteration. If you have any concerns (or people close to you do) that your desire for surgery is symptomatic of one of the disorders discussed in the beginning of this chapter, seek a professional psychiatric assessment before you go through with it. In BDD sufferers, surgery often produces the opposite of the desired effect. The sufferer is dissatisfied with the results, believing that they've made the problem worse. Or the focus of dissatisfaction is transferred to another aspect of their face or body. Many reputable cosmetic surgeons refuse treatment until they've ascertained that the patient is not suffering from BDD or some other psychological disorder.

Highlighting health

Improving and safeguarding your health (as far as is reasonably possible) is an excellent reason for making changes to your lifestyle and – as an inevitable side effect – your appearance. Without exception, we all look better when fitter and healthier.

Health scares delivered to people of any age typically spur the individual into better eating, reduced alcohol consumption, giving up smoking and taking more regular exercise. That's no bad thing. Improved health and fitness typically makes life more enjoyable. Even if you're in fine fettle you may still decide to make changes to your lifestyle in order to maintain your physical health long into the future. Leading a healthy lifestyle can also have fringe benefits like reducing the signs of aging and keeping your figure trim.

Health and happiness show in your looks. Strong teeth, shining eyes, glossy hair, clear skin and a wide smile are all very attractive features. Most of these are the by-products of overall good health and general contentment. So you can enhance your appearance by making improvements to your lifestyle and doing what you can to foster personal happiness (more on this in Chapter 18).

Maximising enjoyment

Making physical changes (such as gaining or losing weight) in order to enjoy life more is a healthy motivation. Changes to body weight can help increase energy and reduce pain in many instances, enabling you to take part in activities that may have not been possible before weight change. Improved physical fitness also can have a positive impact on sleep, digestion, concentration, circulation and blood pressure, and alleviate many other minor or major ailments.

Improving muscle tone can also help with back and joint pain and increase flexibility. So, by becoming fitter, you're likely to find new avenues for enjoyment like walking, dancing or horse riding. You may even just be able to climb stairs without pain or breathlessness, thereby rendering daily life easier. Try to consider what additional benefits other than looking better are likely to ensue from improved fitness.

Bringing out your best

You may decide to make changes to your appearance because you want to look your best. A subtle but pertinent difference exists between being motivated to make physical changes in order to *increase your sense of worth* and simply *to optimise your appearance.* The former motivation suggests that you link your intrinsic human worth to outward appearance, which can compound low self-esteem and unhealthy relations with your body (as discussed earlier in this chapter). The latter motivation, however, implies that you value yourself generally and therefore can consider improving your physical appearance as part of a self-care regime. To make this distinction clearer, look at the two examples of motivational attitudes offered here.

Jenny is in her late thirties and has started to go prematurely grey. Cheryl is roughly the same age as Jenny and is also going grey. Both women are of average good looks and are similarly built. Both women have black hair and the grey shows a lot so they decide to have it dyed. Thus far pretty much no difference exists between Jenny and Cheryl with regard to choosing to have their hair dyed. The hidden difference lies in their motivation.

Jenny thinks the following: 'If I dye my hair it might make me look better and other people will find me more attractive. I need other people's approval to feel okay about myself.'

Cheryl thinks like this: 'This grey is aging me, I reckon, and I do like to look my best. I'll have it dyed and that will help me look my age again. I'll feel more positive about my appearance without the grey.'

Jenny, unlike Cheryl, believes that she needs other people's approval of her looks to feel okay about herself; to feel like a worthwhile person. Cheryl instead focuses on her *own* satisfaction with her appearance and makes no connection between that and her overall sense of self-worth. Cheryl also leaves other people's possible evaluations of her appearance out of the equation entirely.

Use this example to help you clearly assess your motivation for making even minor physical changes, such as changing your hair colour or trying contact lenses. By all means have your hair dyed if you wish to – but try to challenge unhealthy thinking like Jenny's in favour of adopting healthy thinking like Cheryl's. Make changes for the right reasons!

Being daring

Working out, having your teeth cleaned professionally, being pampered with a facial or massage can help you feel more physically comfortable and confident. When you feel like you're looking your best, your physical confidence is on the up.

Sometimes making even small physical improvements can encourage you to be a bit more daring in your dress sense, activity choices, and self-expression in general. You may get a new hairstyle and suddenly feel confident enough to ask out that girl at reception you've been noticing for the past few months. A little weight loss may spur you to wear a fitted dress and join the local salsa dancing class. Regular exercise might lead you into taking part in your child's football coaching. You may well feel more prepared to embark on many new ventures once you've begun a physical improvement regime of some kind.

But bear in mind the basic principle of healthy body image, namely:

> Improved appearance and/or fitness = Increased enjoyment and confidence

Not:

> Improved appearance and/or fitness = Better, more worthwhile and valuable human being

Changing with time

We all change physically, emotionally, and perhaps spiritually and philosophically, as we grow older. Even if nothing exceptionally dramatic or notable happens to us, certain changes are inevitable. Our hair will grey; our facial features will adopt deep expressive wrinkles. Some of us actually even improve physically with age (not to mention in other, more pertinent, personality-based ways, such as mellowing or becoming more accepting), but in the main, we just get older – and it shows.

Being able to acknowledge, adapt to and accept the way your body's abilities and physical attributes change over time can help you to maintain a healthy body image for life. Being older doesn't equate to being 'uglier' or 'less useful'. It just means that you're naturally aging and your looks are changing. Your ability to climb up a mountain or dance the night away may diminish – but that's only natural and normal. Aging gracefully involves accepting the physical changes associated with getting older and adapting to new limitations whilst making the most of your capabilities. Many men and women come to terms with their changing appearances as they grow older and manage to maintain a healthy and robust body image. You can do the same if you apply a healthy attitude to growth, age and change. As humans we're not stagnant. We evolve and develop over time. No one can be defined absolutely on the basis of how they appear externally, however old they are.

So try to embrace rather than reject the ways in which your body and face change over time.

Try to appreciate every smile line and worry wrinkle. They're the traces of a life fully lived.

Other events, such as accidents and illness, can also impact on your appearance and physical abilities. Adjusting to drastic or unpredicted changes to your face and body can be very difficult at any stage of life. Sometimes you may need some extra professional help. It can be inspiring to note that ordinary people do go on to lead satisfying lives even after serious accidents or illness. The actor Christopher Reeve (1952–2004) is probably one of the best-known examples of famous people who've suffered this type of adversity. Reeve, famous for playing the role of Superman in a whole series of films, became a quadriplegic in 1995 after being thrown from his horse during a sporting competition. He then lobbied on behalf of people with spinal cord injuries, and in support of human embryonic stem cell research.

Even if an accident or illness hasn't resulted in serious physical disability, comparatively minor issues, such as facial scarring or walking with a limp, can still be challenging. Adjusting to the loss of a limb, altered facial and bodily appearance due to an accident, loss of sight or hearing and diminished mobility in response to disease can have a profound impact on your personal sense of identity and on your overall body image. Happily, many people adapt to these sorts of difficulty and lead full, enriched lives. If you've experienced any of the difficulties discussed here and feel you'd like some extra support, seek some professional and expert help (see Chapter 21).

Chapter 12

Deconstructing and Demolishing Depression

In This Chapter

▶ Understanding depression

▶ Identifying thinking and behaviour patterns that keep your depression going

▶ Recognising and reducing ruminative thinking

▶ Confronting and solving practical problems

▶ Using activity as an antidepressant

▶ Getting your sleeping pattern back on track

*S*tatistics show that as many as one in two people are estimated to experi-ence depression at some point in their lives. Luckily, the problem is well-recognised and treatable.

If, for the past month, you've felt down, lacked energy, been pessimistic or hopeless about the future, and lost interest or enjoyment in doing things, then you may be suffering from depression. If you've also had difficulty con-centrating, had a poor appetite, been waking early, and experienced a low mood, anxious thoughts or feelings of dread in the morning, then you're even more likely to be depressed. If you have three or more of these symptoms, your symptoms have been present for two weeks or more, and are intense enough to interrupt your usual day-to-day activities, then we recommend that you visit your doctor and investigate the possibility that you're suffering from depression.

Antidepressant medication can help to alleviate some of your depressive symptoms, although not every person diagnosed with depression needs to take medication. Depending on the severity of your depression, a course of CBT treatment may be enough to help you get better. CBT for the treatment of depression is well researched and the results show that it produces good outcomes. CBT and antidepressant medication are often used in conjunction to treat more severe forms of depression. Ask your doctor or psychiatrist to explain your medication and any possible side effects.

Antidepressant medications are often referred to as 'SSRIs', which stands for *selective serotonin reuptake inhibitors.*

This chapter provides you with a guide to assess yourself for possible depression and offers some classic CBT strategies for defeating depression.

Understanding the Nature of Depression

The sort of depression we're talking about in this chapter is different to feeling down or blue in response to a bad event. We're talking about an illness now ranked as one of the most common reasons for people having to take time off work.

Specifically, depression has the following symptoms, usually lasting for at least two weeks:

- Appetite variation, such as eating far less or more ('comfort eating') than usual

- Sleep disturbance, including having difficulty sleeping, wanting to sleep too much or experiencing early-morning wakefulness

- Lack of concentration and poor memory

- Irritability

- Loss of libido

- Loss of interest in activities previously enjoyed; engaging in these activities no longer produces pleasure

- Social isolation and withdrawal from others

- Self-neglect with respect to feeding or grooming

- Neglecting to take care of your living environment

- Decreased motivation and activity levels, often described as a feeling of lethargy

- Feelings of hopelessness about the future and thinking bleak thoughts, such as 'What's the point?'

- Strong and enduring negative thoughts about yourself

- Feelings of guilt

- Inability to experience feelings of love, often described as a flattening of emotions or feeling numb

- Suicidal thoughts, such as feeling that you no longer care whether you live or die

Another common form of depression is *bipolar affective disorder*, formerly called 'manic depression'. People who have bipolar disorder experience periods of severe depression alternating with periods of *hypomania* (feelings of euphoria accompanied by impulsive and often risky behaviour). If you think that you have this disorder we advise you to seek an assessment from a psychiatrist. A psychiatrist will be able to prescribe appropriate medication and can refer you to a CBT therapist.

The techniques covered in this chapter for overcoming *unipolar depression* (depression that's not accompanied by periods of hypomania) are also useful for bipolar sufferers. Keeping up a consistent day-to-day level of activity is one of the main CBT strategies for managing bipolar affective disorder. You can use the techniques in the following sections, which cover improving the quality of your sleep, solving problems, scheduling your activities and interrupting rumination, to stabilise your mood and help you to minimise or avoid excessive highs and lows.

Looking at what Fuels Depression

Unfortunately, certain things that you do, in an attempt to alleviate your feelings of depression, may actually be making your symptoms worse. When people are depressed, they often make the mistake of doing what their mood dictates.

CBT helps depressed individuals learn to override their depressed mood and to do the *opposite* of what their depression makes them *feel like doing*. Here are some of the main actions and thoughts that actually stoke depression:

- **Rumination:** Getting hooked into a repetitive, cyclical process of negative thinking, repeatedly going over problems in the past or asking yourself unanswerable questions. (We discuss rumination in detail in the next section.)

- **Negative thinking:** In depression, your negative thoughts about yourself are often based on beliefs that you're helpless and worthless. Thoughts about the world being an unsafe and undesirable place to live in are also a common feature of depression.

- **Inactivity:** Feeling that you can't be bothered to do day-to-day tasks, not participating in activities that previously you enjoyed and staying in bed because you don't believe you can face the day.

- **Social withdrawal:** Avoiding seeing other people and not interacting with the people around you.

- **Procrastination:** Avoiding specific tasks, such as paying bills, booking appointments and making phone calls, because you think they're too difficult or scary to confront.

✔ **Shame:** Feeling ashamed about your depression, and telling yourself that other people would judge you harshly if they knew how much your effectiveness and productivity had decreased.

✔ **Guilt:** Feeling guilty about your depression, and overestimating the degree to which your low mood causes inconvenience and suffering for your loved ones.

✔ **Hopelessness:** Thinking that you'll never feel better or that your situation will never improve.

Doing only what you feel like doing when you're depressed is likely to maintain or worsen your symptoms. Instead, try doing the opposite of what your depression directs you towards doing. For example, if you feel depressed and want to stay in bed all day avoiding phone calls and seeing friends, do the opposite. Try to make the colossal effort (and it can really feel colossal!) of getting up and dressed, answering the phone and going out of the house to meet friends. Doing so limits you ruminating on your bad feelings and thoughts, and forces your attention onto external things, such as other people and your environment.

Most people find that they feel better for having done *something*, even if they don't experience enjoyment from social interaction like they did before they became depressed.

Depression typically dulls your ability to glean enjoyment from previously enjoyed activities. Be patient with yourself and trust that your feelings of enjoyment can return over time. In the first instance, it's enough to simply do the things that you've been avoiding *for the sake of it*. Doing something is better than doing nothing. Don't put pressure on yourself to 'have a good time' at this early stage in your recovery.

Going Round and Round in Your Head: Ruminative Thinking

Rumination is an integral process in maintaining your depression. Most people with depression are likely to engage in some rumination, even if they're not aware that they do.

Rumination is a circular thought process in which you go over the same things again and again. Often, the focus is on how bad you feel or doubting that you can ever feel differently or better. Your rumination may also focus on trying to work out the root cause of your depression, or on the events that have contributed to you being depressed. You may ask yourself questions like the following, over and over again:

> ✔ Why is this happening to me?
>
> ✔ What could I have done to stop this happening?
>
> ✔ If only *x*, *y* or *z* hadn't happened, I'd be okay.

Depression makes people feel compelled to ruminate. In a sense, rumination is like a faulty attempt to solve problems. Rumination is compelling because your depressed mood tells you that you must try to get to the bottom of why you feel bad. But rumination simply doesn't work: you end up trying to solve your depression by going over the same old ground and looking for answers inside the problem. You focus your attention on how depressed you feel, which leads to you feeling more depressed.

Fortunately, you can catch yourself going into a ruminative state by using the techniques we discuss in the following sections to interrupt the process.

Catching yourself in the act

Rumination is all-consuming. It will typically absorb you quite totally. You may look like you're simply staring blankly into space, but in your head your thoughts are going ten to the dozen. The key is to know when you're going *into* rumination, so you can take steps towards *getting out* of rumination.

Early warning signs of rumination taking hold include the following:

> ✔ **Getting stuck.** You may be in the middle of doing something and find that you've stopped moving and are deep in thought. For example, you may be perching on the side of the bed for several minutes (or even much longer!) when actually you intended going for a shower.
>
> ✔ **Feeling low.** Beware of times when your mood's at its lowest ebb: this is when you're most likely to engage in rumination. Most people ruminate at particular times of the day, more often than other times (although rumination can happen at any time).
>
> ✔ **Slowing down.** You may be doing something and then start to move more slowly, like pausing in the aisle at the supermarket. You start to slow down because your concentration's heading elsewhere.
>
> ✔ **Getting repetitive.** The same old thoughts and questions drift into your head, time and time again. You get a familiar niggling feeling that these vague questions must be answered.

The content of your ruminations isn't the problem – the process of rumination itself is. You don't need to do anything with your thoughts other than disengage from them, as we explain in the following section.

Arresting ruminations before they arrest you

Several different tricks can help you stop the rumination process. Try some of the following:

- ✔ **Get busy.** Perhaps one of the most effective strategies you can adopt is to make your body and mind busy with something outside yourself. If you're vitally absorbed in an activity, you may find it harder to engage in rumination. These types of activity may include doing the house-work with the radio on to hold your attention away from your internal thoughts, making a phone call, surfing the Internet, running errands, taking the dogs for a walk, and so on.

- ✔ **Work out.** Hard aerobic exercise can exorcise those toxic thought processes. Be sure to exercise during the day or in the early morning, because exercising too near bedtime can disturb your sleep.

- ✔ **Get up and out.** Rumination's more difficult when you're outside of your home or in the company of others. If you know that you're most vulnerable to ruminating at certain hours of the day, make sure that you schedule activities for these times.

- ✔ **Let your thoughts go.** Practise letting your negative thoughts pass by and simply observe them like pictures across a television screen. Don't engage with your negative thoughts, judge them or try to answer any questions – just accept their existence and let them slip by. (Check out Chapter 5 for more on this technique.)

- ✔ **Get good at redirecting your attention.** You can strengthen your atten-tion muscles and deliberately focus on less depressing things. Try using *task concentration training*, a method of attending to external aspects of your environment, as it can successfully interrupt rumination. (See Chapter 5 for more on task concentration training.)

- ✔ **Be sceptical.** Your depressed thoughts are a symptom of your depres-sion, so try to take them with a sizable pinch of salt. You can resist the urge to ruminate about your depressed thoughts by deciding that they're neither true nor important. Even though they *feel* important and worthy of scrutiny – they aren't. You won't learn anything new about your depression by focusing on negative repetitive thoughts.

Keeping busy is a great technique for interrupting ruminative thinking. However, you can still end up ruminating while you're engaged in an activity. Be aware of paying attention to whatever you're doing. Be mindful of your actions when you're ironing, cleaning, stringing beads, weeding the garden, or whatever. Rumination can take hold during activities if you're acting *mind-lessly* rather than *mindfully* (refer to Chapter 5 for more on this distinction).

Activating Yourself as an Antidepressant

Withdrawal and inactivity are the two most fundamental *maintaining factors* in depression – they keep you in a vicious cycle of isolation and low mood. For example, to counteract feelings of fatigue, you may be tempted (very tempted) to spend more time in bed. Unfortunately, remaining in bed means more inactivity and less energy.

If you feel ashamed of being 'flat', about having nothing to say, or feel guilty about burdening your friends, then keeping to yourself may seem sensible. The problem is that the less you do and the fewer people you see, the less pleasure and satisfaction you'll get out of life, the less support you'll receive, and the more your problems will pile up and weigh heavy on your mind. Staying away from others may *seem* like the right thing to do when your mood is low. You may believe that you've got nothing to offer others. You may even have thoughts about being undeserving of friendship or love. However, the more you act on these destructive ideas, the more you rein-force them and convince yourself that they're true. Following your depres-sive tendency to isolate yourself can lead into true loneliness.

You don't necessarily have to talk about your low feelings when you see friends; in fact, it's often a good idea not to. Talking about superficial things and listening to what others have been up to can give you a welcome break from your own thoughts. Moreover, noticing that others treat you pretty nor-mally can actually help you to feel a bit more 'normal' rather than afflicted. Try not to worry about making interesting conversation and just allow your-self to absorb the company of those you're with.

A good rule of thumb for recovery from many psychological problems is: 'if you want to *feel* normal again, you need to start *acting* as you would normally.'

Because depressive illness trains you to be such a skilled self-saboteur, you may end up doing negative self-comparisons when in company. Be wary of letting stealthy depressed thoughts such as 'I should be getting on with my life like my friends are' or 'Why can't I be happy like so and so?' take hold. Pretty much the worst time to try to self-evaluate is when you're depressed. So resist making comparisons and instead gently urge yourself to engage in social interaction.

Tackling inactivity

One of the best ways of starting to overcome depression is to gradually become more active, to steadily re-engage with other people, and to start tackling daily chores and other problems.

Use the activity schedule in Table 12-1 to start to plan each day with a realistic balance of activities and rest. Build up your activities gradually. If you've been in bed for days, getting out of the bedroom and sitting in a chair is a big move in the right direction. Remember: take it step by step. Using the activity schedule is really simple; it merely involves allocating a specific time to do a specific activity. You can photocopy the blank schedule in Table 12-1 and fill it in.

Don't overload your activity schedule, otherwise you may feel overwhelmed, sink back into inactivity, and probably berate yourself for being ineffective. It's crucial to *realistically* plan a gradual increase in activities, starting from where you are *now*, not from where you think you *should* be.

Table 12-1			Activity Schedule				
	Monday	**Tuesday**	**Wednesday**	**Thursday**	**Friday**	**Saturday**	**Sunday**
6–8 a.m.							
8–10							
10–12							
12–2 p.m.							
2–4							
4–6							
6–8							
8–10							

Dealing with the here and now: Solving problems

As with other aspects of your daily or weekly activities, you need to be steady and systematic in your attempts to deal with practical problems, such as paying bills, writing letters, and completing other tasks that can pile up when you're less active.

To get started, set aside a specific amount of time each day for dealing with neglected chores. Allocating your time can help things seem more manageable. Try the following problem-solving process:

1. **Define your problem.**

   At the top of a sheet of paper, write down the problems you're struggling with. For example, you might consider problems with the following:

   - Relationships

   - Isolation

   - Interests and hobbies

   - Employment and education

   - Financial issues

   - Legal issues

   - Housing

   - Health

Apply the following steps to each of your identified problems. You may need to do Steps 2 to 5 on each of your different problems.

2. **Brainstorm solutions to your problem.**

   Write down all the possible solutions you can think of. Consider the following questions to help you generate some solutions:

   - How did you deal with similar problems in the past?

   - How have other people coped with similar problems?

   - How do you imagine you'd tackle the problem if you weren't feeling depressed?

   - How do you think someone else would approach the problem?

   - What resources (such as professionals and voluntary services) can you access for help with your problems?

3. **Evaluate your solutions.**

Review your 'brainstormed' list. Select some of your most realistic seeming solutions, and list the pros and cons of each.

4. **Try out a solution.**

On the basis of your evaluation of pros and cons, choose a solution to try out.

You can easily feel overwhelmed when your mood is low. Even the best of solutions can seem too difficult. To deal with this, break down your solution into a series of smaller, more manageable steps. For example, if you're dealing with financial problems, your first step may be to ask friends to recommend an accountant, or to visit a financial consultant in your area. A second step may be to get your tax returns, proof of income and so on, together. A third step may be selecting an accountant, and contacting them for information about their fees and the services they provide.

5. **Review.**

After trying out a solution, review how much it has helped you to resolve your problem. Consider whether you need to take further steps, try another solution or move on to tackling another problem.

Taking care of yourself and your environment

One of the hallmarks of depression is neglecting yourself and your living environment, which in turn leaves you feeling more depressed.

Instead of allowing your depression to be mirrored in your appearance and your home, make an extra effort to spruce things up. Your environment can have an astounding effect on your mood, both positive and negative.

Include bathing, laundry, tidying and cleaning as part of your weekly activity schedule.

Getting a Good Night's Sleep

Good night, sleep tight, don't let the bedbugs bite!

Sleep disturbance, in one form or another, can often accompany depression. Here are some tips you can use to improve your chances of greeting the sandman:

✔ **Get some exercise.** We cannot overstate the benefits of taking regular exercise. Exercise is good for your mood and good for your sleeping. You can take vigorous exercise during the day or even first thing in the morning to get your *endorphins* ('feel good' chemicals in your brain) charging. If you want to take some exercise in the evenings to help you wind down and de-stress, keep it gentle and not too close to your bedtime. A stroll, or an easy cycle ride, is an ideal choice.

✔ **Establish a schedule.** Getting up at the same time every day and avoiding daytime naps can help you get your sleeping back on track. Catnapping may be very tempting, but ultimately it interferes with your bedtime and can actually lower your mood. If you know that you get the urge for a siesta around the same time every day, make plans to be out of the house at this time. Make yourself busy to keep yourself awake.

✔ **Avoid lying in bed awake.** If you find dropping off to sleep difficult, don't lie in bed tossing and turning. Get out of bed and do something – ideally, something boring like sorting laundry or reading a book on a subject you find dull, drinking something warm and low-in-caffeine, such as milk or cocoa – until you feel ready for sleep. Try to stay up until your eyelids start to feel heavy. The same applies if you wake in the middle of the night and can't get back to sleep easily. Don't stay in bed for longer than ten minutes trying to get back to sleep. Get up and do something like the above ideas, then get back into bed only when you feel sleepy.

✔ **Watch your caffeine and stimulant intake.** Avoid caffeinated drinks from mid- to late afternoon. Caffeine can stay in your system for a long time. Remember that, as well as tea and coffee, many soft drinks, chocolate (although not so much) and various energy drinks contain caffeine. Even some herbal teas contain stimulants, such as matte and guarana.

✔ **Establish a bedtime routine.** Going through the same pre-bedtime procedures each night can help your mind realise that it's getting near to shutdown time. Your routine may include having a warm bath, listening to a soothing radio programme, having a warm, milky drink, or whatever works for you. Sometimes, having a very light, easily digestible snack before bedtime is a good idea to prevent sleep disturbance associated with going to bed hungry.

Setting realistic sleep expectations

During the day and while you try to fall asleep, you may well have thoughts like 'I'll never be able to get to sleep', or 'I'm in for another night of waking up every two hours'. Understandably, you may have these expectations if your sleep has been disturbed for some time, but such thinking is likely to perpetuate your sleep disturbance. Be aware of your worrying thoughts about sleep problems, such as 'I'll never be able to cope on such little sleep', or 'I've got to get some sleep tonight'. Trying to force yourself to go to sleep is rarely successful, and doing so contradicts the concept of *relaxation* because you're making an *effort* to sleep.

 Although it may sound like a tall order, try to take the attitude that you *can* cope with very little, or poor-quality, sleep. Also, answer back your sleep expectations by briefly telling yourself that you don't know for definite how you may sleep tonight and that you're just going to see how it goes.

Making your bedroom oh so cosy

Your bedroom should be used for sleeping and nothing else, apart from sex. When you're trying to settle your sleep pattern, you should avoid even reading in bed. The idea is to help your fatigued mind build helpful, sleep-inducing associations with your boudoir. So, you definitely don't want to be watching telly, working on your laptop, talking on the phone, eating or engaging in any other activity in bed, apart from slumbering or making sweet lurve.

Take care to make your bed and bedroom a relaxing, soothing place to be. Get yourself some very nice bed linen, remove clutter from the room, maybe put out some candles, hang some relaxing pictures on the walls, and make the temperature right for you. Smells can carry strong associations, so consider using a pleasant fabric softener on your linen or a special-purpose pillow spray. Just the smell of a soothing fabric softener on your linen can be enough for you to associate your bed with sleeping.

You can buy several natural essential oils from herbalists and health food shops that are thought to have relaxing properties. Try having an aroma-therapy massage, or add essential oils to your bath, heat them in a burner to fragrance your room or sprinkle them diluted on your bedclothes. Consider trying some of the following oils:

- Chamomile
- Clary sage
- Geranium and rose geranium
- Lavender (always popular)
- Palma rosa (also said to be good for depression)
- Ylang ylang (also claimed to have an aphrodisiac effect)

Always get advice from a qualified herbalist about how to use essential oils correctly and safely. Most good quality health food shops may either have some qualified staff or be able to recommend a herbalist or aroma therapist. Undiluted essential oils are very strong, and you shouldn't apply them directly to your skin. If you're taking medication, are pregnant or have any allergies or medical conditions, you should always consult your doctor before using any aromatherapy or herbal remedies.

ACTing against Depression

Acceptance and commitment therapy (ACT), founded by Stephen Hayes, is one of the 'third wave' developments in cognitive therapy. Basically, ACT is a newer approach to treating depression but still largely based on core cognitive therapy principles. ACT differs in some pertinent ways from standard CBT. The chief difference is that, instead of challenging your negative thoughts directly, you're encouraged to observe them without judgement and let them pass naturally. We touched on this concept earlier on in this chapter (also see Chapter 5 for more on allowing thoughts to pass).

In addition to tolerating and non-judgementally observing negative thoughts, ACT focuses on commitment to personal values. According to ACT, people who recognise their values (and pursue action to reflect those values) avoid depression. (We look at value-based living in Chapter 18.)

The following three sections expand on some basic principles involved in recovery from depression found both in CBT and ACT.

Practising acceptance

The feeling of depression, and the thoughts that go with it, are undeniably deeply unpleasant and unwelcome. We've never met anyone who said they elected to become depressed. You may conclude that you're basically miserable, a 'misery guts' or a fundamentally negative person based on your depression. We find that this is rarely the case. Being depressed is *not* the same as holding a cynical and pervasively negative view of the world generally. In fact, the opposite is typically the case. If you're depressed, one of the things you may find hardest to accept is the change from being a positive person who enjoys life to one who feels utterly defeated and devoid of enjoyment. People who are depressed sometimes express feeling that they no longer recognise themselves.

Because symptoms of depression frequently run so counter to your understanding of your natural temperament, they can be uniquely difficult to accept. We're not suggesting that you learn to *like* being depressed – that *would* be crazy. But it can help to accept your depression for what it is – an illness. Thankfully, depression is usually temporary (even if it does last for a long while) and is not a change of personality. Your personality is still in tact; your depression is merely masking it. Unwittingly, you may be putting extra pressure on yourself by issuing demands such as 'I must not feel this way', 'this is intolerable' or 'I have to get better *now!*' Such demands (though understandable) just reinforce your bad feelings and build bigger obstacles to recovery. They're rather like banging your head against a wall. Try practising these types of accepting attitude instead:

✔ 'I hate being depressed but unfortunately I'm not immune to depression.'

✔ 'Depression is very hard to bear but I *am* tolerating these unpleasant feelings.'

✔ 'I want to get better now but I can't bully myself out of depression so I will be patient but determined.'

Give yourself credit for coping even though you may feel like you're not. You *are* coping; it's just not easy.

Considering compassion

You can't bully yourself out of depression. If that strategy worked, we'd have far fewer clients. Giving yourself a hard time for being low is literally kicking yourself when you're down. So many depressed people both berate and refuse to look after themselves because doing so's part of an insidious cycle. See Figure 12-1.

When you're ill, you want to get well again. That involves looking after yourself, both mentally and physically. When you have flu or some other physical illness, you probably don't tell yourself that you should never have become ill in the first place, or that you're weak and pathetic because you've done so. Depression is a different ball game, as Figure 12-1 illustrates. An essential part of recovery is offering yourself compassion instead of criticism. Try these tips for being kind to yourself:

✔ **Give yourself credit for your efforts to act against depression.** Instead of telling yourself that you should be doing more, start from where you are now. If yesterday you didn't get out of bed and today you did – that's significant progress. The next step may be going to the shops or answering your telephone. Focus on your small daily improvements instead of benchmarking yourself against where you ultimately want to be.

✔ **Compliment and kindly cajole yourself.** Depression inevitably invites you to think of yourself in negative ways and call yourself bad names. Stop yourself from verbalising or mentally constructing self-directed insults. Instead, deliberately call to mind your good points and encourage yourself to do more through the use of praise. Be nice!

✔ **Be wary of false friends.** Using illicit drugs, alcohol or food to alleviate your feelings and thoughts can grant you a brief respite – but at a high cost. You're likely to feel far worse when you 'come down' from drugs and alcohol or after an eating binge. You may end up with a dependency that prolongs a period of depression which may otherwise shortly relent. Alcohol and drug use can also interfere with the effectiveness of antidepressant medication. See Chapter 10 for more information about addictions.

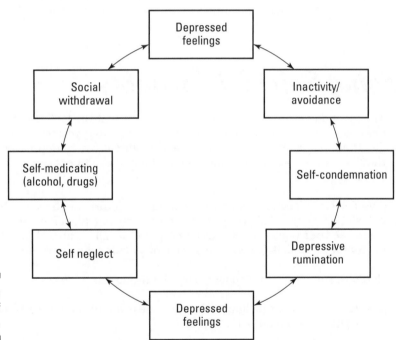

Figure 12-1:
The cycle of
depression.

Obtaining a new outlook

A depressed outlook is typically bleak. The future seems impossible to contemplate because everything seems tinged with grey. Even as you make steps toward recovery, your outlook may remain stubbornly negative for some time. Constructing a new optimistic outlook and practising it daily – even several times each day – can be useful. You may not feel as though you believe it at first but, with time, this bright outlook will probably begin to ring true. Try adopting these new outlooks:

✔ 'I look forward to feeling better soon.'

✔ 'I may not see the light at the end of the tunnel but I know it's there.'

✔ This will pass.'

✔ I'll deal with the future when it comes; I don't need to worry about it now.'

✔ Hanging on is worth it because things will get better.'

The road to recovery from depression is rarely a steady uphill climb. Setbacks and difficult days are part and parcel of a normal recovery. Don't be too disappointed if, after a series of good days, you have a hard one. This difficult day isn't a return to square one or a sign that you're not improving. Just saddle up and get back on the horse.

Managing Suicidal Thoughts

The most dangerous element of depression is that the feelings of hopelessness you can experience may become so strong that you try to take your own life. Don't panic about having suicidal thoughts if you're depressed. Such thoughts are very common and having them doesn't necessarily mean that you'll act on them.

If you've been feeling very hopeless about the future and have started to make plans about how to kill yourself, *you must immediately seek medical assistance.* Go to see your regular doctor as a first point of call, or attend Accident and Emergency (Casualty) if you feel at risk of suicide outside of surgery hours.

Here are some tips on managing suicidal thoughts:

✔ Recognise your feelings of hopelessness about the future as a *symptom* of depression, not a fact.

✔ Remember that depression is a temporary state and there's lots of ways to treat it. Decide to tackle your depression for, say, six weeks, as an experiment to see whether things can improve.

✔ Tell a friend or family member how you're feeling.

✔ See a doctor and/or therapist, or join a support group for further help and support if you're finding it difficult to overcome your depression alone.

✔ Try instigating the problem-solving process we outline in the previous section in this chapter, for any problem you currently see as hopeless.

Famous and depressed

One of the most crucial aspects of recovering from depression is shedding any feelings of shame you may have about the problem. Realising that *no one* has a guarantee that they won't get depressed can help here. Depression has affected all kinds of people, from all walks of life, and of all creeds, colours and levels of intelligence.

Dozens of famous people have publicly reported or discussed their battles with depression during their lives. Celebrities are now 'coming out' about their suffering from depression or bipolar affective disorder (formerly known as manic depression). We hope that their actions can help to remove the stigma of mental health problems and enable more people to identify and seek help for depression.

Here are just a few famous types who've suffered from depression or bipolar affective disorder:

- Buzz Aldrin (astronaut)
- Ludwig van Beethoven (composer)
- William Blake (poet)
- Winston Churchill (British Prime Minister)
- John Cleese (comedian, actor and writer)
- Charles Dickens (writer)
- Germaine Greer (writer and journalist)
- Spike Milligan (comedian, actor and writer)
- Isaac Newton (physicist)
- Mary Shelly (writer)
- Vincent Van Gogh (artist)
- Lewis Wolpert (embryologist and broadcaster)

In our clinical practice we often treat doctors, psychiatrists and other mental health professionals for depression. So it just goes to show that anyone can suffer from psychological illness – even those who earn a living treating it.

Chapter 13

Overcoming Obsessions

- -

In This Chapter

▶ Identifying obsessional problems

▶ Managing upsetting intrusive thoughts

▶ Facing fears and reducing rituals

▶ Decreasing preoccupations with health and appearance

- -

This chapter aims to introduce you to common obsessional problems and how to tackle them using CBT. Specifically, in this chapter we focus on obsessive-compulsive disorder (OCD), health anxiety, and body dysmorphic disorder (BDD). These problems can cause significant levels of distress and interference in daily living. However, if you have one or more of these disorders, you can use the CBT principles we outline in this chapter to reduce your obsessions and preoccupations. If you have a more severe form of these problems you should consider adding some professional help, but the core principles can still be very useful.

Many people have some degree of obsessional behaviour, such as checking or ordering, that doesn't particularly interfere with their lives. This level of problem is usually regarded as *subclinical*. However, problems like OCD are very disruptive and distressing when they reach more severe levels. A report from the World Health Organisation (WHO) states that people with OCD can experience an impact on their lives similar to that of people with HIV infection.

Fortunately, obsessional problems are being diagnosed more accurately than ever before. Problems such as OCD are now among some of the most common psychiatric disorders. This increase is probably due to increased awareness and more accurate assessment measures. CBT is well-recognised as the psychological treatment of choice for obsessional problems, and has far superior relapse rates compared to medication alone.

Identifying and Understanding Obsessional Problems

Obsessional problems are among the most disabling of common emotional-behavioural problems. People with *obsessional problems* can spend many hours a day plagued by upsetting thoughts and feel driven to repeatedly carry out rituals or avoid certain situations. This section outlines three key obsessional problems: OCD, health anxiety and BDD.

Some degree of obsessionality is entirely normal – for example, around half of all people have a particular thing that they check more than they think is necessary, such as whether the gas cooker has been switched off or the door's been bolted. Obsessional problems have their roots in normal experiences, but the rituals and avoidance behaviours serve to make the frequency, severity and duration of obsessions worse. The more you try to rid yourself of doubts, the more they tend to play on your mind.

We define the terms related to obsessions in the list below:

- ✓ An *obsession* is a persistent, unwanted thought, image, doubt or urge that intrudes into your mind and triggers distress. Obsessions are said to have reached a 'psychiatric problem' level when they cause significant levels of distress, interfere with your life and are present for more than an hour a day.

- ✓ *Preoccupation* means being absorbed with something troubling that's on your mind. In this chapter we focus on preoccupations with appearance and health. Preoccupations are usually the result of you frequently focusing your attention on an idea (such as 'I'm seriously ill' or 'I'm repulsive to look at') or doubt ('Did I lock all the windows?') that's distressing to you. Preoccupations are similar to obsessions in that they're regarded as problematic when they cause significant distress, interfere with your life, and last for more than an hour per day.

- ✓ *Compulsions*, also called *rituals*, are the actions you may take in response to your obsessions or preoccupation, but do not particularly help you in your life. Compulsions can be observable behaviours (such as checking or washing your hands) or can be carried out in your mind (such as repeating a phrase in your head or counting). Compulsions are usually attempts to either get rid of a thought, image, urge or doubt; an attempt to reduce danger; or an attempt to reduce discomfort.

- ✓ *Avoidance behaviours* are things you do to avoid triggering your obsession or preoccupation. Your avoidance behaviour may be avoiding driving; avoiding visiting a hospital; or avoiding being seen in bright light.

Rituals and avoidance behaviours are the lifeblood of obsessional problems. Add to these catastrophic thinking (see Chapters 2 and 9), negative emotions (see Chapter 6) and attention bias (see Chapter 5), and you have the anatomy of obsessional problems

Understanding obsessive-compulsive disorder (OCD)

According to the American Psychiatric Association, OCD is:

> *A problem in which the sufferer is plagued by either obsessions or compulsions, or usually both. [They experience] unwanted recurrent intrusive thoughts, impulses, or images that cause marked distress and are not simply excessive worries about real life problems. The sufferer makes attempts to ignore, suppress [or] neutralize the obsessions and recognizes them as the products of their own mind.*

Common obsessions in OCD include the following:

- Fear of contamination
- Fear of accidentally causing harm to yourself or others
- Preoccupation with order or symmetry
- Religious obsessions, for example fear of offending God
- Sexual obsessions, for example fear of being a paedophile
- Fear of losing something important (such as a possession, paperwork or ideas)
- Fear of becoming violent or aggressive

Compulsions frequently associated with OCD include the following:

- Checking (for example, if a light is switched off or the front door is locked)
- Cleaning or washing (such as yourself, others or home)
- Counting
- Repeating actions or special words, images or numbers in one's mind
- Ordering and making things 'just so'
- Hoarding (excessive keeping of possessions such as newspapers that have no real value, interest or function)

✔ Making lists

✔ Replaying or repeating scenes, images or actions in your mind

The prevalence of OCD is estimated to be around 1 per cent of the population, with some studies suggesting more. The severity and impact of OCD varies greatly, and in its most extreme form individuals can become totally housebound, even bedridden. Whilst the severity of symptoms can wax and wane, most people with OCD do function, have relationships, hold down jobs and complete education, but will be under considerable extra strain. Clearly, very many people may recognise some degree of the excessive worries and rituals outlined above. The question is how much choice you feel you have to stop a ritual without distress, and how much interference OCD is causing in your life.

Recognising health anxiety

The American Psychiatric Association defines health anxiety as 'preoccupation with fears of having, or the idea that one has, a serious disease, based on misinterpretation of bodily sensations.' These preoccupations can:

✔ Persist despite medical evaluation and reassurance

✔ Cause significant distress or impairment in social, occupational or other areas of functioning

✔ Last at least six months

People with health anxiety misinterpret body sensations. Examples of common sensations and misinterpretations include the following:

✔ **Heart pounding:** 'I'm going to get heart disease.'

✔ **Lumps under the skin:** 'I have cancer.'

✔ **Tingling or numbness:** 'I have multiple sclerosis.'

✔ **Headache:** 'I must have a brain tumour.'

✔ **All of the above:** 'I'm dying.'

Compulsions commonly associated with health anxiety include the following:

✔ Seeking reassurance from medical professionals about the nature of physical sensations

✔ Seeking reassurance from others

✔ Checking body parts by poking, prodding and touching

✔ Checking for symptoms in medical textbooks or on the Internet

✔ Examining oneself for signs of disease

✔ Monitoring physical sensations

✔ Looking for evidence that the physical sensations are worsening

Common avoidance behaviours associated with health anxiety include the following:

✔ Avoiding health-related stories in magazines or on TV

✔ Avoiding talking or thinking about death

✔ Avoiding touching body parts

✔ Avoiding exposing body parts

✔ Avoiding having medical check-ups

Health anxiety is estimated to affect between 1–2 per cent of the population. It can result in people becoming tormented with fears that they have an illness that has not been properly diagnosed, or that they might become ill. Frequent trips to doctors are not uncommon when the person is gripped by anxiety and a fear that it would be irresponsible of them not to get themselves checked out. This can then result in even more worry that should they really be ill, they'll be dismissed as a hypochondriac. People with health anxiety usually either make repeated trips to medical specialists trying to get an explanation for their symptoms, or avoid seeing doctors because they fear being told something is severely wrong. We've seen many people who've ended up badly bruised from repeatedly prodding an area of their body, or have spent hours doing research in desperate attempts to check to see what may be wrong with them.

Understanding body dysmorphic disorder (BDD)

BDD is defined by the American Psychiatric Association as follows:

> *A preoccupation with an imagined defect in appearance. If a slight physical anomaly exists, the person's concern is markedly excessive. The preoccupation causes clinically significant levels of distress and/ or impairment in social, occupational or some other important area of functioning.*

Don't confuse BDD with an eating disorder, which is when a person restricts their weight, or binges and purges food. If you're very preoccupied with your overall size and shape and have difficulties with eating regular meals, consult your doctor about whether you have an eating disorder. If this is the case, you may need help to tackle your eating behaviours as well as your preoccupation with how you look.

BDD preoccupations can focus on any part of the body and often affect multiple areas. The face is the most common area of preoccupation, particularly the nose, skin, hair, eyes, teeth, lips and chin. People with BBD believe that one or more of their features is too small or too big, or that their face doesn't 'fit together', is out of proportion, isn't symmetrical or is just plain ugly.

Typical compulsions associated with BDD include the following:

✔ Gazing and checking in mirrors or other reflective surfaces

✔ Avoiding mirrors or other reflective surfaces

✔ Seeking from other people reassurance of attractiveness or how noticeable a 'defect' in appearance is

✔ Checking features by frequent touching or measuring

✔ Camouflaging features using clothing, padding, hairstyle or make-up

✔ Attempting to distract others from the supposed defective feature with jewellery or by accentuating other body parts

✔ Frequently looking for and trying out new skincare, beauty and haircare products

✔ Researching or seeking cosmetic surgery

✔ Doing excessive exercise

✔ Abusing steroids

Some common avoidance behaviours in people with BDD include the following:

✔ Avoiding social situations

✔ Avoiding 'attractive' people

✔ Choosing lighting carefully in social situations or near mirrors

✔ Carefully positioning yourself around (or avoiding) mirrors

✔ Changing posture or covering flaws with hands or other items

Frequently starting in adolescence, BDD affects around 1 per cent of the population, and has a relatively high suicide rate compared to many other emotional problems, proving that the disorder is much more than mere vanity. BBD affects men and women roughly equally. Individuals can often spend many hours a day preoccupied with their appearance, perhaps having to get up hours early in order to work it just to feel less unacceptable.

Identifying Unhelpful Behaviours

As we note in Chapter 7, the things humans do to reduce their distress in the short term often maintain problems in the long run – so the solution becomes the problem! In the case of obsessional disorders, behaviours such as avoidance, checking, washing, seeking reassurance, comparing, readjusting and repeating (to name but a few) are the maintaining mechanisms.

Most clients we work with on their obsessional problem agree *intellectually* that their behaviours perpetuate and aggravate their problems, but very often they say 'Now I really see what you mean!' after they experiment with them. Check out Chapter 4 for more information on designing CBT experiments to challenge your thinking.

The first step is to understand the concept of problem maintenance. The next step is to really experience how your behaviours affect your obsessions and preoccupation, by doing experiments.

In the broadest sense, you can try two kinds of experiment with your obsessional thinking:

- ✔ *Reduce* (or stop) a particular ritual and see how this affects the frequency, intensity and duration of your upsetting thoughts.

- ✔ *Increase* a ritual or avoidance for a day and see what effect this has on the frequency, intensity and duration of your upsetting thoughts.

Increasing a ritual or avoidance is often easier to do in the short term and often yields more results more rapidly.

 Say you worry frequently about your house being burgled and you repeatedly check your doors and windows before leaving the house or going to bed. To find out whether your checking is part of the problem rather than the solution, record the frequency, duration and intensity of your worry about burglary on a usual day of checking. Then spend another day trying as hard as you can to double your checking, and record the results. If you note a clear increase in your worry on the day of extra checking, the ritual behaviour's clearly part of your problem.

Acquiring Anti-Obsessional Attitudes

Research and clinical observation shows that a number of thinking styles are related to the development of obsessional problems. Fortunately, you can also use thinking to combat obsessional problems. The following sections offer alternative ways of thinking that can help you in your fight against your obsessional problem.

Tolerating doubt and uncertainty

In our and many other therapists' experience, one of the main protestations that clients make about stopping rituals or avoidance behaviours is along the lines of 'How can you guarantee that what I'm afraid of won't happen?'

The truth is, of course, that we can't. But no one without obsessional problems gets those kinds of guarantees either, so clearly the problem *isn't* a lack of certainty. We can offer a different kind of guarantee, however: as long as you continue to demand a guarantee or certainty that your fears won't come true, you're likely to have your obsessional problem.

Instead, practise *consistently* and *repeatedly* tolerating doubt and uncertainty without resorting to checking, washing, reassurance-seeking, or whatever you do compulsively. Your rituals only fuel your belief that you need certainty. Initially, staying with doubt may well feel uncomfortable, but if you stick with it your anxiety can reduce. Deliberately seek out triggers for your doubt and practise resisting the urge to carry out rituals, seek reassurance or work things out in your mind.

Trusting your judgement

In an attempt to explain why individuals with obsessional problems check so much more than those without these problems, scientists explored the hypothesis that people with OCD have poorer memories. The rationale here was, perhaps, that people with OCD check or seek reassurance because they can't remember properly. The scientists do make an important discovery: people with obsessional problems have no memory deficiency. What they do have, however, is poor confidence in their memory.

Poor confidence in one's memory may be related to unrealistic demands for certainty (see the preceding section on how to tolerate doubt and uncertainty), because no amount of checking removes that grain of doubt from your recall.

The best thing you can do to boost your confidence in your memory is to act as if you are more confident and cut back on rituals. Doing so consistently and repeatedly gradually helps you to build your confidence.

Treating your thoughts as nothing more than thoughts

One of the main thinking errors in obsessional problems is overestimating the importance of the intrusive doubts, thoughts and images that occur naturally in your mind. Experts in OCD have shown that the following three key misinterpretations contribute to obsessional problems:

- **The probability misinterpretation:** The idea that having a thought about an event in your mind affects the probability of that event occurring. For example, 'If I allow myself to picture myself hurting someone, then it's more likely that I'll do it.'

- **The moral misinterpretation:** The idea that an unpleasant thought entering your mind reveals something unpleasant about yourself. For example, 'Having thoughts of causing harm means I'm a bad and dangerous person.'

- **The responsibility misinterpretation:** The idea that having a thought about an event means that you have responsibility for it happening or for preventing it from happening. For example, 'Having an image of myself ill in a hospital bed means that I need to be more vigilant for signs of illness.'

Intrusive thoughts, images, doubts and impulses are entirely normal. Your assumption that the thoughts that you're having aren't normal is the problem. The solution is to allow these thoughts to pass through your mind without engaging with them or trying to change, suppress or hurry them along. As the song says, let it be! See Chapter 5 for more suggestions on managing your mind without interfering with it.

Being flexible and not trying too hard

If you have an obsessional problem, you're almost certainly trying too hard at something. You may be trying too hard to get your appearance or desk looking just so. Or you may be trying to ensure that you or someone you feel responsible for is safe from harm or disease. Or perhaps you're inclined to follow moral or religious instruction to the letter, rather than living within the spirit of these ideals.

Flexibility is one of the hallmarks of psychological health because it helps you adapt effectively to the real world. Consider carefully the real-life consequences of holding standards or ideals too rigidly. Do these ideals really help you live the kind of life you want? Are the costs to yourself and others worth the benefits? If not, try to define how you'd behave if you were free from your obsessional problem, or take a leaf from someone else's book and try acting accordingly. Refer to Chapter 8 for more on doing a cost–benefit analysis.

Using external and practical criteria

A crucial difference between people with and without obsessional problems is regarding the criteria they use to decide when to stop a particular behaviour. People without obsessions tend to use external observations, or practical criteria, to evaluate situations and make decisions.

In contrast, people with obsessional problems tend to use *internal criteria* – such as something feeling 'right', 'better' or 'comfortable' – to make decisions. Here are two examples of internal criteria with their external alternatives:

- ✔ A person with contamination OCD may wash her hands until she *feels* that her hands are clean enough. Someone without this problem may tend to stop washing when she can *see* her hands are clean or when she's been through a quick and convenient routine.

- ✔ A person with BDD may readjust her hair, trying to reduce her *feelings* of anxiety and to *feel satisfied inside* with how she looks. Someone without excessive concerns about her appearance may stop styling her hair when it *looks the same as usual* or isn't sticking up.

Strive to use normal criteria to decide when to stop an activity. Instead of stopping when you feel comfortable, force yourself to stop washing your hands or fixing your hair *before* you feel comfortable. Making this change can help reinforce the fact that your criteria for stopping rituals are the problem and proves to you that your discomfort and anxiety can diminish spontaneously. Importantly, this technique can also show you that you *can* tolerate the discomfort of resisting your rituals.

Allowing your mind and body to do their own things

Complete control of your thoughts and body is:

- ✔ **Impossible:** No one has it, not even highly trained doctors, athletes, monks or psychologists!

✔ **Counterproductive:** Attempting to completely control your thoughts results in more of the thoughts and sensations you were trying to get rid of. You may seem even more out of control as a result.

✔ **Undesirable:** Being able to completely choose the thoughts that enter your mind effectively puts a stop to any originality and creative problem-solving. Being in control of your body would almost certainly result in your demise – after all, do you really know how to run a body?

Allowing your body and mind to go on autopilot is so much easier and more helpful than trying to control your thoughts and bodily sensations.

Normalising physical sensations and imperfections

Obsessional problems like OCD, BDD and health anxiety can lead you to focus too much on your thoughts, physical sensations and minor physical imperfections. These problems also lead you to attach undue importance and meaning to your sensations, physical imperfections and upsetting thoughts.

✔ Health anxiety leads you to attach too much importance to normal physical sensations.

✔ OCD leads you to attach too much meaning to normal thoughts that intrude into your mind.

✔ BDD leads you to attach too much meaning to your appearance.

 Your problem isn't the content of your thought, the flaws in your complexion or the variation in your heart rate. Your problem is *your belief* that these experiences are abnormal. To help yourself overcome your obsessional problems, take the view that your thoughts, flaws and imperfections are *normal*. Conducting surveys (which we talk about in Chapter 4) is an excellent way of gathering evidence that many of the things you focus on and worry about are normal human experiences.

Facing Your Fears: Reducing (and Stopping) Rituals

In CBT, facing your fears and resisting the urge to carry out compulsions is called *exposure and response prevention*. This term has two important components:

✔ **Exposure:** Deliberately facing up to the places, people, situations, substances, objects, thoughts, doubts, impulses and images that trigger off your feelings of anxiety and discomfort.

✔ **Response prevention:** Reducing and stopping the rituals and any other safety precautions that you adopt.

In order to reduce or potentially stop your reliance on rituals, you must tackle your obsessions head-on. To accomplish this, you need to get better at tolerating doubt, allow thoughts and images to come and go from your mind, and be realistic about responsibility. And yes, you need to practise these skills!

You can make faster progress if you *deliberately* trigger off your upsetting thoughts and anxiety in a regular and consistent way. See Chapter 9 for more detail on designing an exposure programme to help combat your anxieties.

Facing your fears when overcoming an obsessional problem is different from dealing with many other kinds of anxiety problem because the object of your fear may be more *internal* than *external*. For example, facing the *mental image* of pushing someone on to a train track is just as important as actually standing on the platform.

Putting up firm resistance

To overcome an obsessional problem, you need to develop a list of your main fears as well as your typical rituals and safety behaviours.

Keeping a daily record of the frequency of the rituals you wish to reduce helps you to keep track of your progress and motivates you to keep reducing. You can record the frequency on paper or buy a 'tally counter' (a 'clicker' that counts each time you press it) from a stationery shop.

When you've written your list, you need to systematically expose yourself to your main fears, while simultaneously reducing and dropping your rituals and safety behaviours.

Stopping your rituals is not sufficient to overcome your obsessions. You need to incorporate deliberate exposure to your fears in order to get the practice you need.

Delaying and modifying rituals

Delaying and modifying a ritual can also be a useful lead up to dropping it entirely:

✔ **Delaying rituals.** If you find stopping your rituals difficult, start off by delaying them for a few minutes. Gradually build up the time delay until you can resist a ritual long enough for your anxiety to reduce of its own accord.

✔ **Modifying rituals.** If you can't gear yourself up to stop your ritual entirely just yet, modify it. Instead of going for the full-blown version of a ritual, allow yourself to perform only a shortened version. For example, if you normally vacuum every corner of a room, try making yourself stick to the areas that you can see, without moving any furniture or other objects.

Overcoming your obsessional problems is supposed to be an uncomfortable experience. If you're working through the exercises in this chapter and not experiencing a temporary increase in your discomfort, then either you're not exposing yourself sufficiently or you're not resisting your rituals sufficiently.

If you plan to stop a particular ritual but end up doing it anyway, *re-expose* yourself rather than letting your obsessional problem win. For example, if you have a fear of contamination, touch the floor to re-expose yourself after washing your hands.

You may be very tempted to err on the safe side and allow yourself to carry out more rituals or safety measures than the average person. Retaining avoidance and rituals can leave you very prone to your obsessions returning. Keep working at your ritual reduction until your rituals are at least as low as those of the average person on the street. Think of rituals and avoidance as the roots of a weed you're trying to get rid of from your garden. If you don't get weeds up by the roots, they're sure to grow back.

Being Realistic about Responsibility

One of the hallmarks of obsessional problems is a tendency to take too much responsibility. Individuals with OCD, for example, often take excessive responsibility for causing or preventing harm to themselves or others. A person with health anxiety may have an overdeveloped sense of responsibility for spotting possible health problems. Someone with BDD may have an excessive sense of responsibility for not causing offence or being humiliated because of her appearance. In all cases, this sense of responsibility can drive the person to carry out rituals and leave them feeling guilty if they don't.

Dividing up your responsibility pie

A helpful technique for developing a more realistic perception of your personal responsibility is to create a *responsibility pie chart*, as follows:

1. **Identify an event you fear being responsible for** (such as the house being burgled, causing harm, falling ill, being rejected).

2. **Write down the level of responsibility you would feel for the event if it occurred as a percentage.**

   You can have between 0 and 100 per cent of the responsibility for an event occurring.

3. **List all the possible contributing factors to your feared event occurring, including yourself.**

4. **Create a responsibility pie chart.**

   Use a large empty circle to represent 100 per cent, or all the responsibility for an event occurring. You can draw a circle yourself or use the circle provided in Figure 13-1.

   Proportionally divide the pie into wedges, based on how much responsibility you assign to each of the factors you list in step 3. Be sure to put yourself in last.

Figure 13-1:
The starting point for your responsibility pie chart.

5. **Re-rate your estimation of your responsibility for your feared event.**

   Use the 0 to 100 per cent scale described in step 2.

   For example, Figure 13-2 shows the responsibility pie chart for Theresa, a mother with OCD who obsesses about harm coming to her children from poisonous substances. Initially, Theresa believes that she'd be totally to blame if any harm befell her children. However, after working through the responsibility pie chart activity, she's able to gain a more realistic perspective on her level of personal responsibility.

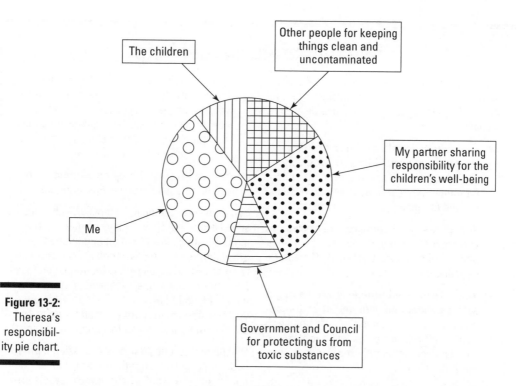

The children

Other people for keeping things clean and uncontaminated

My partner sharing responsibility for the children's well-being

Me

Government and Council for protecting us from toxic substances

Figure 13-2:
Theresa's responsibility pie chart.

You can also use the responsibility pie chart with negative events that *have actually happened* and that you're blaming yourself for, for example losing a job, a failed relationship, someone treating you badly, or a loved one becoming ill.

The purpose of the responsibility pie is to help you see that you're not 100 per cent responsible for an event happening. Many obsessional people give themselves more responsibility than is legitimate – or at least more than non-obsessional people do.

Taking *less responsibility* is something that you steadily need to train your mind to do. Actually, you're retraining your mind to break your habit of *taking excessive responsibility.*

Retraining your attention

If you think you're preoccupied with your appearance, health or being responsible for harm coming to yourself or others *because you focus on it too much,* try to create a counterbalance by training your attention elsewhere. Chapter 5 gives you some more guidance.

Seeking professional help

Use the following checklist to determine whether an obsession or compulsion is normal or a problem for which you should seek professional assistance.

✔ **Your obsessional problems are impacting on your physical health.** For example, you're not taking prescribed medication, attending medical appointments, or feeding and grooming yourself sufficiently.

✔ **Your obsessional problems are preventing you from leaving your home.** Sometimes people with severe OCD or BDD become housebound.

✔ **Your obsessional problems are having a serious impact on your social and occupational life.** For example, you're unable to continue working, you've lost a job, you're avoiding contact with friends or your partner has left you.

✔ **Your obsessional problems are preventing you from caring adequately for your children.** This is a particularly painful point for many people with OCD. People with OCD typically take too much responsibility for the welfare of their loved ones. However, if you contemplate the needs of your children and decide *impartially* that your problems are stopping you from meeting those needs, get in touch with a professional.

✔ **You've given self-help an earnest try but are unable to overcome your problem.**

Your family doctor might be familiar with obsessional disorders, but you may be better off seeking out a specialist. Make an appointment with a psychiatrist for assessment. If your problem is so severe that you're housebound, you may be able to get a home assessment via a community mental health outreach team. However, you may need to prepare yourself for going out of your safety zone and into a hospital or clinic.

Getting the best help for your obsessional problems isn't always straightforward, but we do encourage you to not give up. If you meet the criteria on the checklist above, please do seek help. Appendix A lists relevant organisations you can consider contacting for more information.

Chapter 14

Overcoming Low Self-esteem and Accepting Yourself

- -

- -

Disturbing feelings, such as depression, anxiety, shame, guilt, anger, envy and jealousy, are often rooted in low self-opinion. If you're prone to experiencing these feelings, then you may well have a problem with your self-esteem. You may assume that you're only as worthwhile as your achievements, love life, social status, attractiveness or financial prowess. If you link your worth to these *temporary conditions* and for some reason they diminish, your self-esteem can plummet too. Alternatively, you may take a long-standing dim view of yourself: However favourable the conditions mentioned above, your self-esteem may be chronically low. Whatever the case, you can follow the philosophy of self-acceptance that we outline in this chapter, which can significantly improve the attitude you hold towards yourself.

Identifying Issues of Self-Esteem

Implicit in the concept of self-esteem is the notion of *estimating*, or rating and measuring, your worth. If you have high self-esteem, then your measure of your value or worth is high. Conversely, if you have low self-esteem, your estimate of your value is low.

Condemning yourself globally is a form of overgeneralising, known as *labelling* or *self-downing* (we talk about overgeneralisation in more detail in

Chapter 2). This thinking error creates low self-esteem. Labelling yourself makes you feel worse and can lead to counterproductive actions, such as avoidance, isolation, rituals, procrastination and perfectionism (which we talk about in Chapters 7, 12 and 13), to name but a few.

Examples of labelling or self-downing include statements such as the following:

I'm disgusting	I'm a failure	I'm stupid
I'm inferior	I'm useless	I'm less worthwhile
I'm inadequate	I'm not good enough	I'm bad
I'm unlovable	I'm worthless	I'm defective
I'm incompetent	I don't matter	I'm pathetic
I'm weak	I'm no good	I'm a loser

When you measure your worth on the basis of one or more external factors, you're likely to go up and down like a yo-yo in both mood and self-concept because life is changeable.

Developing Self-Acceptance

One approach to tackling your low self-esteem is to boost the estimate you have of your worth. The underlying problem, however, still remains; and like an investment, your self-esteem can go down, as well as up.

Self-acceptance is an alternative to boosting self-esteem and tackles the problem by removing self-rating. If you don't have a sturdy belief that your value is *intrinsic*, or built-in, you may have difficulty concluding that you have any worth at all when things go wrong for you.

Unconditional self-acceptance means untangling your self-worth from external 'measures' or 'ratings' of your value as a person. Eventually, you can become less likely to consider yourself defective or inadequate on the basis of failures or disapproval, because you view yourself as a *fallible human being*, whose worth remains more or less constant.

Self-acceptance involves making the following assertions:

✔ As a human being, you're a unique, multifaceted individual.

✔ You're ever-changing and developing.

✔ You may be able, to some degree, to measure specific aspects of yourself (such as how tall you are), but you'll never manage to rate the whole of yourself because you're too complex and continuously changing.

✔ Humans, by their very nature, are fallible and imperfect.

✔ By extension, because you're a complex, unique, ever-changing individual, you cannot legitimately be rated or measured as a whole person.

The following are the principles of self-acceptance. Read them, re-read them, think them over and put them into practice in your daily life to significantly enhance your self-acceptance. The principles are good sense, but we're leaving it up to you to decide how 'common' this kind of sense is. The principles are derived from the rational (self-helping) thinking methods developed by Albert Ellis and Windy Dryden.

Understanding that you have worth because you're human

Albert Ellis, founder of rational emotive behaviour therapy – one of the very earliest approaches to CBT – states that *all human beings* have *extrinsic* value to others and *intrinsic* value to themselves. But we humans gamely confuse the two and classify ourselves as 'worthy' or 'good' on the basis of assumed value to others. We humans too easily allow our self-worth to be contingent upon the opinions and value judgements of others. Many cognitive behaviour therapists (and indeed other kinds of psychotherapists) hold the implicit value of a human being at the very heart of their perspective.

Imagine how much easier your life will be, and how much more stable your self-esteem will be, if you realise that you have worth as a person *independently* of how much other people value you. You can appreciate being liked, admired or respected without feeling a dire necessity to prompt these responses, or living in fear of losing them.

Appreciating that you're too complex to globally measure or rate

You may mistakenly define your whole worth – or even your entire self – on the basis of your individual parts. Doing so is pointless, because humans are ever-changing, dynamic, fallible and complex creatures.

Humans have the capacity to work on correcting less desirable behaviours and maximising more desirable behaviours. You have the distinctive ability to strive for self-improvement, to maximise your potential and to learn from your and others' histories, mistakes and accomplishments. In short, you have the capacity to develop the ability to accept yourself as you are, while still endeavouring to improve yourself if you so choose.

Consider a bowl of fresh, hand-picked fruit, beautiful in almost every respect. Now imagine that one of the apples in the fruit bowl is bruised. Do you consider the whole bowl of fruit to be worthless? Of course not! It's a beautiful bowl of fruit, with a single bruised apple. Avoid overgeneralising by seeing that your imperfections are simply *facets* of yourself and do not define the whole of you.

Letting go of labelling

Self-acceptance means deciding to resist labelling yourself at all and rather to entertain the idea that ratings are inappropriate to the human condition. For example:

✔ You lied to a friend once. Does that make you a liar forever and for all time?

✔ You used to smoke cigarettes but then you decided to give them up. Are you still a smoker because you once smoked?

✔ You failed at one or more tasks that were important to you. Can you legitimately conclude that you are an utter failure?

✔ By the same token, if you succeeded at one important task, are you now a thoroughgoing success?

As you can see by reviewing these examples, basing your self-esteem on one incident, one action or one experience is a gross overgeneralisation.

Believing you're more than the sum of your parts

Take a look at Figure 14-1. The big *I* is comprised of dozens of little *is*. So, what's the point of the figure? When you evaluate yourself *totally* on the basis of one characteristic, thought, action or intention, you're making the thinking error that a single part (the little *i*) equals to the whole (the big *I*).

iiiiiiiiiiiiiiiiiiiiiiiiiiiiiiiiiiiiiiiiiiiiiiiiiiiiii
iiiiiiiiiiiiiiiiiiiiiiiiiiiiiiiiiiiiiiiiiiiiiiiiiiiiii
iiiiiiiiiiiiiiiiiiiiiiiiiiiiiiiiiiiiiiiiiiiiiiiiiiiiii
              iiiiiiiiiiiiii
              iiiiiiiiiiiiii
              iiiiiiiiiiiiii
              iiiiiiiiiiiiii
              iiiiiiiiiiiiii
              iiiiiiiiiiiiii
              iiiiiiiiiiiiii
              iiiiiiiiiiiiii
              iiiiiiiiiiiiii
iiiiiiiiiiiiiiiiiiiiiiiiiiiiiiiiiiiiiiiiiiiiiiiiiiiiii
iiiiiiiiiiiiiiiiiiiiiiiiiiiiiiiiiiiiiiiiiiiiiiiiiiiiii
iiiiiiiiiiiiiiiiiiiiiiiiiiiiiiiiiiiiiiiiiiiiiiiiiiiiii

Figure 14-1:
Which do you see first: the big *I* or all the little *is*?

Along similar lines, consider a finely woven tapestry comprised of countless variations of texture, colour and pattern. Within this tapestry, you may find one or more flaws, where the colours fail to meet or the patterns are slightly out of sync. The flaws in the tiny details don't cancel out the beauty or value of the overall piece. And what about the *Venus de Milo*? Over the years, she's lost a limb or two, but the officials at the Louvre don't say, 'Um, sorry, she's flawed; put her in the bin!' The fact that the statue is damaged doesn't diminish or *define* its overall worth. The statue is valued *as it is*, and the absence of arms doesn't negate the impact it has on our understanding of the evolution of art.

If your child, sibling or nephew failed a spelling test, would you judge them a total loser? Would you encourage them to think of themselves as a global failure, based entirely on one action? If not, why are you doing this to yourself?

Start acting in accordance with the belief that your parts do not define your wholeness. If you truly believe this idea, what do you do when you fail at doing something, behave badly or wickedly, or notice that you have a physical imperfection or character flaw? How do you expect to feel when endorsing this belief?

Take a pack of self-adhesive notes and a large, flat surface. A wall or a door works well – or try a mate if he has a few spare minutes. Write down on one of the notes a characteristic that you, as a whole person, possess; then stick the note on the wall, door or volunteer. Keep doing this, writing down all the aspects of yourself that you can think of until you run out of characteristics, or sticky notes. Now step back and admire your illustration of your complexity as a human being. Appreciate the fact that you cannot legitimately be rated globally.

Acknowledging your ever-changing nature

As a human being, your nature is to be an ever-changing person. Even if you measure all your personal characteristics today and come up with a global rating for yourself, it'll be wrong tomorrow. Why? Because each day you change a little, age very slightly and gather a few new experiences.

Consider yourself as work-in-progress and try holding a *flexible* attitude towards yourself. Every skill you acquire or interest you develop effectively produces a change within you. Every hardship you weather, every joyous event that visits you and every mundane occurrence you endure causes you to develop, adapt and grow.

Ellis theorises that your essential value or worth cannot be measured accurately because your *being* includes your *becoming*. Ellis suggests that each human is a *process* with an ever-changing present and future. Hence, you cannot conclusively evaluate yourself while you're still living and developing.

Forgiving flaws in yourself and others

Interestingly, you may overlook some imperfections in yourself while condemning the same shortcomings in others, or vice versa. To some degree, this relates to what you consider important, your flexibility and your level of self-acceptance. Consider the following scenarios:

✔ Julian works in a computer shop. Whenever he's about to close a sale, he gets excited and trips over some of his words. He feels a bit foolish about this, although none of his customers has ever mentioned it.

✔ Margarita has a poor sense of direction. Sometimes she forgets which way is left and which is right. When she's driving, Margarita has difficulty following directions and frequently finds herself lost.

✔ Carlos is a good student, but has difficulty in exam situations. He studies earnestly but, come the day of the test, he forgets what he's read and performs poorly.

You can't always change things about yourself. Sometimes you can improve a bit, but sometimes you can't change at all. If you're a fully developed adult and five-foot tall, you're unlikely to be able to make yourself grow to six foot through sheer determination. The trick is to begin to recognise where you can make changes and where you can't. Living happily is about accepting your limitations without putting yourself down for them and capitalising on your strengths. So, taking the three examples above:

✔ Julian may be able to make himself less anxious about a potential sale; therefore, he may speak more coherently. By accepting that he mangles his words sometimes, but not condemning himself for it, he may come some way towards overcoming this aspect of his behaviour.

✔ Margarita may simply be someone who's not particularly good at navigation. She may improve with practice, but she may also do well to accept that she's the person who turns up late for parties two streets away from her home.

✔ Carlos can look at his studying habits and see whether he can study more effectively. However, he may simply be someone who does better on practical assignments rather than tests.

Overall, Julian, Carlos and Margarita can choose to accept themselves as fallible human beings and work to improve in the areas described, while also accepting their personal limitations. They can choose to embrace their inherent fallibility as part of the experience of being a human, and understand that their 'less good' traits are part of their individual composition as much as their 'good' traits.

Alternatively, they can choose to evaluate themselves on the basis of their 'less good' traits and judge themselves as worthless, or less than worthy. But where, oh where, do you go from there?

Accepting your fallible nature

Sorry if we're the ones to break it to you, but human beings are flawed and imperfect. You may be the pretty impressive product of evolution, but essentially you're just the smartest animal on the planet. Even if you believe you're the creation of a divine entity, do you really think the design brief was perfection? Maybe being complex, different and with an in-built tendency to make mistakes are all part of the plan. When people say 'You're only human,' they have a point: never, ever, can you be flawless or stop making mistakes. And neither can anyone else. It's just how we're built.

During the process of accepting yourself, you may experience sadness, disappointment, or remorse for your blunders. These healthy negative emotions may be uncomfortable, but usually they can lead to self-helping, corrective and 'adaptive' behaviours. Self-condemnation or self-depreciation, on the other hand, are likely to lead to far more intense, unhealthy negative emotions, such as depression, hurt, guilt and shame. So, you're more likely to adopt self-defeating, 'maladaptive' behaviours, such as avoidance or giving up.

Valuing your uniqueness

Who else do you know who's exactly – and yes, we do mean *exactly* – like you? The correct answer is no one, because the human cloning thing hasn't really taken off yet. So you are, in fact, quite unique – just like everyone else!

You alone are possessor of your own little idiosyncrasies. So learn to laugh it up, because the mistakes and foot-in-mouth moments will just keep on coming, whether you like it or not.

Taking yourself overly seriously is not a successful path to obtaining good mental health (which we talk about in Chapter 24). Your individual human fallibility can be both amusing and illuminating. Think about comedy programmes and films. Much of what makes these shows funny is the way the characters *behave*, the mistakes they make, their social blunders, their physicality, their personal peculiarities, and so on. When you laugh at these characters, you aren't being malicious – you just recognise echoes of yourself and of the entire human experience in them. Furthermore, you're unlikely to put down these characters on the basis of their errors. Give yourself a similar benefit of the doubt. Accepting the existence of personal shortcomings can help you to understand your own limitations and identify areas that you may wish to target for change.

For example, we have a couple of our own quirks that we try to accept, and even celebrate, as unique. Rob possesses no sense of direction, which can leave him lost in an empty car park for hours; believe us when we say that no map or sat nav helps. Sometimes we wonder if he even knows where he lives. Rhena has her own *special* pronunciation for many words, (that's to say, she gets them wrong). These are only two of our personal foibles that we're prepared to commit to print!

You're unique because no one is a facsimile of you. At the same time, you're also not special or unique in any way because *everyone* is an individual and, hence, unreplicable. Your uniqueness means that you're *different* from all others and paradoxically that you're the *same* as all others.

Why self-acceptance beliefs work

At first glance, self-acceptance and self-acceptance beliefs may seem like a tall order or 'not what people think'. However, incorporating self-accepting beliefs into your life can really make a difference in your life, and we recommend it for the following reasons:

✔ **Self-acceptance beliefs are helpful.** You're inspired to correct your poor behaviour or address your shortcomings on the basis that you give yourself permission to be flawed. You allow yourself a margin for error. When problems occur or you behave poorly, you can experience appropriate and proportionate negative emotions and then move on. People are generally more effective problem-solvers when they're not severely emotionally distressed.

✔ **Self-acceptance beliefs are consistent with reality.** Do you know anyone who's entirely flawless? If you have only conditional self-acceptance, you're subscribing to a belief that you cease to be acceptable, or worthwhile, when you fall short of those conditions or ideals. Basically, you're telling yourself that you must succeed at any given task. Because you can (and do) both fail and succeed, the evidence suggests that your demand to always succeed is erroneous.

✔ **Self-acceptance beliefs are logical.** Just because you *prefer* to behave in a certain way, doesn't mean that you *must* behave in a certain way. Nor does your failing to act in that manner logically render you a failure in all respects. Rather, this 'failure' supports the premise that you're a fallible human capable of behaving in differing ways at various times. To broaden the point, this 'failure' highlights your humanness and your inherent capacity to do both 'well' and 'less well'.

Using self-acceptance to aid self-improvement

As we touch upon in the nearby sidebar, which covers accepting flaws in others and yourself, self-acceptance can lead to healthy and *appropriate* negative emotional responses to adverse experiences. This type of emotional response tends to lead to functional or *adaptive* behaviours. Self-denigration, on the other hand, leads to unhealthy, *inappropriate* emotional responses, which in turn tend to produce unhelpful or *destructive* behaviours. Look at the following situation:

Wendy's been a full-time mum for the past ten years. Before she had her children, she worked as a legal secretary. Now that her children are older, she wants to return to work. Wendy attends a job interview. During the interview, she becomes very nervous and is unable to answer some of the questions adequately. She notices that she's becoming flustered and hot. It also becomes clear to her that secretarial work has evolved in the past ten years and that she lacks the computer skills necessary for the post. Unfortunately, she doesn't get the job.

Now consider two very different responses to the interview:

> **Response A:** Wendy leaves the interview, ruminating on her poor performance all the way home. 'I looked such an idiot,' she tells herself. 'They must have thought me a real amateur, blushing and stuttering like that. I'm such a failure. Who'd want to hire someone as lacking in skills as me? I don't know what made me think I'd be able to get into work again anyway. I'm clearly not up to standard at all.' Wendy feels depressed and hopeless. She mopes around the house and continues to think about what a failure she is. She feels so ashamed about failing the interview that she avoids talking about it to her friends, thus denying herself the opportunity to receive feedback, which may be useful or help her feel more balanced. Wendy stops looking in the employment pages.

> **Response B:** Wendy leaves the interview and thinks: 'I really didn't present very well in there. I wish I hadn't been so obviously nervous. Clearly, I need to get some computer skills before I'm likely to get a job offer.' Wendy feels very disappointed about not getting the job, but she doesn't conclude that failing one important task makes her a failure. She feels regretful, but not ashamed, about her performance and talks to a few friends about it. Her friends give her some encouragement. Wendy then enrols on an IT course at her local college. She continues to look through the job ads in the paper.

In response B, Wendy is understandably disappointed with how the interview turned out. She's able to recognise her skills' deficit. Because she accepts herself with this *specific deficit*, she takes concrete steps towards improving her skills base.

In response A, Wendy is not thinking about how to do better at the next interview. She's thinking about how she'd like to crawl under the carpet and spend the rest of her days there. A bit of an extreme reaction considering the circumstances, but Wendy isn't considering the circumstances. She's decided that messing up an interview equals total failure, and she's feeling far too depressed and ashamed to start problem-solving.

Generally, your failures and errors aren't as important or calamitous as you think they are. Most of the time, your failures mean a lot more to you than they do to other people.

Understanding that acceptance doesn't mean giving up

In the example of Wendy, we don't suggest that she must resign herself to a life of unemployment simply because she lacks computer skills. Why should she? Clearly, she can do things to ensure that she stands a good chance of getting back into the job market.

In Wendy's case, self-acceptance means that she can view herself as worthwhile, while getting on with self-improvement in specific areas of her life. By contrast, if Wendy refuses to accept herself and puts herself down, she's far more likely to resign – perhaps even condemn – herself to her current state of unemployment.

Resignation requires little or no effort, but self-acceptance can involve a lot of personal effort.

- ✔ **High frustration tolerance** (HFT) is the ability to tolerate discomfort and hard work in the *short term*, en route to achieving an identified *long-term* goal. In response B in the job interview example, Wendy accepts herself and holds an HFT attitude. She's prepared to do the work necessary to reach her goal of getting a job.

- ✔ **Low frustration tolerance** (LFT) is unwillingness to tolerate *short-term* pain for *long-term* gain. An LFT attitude is present in statements such as 'It's too difficult to change – this is just the way I am' and 'I may as well just give up'. Resignation and LFT go hand in hand. In Wendy's response A, she refuses to accept herself in view of her recent experience and resigns herself to unemployment.

Resignation may seem like an easier option than self-acceptance because it means that you have to *do* less. However, people tend to feel pretty miserable when they resign and condemn themselves, refusing to put effort into improving their situation.

Being Inspired to Change

You may think that self-acceptance is all fine and well when talking about human error, social gaffes and minor character flaws, but the dice are more loaded in instances where you've transgressed your personal moral code.

If you've behaved in an antisocial, illegal or immoral manner, you may have more difficulty accepting yourself. But you can! Accepting *yourself* doesn't mean accepting the negative behaviour and continuing to do it. On the contrary, accepting yourself involves recognising that you – an acceptable human being – have engaged in a poor, or unacceptable, behaviour. Accepting yourself makes you more likely to learn from your mistakes and act more constructively – which is in both your interest and in those around you.

Consider the following two scenarios:

- ✔ Malcolm has an anger problem. He puts unreasonable demands on his wife and children to never get on his nerves. He has a bad day at work and comes home to find no dinner on the table and his two young children playing noisily in the sitting room. Malcolm shouts at his wife and slaps her. He calls his children names and hits them. His family is afraid and upset. This happens on a regular basis.

- ✔ Fiona works in a shoe shop. She's been stealing money from the till to buy alcohol and codeine-based painkillers. Usually, she takes the tablets throughout the day and drinks heavily in the evenings, until she passes out. Lately, she's called in sick to work more often because she has terrible hangovers and feels very depressed. Fiona often calls herself a 'useless drunk' and 'a low-life thief', and then drinks more to stop herself thinking. She works hard to hide her drinking and stealing, and feels ashamed of herself most of the time.

Are Malcolm and Fiona bad people, or are they just currently exhibiting bad behaviours? If you condemn Malcolm or Fiona – or, indeed, yourself – as a 'bad person' on the basis of bad behaviour, you're missing the point that a person is more complex than a single act.

In order to overcome destructive or socially unacceptable behaviours, you need to do the following:

- ✔ **Take personal responsibility for your bad behaviour.** Rather than deciding you're just a bad person who has no control or responsibility for your actions, accept that you're doing bad things.

  In the example above, Malcolm's doing very bad things when he takes out his anger on his family. But, if he decides that he's a bad person overall, he relinquishes his responsibility to change. Basically, he's saying: 'I beat my family because I'm a bad person through and through and therefore I can't change.' He's also more likely to attribute his violence to external factors rather than to his own unreasonable demands: 'They know what I'm like and they should damn-well stay out of my way when I come in from work.'

✔ **Identify clearly what you're doing that's wrong or unacceptable.** You must be specific when pinpointing bad behaviours.

For example, Fiona has two definite serious problems or 'bad' behaviours. First, she has an addiction; second, she's stealing to support that addiction. Fiona's shame and self-condemnation are very likely going to get in the way of her overcoming her problems. She cannot put in the hard work needed to recover from her addiction (which includes seeking professional help) if she can't accept herself as worth the effort.

To move on in life in a way that contributes to the kind of world you'd like to live in, assume personal responsibility and keep working on your self-acceptance.

Actioning Self-Acceptance

Just like virtually all skills worth acquiring, you're going to have to work hard and practise in order to achieve successful self-acceptance skills. This section focuses on ways to start integrating self-acceptance into your daily life.

Self-talking your way to self-acceptance

What's in a name? Rather a lot, actually. As we discuss in Chapters 3 and 9, most people largely *feel* the way they *think*. In other words, the meanings you assign to events have a great deal to do with how you ultimately feel about those events.

Similarly, meaning is attached to the names you call yourself. If you use abusive, harshly critical or profane terminology to give utterance to your behaviours or traits, then you're heading towards emotional disturbance.

The notion that you may start to believe something if you tell yourself it enough times, is partly true. Fortunately, you can *choose* what messages you give yourself and, therefore, choose how you think and feel about yourself.

How you talk to yourself impacts immediately, or obliquely, on your self-concept. Try the following self-talk strategies to make the best impact on yourself:

✔ **Desist with global labels.** Humans often call themselves losers, idiots, failures, stupid or unlovable because of certain events or actions they've been involved in or done. You may use even worse language on yourself in the privacy of your own head. Why? Because you're caving in to the temptation to rate your entire selfhood on the evidence of one, or more, isolated incidents.

✔ **Be specific with your self-assessments.** Before you classify yourself as a failure, ask yourself the following questions: 'In what specific way have I failed?' 'In what specific way have I acted stupidly?' It's far less easy to fall into global self-rating when you force yourself to be specific.

✔ **Say what you mean and mean what you say.** You may be saying to yourself right now: 'Oh, but I don't *mean* it when I call myself those bad names.' No? Then don't say them! Get into the practice of using language that describes accurately your behaviour and is in keeping with self-acceptance beliefs. Instead of muttering 'I'm such an idiot for missing that deadline,' try saying: 'Missing that deadline was a really bad move. I'm really disappointed about it.'

Resisting self-abusive language cuts two ways. This chapter focuses on self-acceptance, but much of the advice applies to acceptance of others, too. Generally, people are nicer and more forgiving to their mates than they are to themselves. But, people are still capable of damning others and calling them ugly names. Start exercising a different type of consistency: stop name-calling, full stop. When you do put a halt on name-calling, it can lead you to feel less intense anger and hurt when others behave poorly, which helps to reinforce your self-acceptance beliefs. If you're practising not globally rating others, then you're also minimising the tendency to globally rate yourself.

Following the best-friend argument

Out of habit, most humans employ double standards: you judge your friends by an entirely different, often more accepting, standard than you use on yourself.

Try to take the same attitude of acceptance towards yourself that you take towards your friends and family. Consider the following:

✔ **Act like your best friend by judging your behaviour but not judging yourself.** Eustace has been having difficulties in his marriage. He has been staying out late, drinking with his mates, before going home and being verbally abusive to his wife. His best mate, Lucian, has highlighted Eustace's poor behaviour in their conversations but he's maintained an understanding attitude towards his friend's unhappiness. Lucian isn't about to define Eustace as a complete pig on the strength of his recent, excessive drinking and arguments with his wife.

✔ **Accept your failings as you would those of a dear friend.** Laura just failed her driving test for the fourth time. She feels very down about it. Her best friend, Maggie, tells her to try again and to be less hard on herself. Maggie wants Laura to do the driving test again. She doesn't view Laura as a total failure based simply on her difficulty in passing a test. Even if Laura never drives, Maggie will likely remain her friend because of other things she likes and appreciates about Laura.

✔ **View your behaviour within the context of your circumstances, and above all, be compassionate.** Rivka had an abortion following a short affair. She feels very guilty and can't imagine putting the event behind her. Rivka's close friend, Carla, reminds her of the unfortunate circumstances she found herself in at the time, and tells her that she's still someone that she likes and respects very much. Carla can see that Rivka has made a difficult decision. She compassionately considers that Rivka has acted out of a degree of desperation. Rivka may have been unlucky, or a bit careless, with respect to birth control, but Carla does not judge her on the basis of the abortion.

Ask yourself whether the punishment fits the crime. Are you being fair on yourself? What punishment would you dole out to your best friend for the same behaviour? Be aware that you may be making yourself feel extremely guilty, or ashamed, inappropriately. If you wouldn't like to see anyone else feeling such extreme emotions in response to the same transgression you've committed, then you're applying a double standard that's loaded against you.

Are you created so differently that you must subscribe to an exceptional code of conduct? (Consider this an inverted inferiority complex.) Having some exceptional code of conduct implies that you, and you alone, are somehow designed exclusively to transcend the ubiquitous human essence of fallibility. However, you are human. You don't fail any more extravagantly than any of your peers – nor do you succeed more dramatically than they do. If you're going to exercise compassion towards your friends' failures and wobbles, you need to consistently apply the same rules of compassion and understanding to yourself.

Dealing with doubts and reservations

Many people feel that, by accepting themselves, they're simply letting themselves off the hook. But self-acceptance is about taking personal responsibility for your less good traits, actions and habits. Self-acceptance is about targeting areas that you both *can* and *wish to* change and then taking the appropriate steps towards change. Self-acceptance is not saying: 'Hey, I'm human and fallible! Therefore, I just am the way I am and I don't need to think about changing anything.'

You are, at baseline, worthy and acceptable, but some of your behaviours and attitudes may be simultaneously unacceptable.

Another common fear is that by accepting yourself, you're actually condoning undesirable aspects of yourself: 'Hey, I'm an acceptable human being and, therefore, all I think and do is acceptable.' Not so.

Work on accepting your overall self on the basis of your intrinsic human fallibility, and be prepared to judge *specific aspects* of yourself. You can both condone your personhood and also condemn, or reject, certain things that you do.

Selecting the Self-Help Journey to Self-Acceptance

A common reason for people persistently putting themselves down is that they hope to become better by calling attention to their mistakes, flaws and failings. Unfortunately, this process frequently includes feeling depressed or anxious, which may well already be underpinned by low self-esteem.

Trying to solve an emotional problem at the same time as calling yourself useless, worthless and pathetic is much like trying to learn a foreign language while hitting yourself over the head with a textbook – your actions are likely to make both jobs much harder. Self-esteem is such an important issue for so many people that we've written an entire book on the subject: *Boosting Self-Esteem For Dummies* (Wiley).

Accepting yourself has two interesting implications for overcoming emotional problems and personal development. First, you're equal in worth to other human beings just as you are, which helps to reduce emotional pain. Second, because you're not distracted by beating yourself up, you can focus better on coping with adversity, reducing disturbance, and self-improvement.

Imperfect self-acceptance

As you're a fallible human being, you won't be perfect at self-acceptance either. You'll very probably slip into putting yourself down from time to time, as everyone does – us included. The aim is to accept yourself more often and to accept yourself again more quickly, if you notice that you're putting yourself down. Such acceptance definitely gets easier and more consistent with practice.

Broadly speaking, you may be using one of two common strategies to manage low self-esteem:

avoiding doing things, or doing things excessively. For example, a person who believes they're worthless unless they're liked by everybody may try extra hard to avoid rejection or to win people's approval; while a person who regards themselves as a 'failure' may try to avoid situations in which they might fail. Have a look at Chapter 23 for more on avoiding potential self-esteem pitfalls.

Chapter 15

Cooling Down Your Anger

In This Chapter

▶ Knowing when your anger's problematic

▶ Developing healthy anger

▶ Taking healthy anger to work

▶ Communicating effectively to combat unhealthy anger

A nger's a pretty common emotion. However, anger is also increasingly recognised as an important emotional problem. Anger can be bad for your relationships, your health and your self-esteem.

In the bad old days of psychological treatment for anger, people were encouraged simply to 'get it out', often by beating pillows to vent their fury. The result? Just like anything you practise, these people got better at being angry. The notion that expressing your rage can 'get it out of your system' is something of a myth. More often, you wind yourself up further, generating even more anger. A better solution is to get to grips with managing your angry feelings responsibly, and to master skills that can help you to feel less angry, less often.

CBT offers clear and effective management of anger by tackling the thinking that underpins your anger and helping you express it in a healthy manner. This chapter focuses on CBT techniques that can help you deal directly with your feelings of anger.

Discerning the Difference between Healthy and Unhealthy Anger

Essentially, two different types of anger exist – healthy and unhealthy:

✔ **Healthy anger is helpful annoyance and irritation.** This is the kind of anger that spurs you on to assert your rights when it is important that you do so.

✔ **Unhealthy anger is unhelpful rage, and hate.** This type of anger leads you to behave aggressively or violently even in response to mild or unimportant provocation. Unhealthy anger can also mean you bottle things up and vent your anger indirectly (sometimes called 'passive aggression') or take it out on innocent parties.

All emotions have *themes* – that is, sets of circumstances or triggers from which they arise (we explain this a bit more in Chapter 6). Themes for anger include someone breaking one of your personal rules, or threatening your self-esteem through word or deed. Another anger theme is frustration, when someone or something gets in the way of you reaching a goal.

The triggers for healthy and unhealthy anger are the same, but the behavioural responses they typically produce are very different. Both anger types are also associated with different ways of thinking and attention focus.

Key characteristics of unhealthy anger

Unhealthy anger is far more likely than healthy anger to cause fractures in your personal relationships, create trouble in your workplace or land you in prison. You're also likely to feel more physically and emotionally uncomfortable when you're unhealthily angry.

Several ways of thinking typically underpin unhealthy anger:

✔ Making rigid demands and rules about the way other people must or must not behave

✔ Insisting that other people do not insult or ridicule you

✔ Demanding that life conditions and other people don't get in the way of you getting what you want

✔ Overestimating the degree to which people deliberately act in undesirable ways towards you

✔ Assuming automatically that you're right and the other person's wrong

✔ Refusing to consider another person's point of view

Common behavioural characteristics associated with unhealthy anger include the following:

✔ Attacking or wanting to attack another person physically or verbally

✔ Attacking another person in an indirect – also known as *passive-aggressive* – way, for example trying to make someone else's job difficult

✔ Taking out your anger on innocent parties, such as another person, an animal or an object

- ✔ Plotting revenge

- ✔ Holding a grudge

- ✔ Attempting to turn others against the person you believe has behaved undesirably

- ✔ Sulking

- ✔ Looking for evidence that someone has acted with malicious intent

- ✔ Searching for signs of an offence being repeated

- ✔ Being over-vigilant for people breaking your personal rules or acting disrespectfully towards you

Common physical signs of unhealthy anger include the following:

- ✔ Clenched fists

- ✔ Muscular tension, especially in the neck and shoulder muscles

- ✔ Clenched jaw

- ✔ Trembling or shaking

- ✔ Raised heart rate

- ✔ Feeling hot

For many people, anger can come on hot and fast. Familiarising yourself with your own early warning signs of anger can help you to intervene earlier.

Hallmarks of healthy anger

In general, people experience healthy anger as intense but not overwhelming. You can feel intensely angry in a healthy way without experiencing a loss of control. Healthy anger does not lead you to behave in antisocial, violent or intimidating ways.

In addition, healthy anger is typically underpinned by the following ways of thinking:

- ✔ Holding strong preferences rather than rigid demands about how people should act

- ✔ Having flexibility in the rules you expect people to abide by

- ✔ Strongly preferring that others don't insult or ridicule you

- ✔ Desiring that other people and life conditions don't get in the way of you getting what you want

- ✔ Thinking realistically about whether other people have deliberately acted undesirably towards you

✔ Considering that both you *and* the other person may be right *and* wrong to a degree

✔ Trying to see the other person's point of view

Behavioural characteristics typical of healthy anger include:

✔ Asserting yourself with the other person

✔ Staying in the situation with the intent of resolving any disagreement

✔ Requesting the other person to modify her behaviour – and respecting her right to disagree with you

✔ Looking for evidence that the other person may not have behaved with malicious intent

✔ Being able to forgive and forget

Assembling Attitudes That Underpin Healthy Anger

If you're serious about overcoming your unhealthy anger, you have to take a long, hard look at some of the attitudes you hold. This involves honestly looking at the way you believe that other people and the world at large *must* treat you. You may hold some common toxic beliefs that frequently lead to unhealthy anger in people. Some of these toxic thoughts include:

✔ 'No one must ever treat me poorly or disrespectfully.'

✔ 'The world must not be unjust or unfair and *especially* not to me!'

✔ 'I must get what I want when I want it and nothing should get in my way.'

✔ 'I must never be led into feeling guilty, inadequate, embarrassed or ashamed by other people or life events.'

✔ 'No one and nothing must ever expose my weaknesses or errors.'

Having looked long and hard at your attitudes, you need to make your toxic attitudes more helpful and realistic (see Chapter 3 for more on tackling toxic thoughts in general). Yes! Once again, positive emotional change comes from changing the way you think about yourself, other people and the world in general. If you want to be emotionally healthy and high-functioning, you need to start developing flexible, tolerant and accepting attitudes. High-functioning individuals experience fewer disturbing emotional responses, they are able to enjoy life, and they bounce back fairly readily from everyday hassles and annoyances. It's all in the way you look at life and the kind of attitude you take toward life's ups and downs (particularly with regard to anger).

We can explain the types of attitude that are likely to help you overcome unhealthy anger. However, *you* must decide to agree with these attitudes and ultimately *act in accordance with them* if you want to see a change in the amount of anger you experience.

The following sections describe the healthy attitudes that you need to take in order to overcome your unhealthy anger.

Putting up with other people

Other people exist in the same universe as you. Sometimes, this can be a rather pleasant state of affairs, but on occasions you may find that these other people are a damnable inconvenience. Whether you like it or not, other people can exist, do exist and will continue to exist in your universe for the foreseeable future. Accepting that these other people have as much right as you to inhabit the planet just makes sense. And while cohabitating, you may as well accept the reality that sometimes other people may get on your nerves. As you're not in charge of the universe, you'd better accept that other people are *allowed* to act according to their rules and values – not yours.

You've probably noticed that humans come in a variety of shapes, sizes and colours. No doubt you've seen that not all people share the same religion, culture, political opinions, moral codes or rules of social conduct. Now, without going into a long-winded speech about the value of diversity, accepting individual difference is terribly important. Acknowledging that other people have a right to their own ideas about how to live their lives – even when you flatly disagree with their ideas – can save you a lot of emotional upset. People will continue to exercise these rights, whatever your opinion.

Accepting others can save you a world of unhealthy anger. Consider this: every morning Jill and Tim travel to work together by bus. Every time she boards the bus, Jill says a pleasant 'Good morning!' to the driver, who always ignores her completely. One day, Tim asks Jill why she persists in greeting the driver, even though he never acknowledges her. Jill says: 'Because I choose to behave in line with my standard of politeness rather than to respond to his standard of rudeness.'

Jill's high tolerance to rudeness from the bus driver means that she can avoid making herself unhealthily angry. She does this by:

- ✔ Accepting that the driver has the right to be rude. No law exists against responding (or not) to another person's greeting.

- ✔ Not taking the driver's rudeness over-personally. The driver doesn't know Jill, so it's highly unlikely that he's actually 'out to get her' specifically. He's probably foul-tempered to many people in addition to Jill.

✔ Exercising her right to behave according to her own standard of polite-ness, even in the face of another person's rudeness. Although the bus driver is rude to Jill, she chooses not to respond in the same way. She can carry on being a generally polite person even in the face of another person's rudeness if she so chooses.

Forming flexible preferences

Wanting others to treat you well and with respect makes sense. Similarly, you probably want other people to do their jobs well and to help you to get what you want. You're likely to want life to roll your way and for world events to gel with your personal plans.

However, expecting and demanding these conditions to be met all the time doesn't make sense!

Keeping your attitudes flexible and based on *preferences*, rather than demands or expectations, can keep your anger in the healthy camp. Rigid and demand-ing attitudes can land you in unhealthy destructive anger, time and time again.

Consider the relationship of Ade and Franco: Ade holds rigid beliefs about other people showing him respect and courtesy. Franco holds the same principal attitudes, but flexibly. Ade and Franco go for lunch together and sit near a table of young men, who drink a bit too much and end up talking very loudly and rudely. Franco and Ade can't hear each other and their lunch is being ruined by the behaviour of these young men. Franco suggests that he and Ade move to another table, where they won't be disturbed by the men's antisocial behaviour. Ade, however, gets up and shouts at the men, ending up in a brawl outside the cafe. He's lucky not to be hurt more seriously than he is.

Ade's rigid attitudes about the situation are:

'How dare these idiots treat me this way?'

'I won't tolerate being disrespected like this.'

'I've got to show these idiots who's boss.'

Franco's more flexible attitudes about the situation are:

'These guys are behaving like idiots.'

'These guys are really annoying me with their disrespectful behaviour.'

'I don't want to put up with this, so I think I'll get away from these guys.'

Flexible preferences for things like respect allow for the possibility of you being treated disrespectfully. Rigid demands don't allow for the possibility of life and other people treating you in ways that you think they shouldn't. Inevitably, you can end up feeling outraged if you always demand that others behave in a specific way. People behave according to how *they* want to behave – not how *you* want them to behave.

Accepting other people as fallible human beings

When you angrily condemn another person as 'useless', 'no good' or 'idiotic', you make a gross overgeneralisation. The other person isn't a thoroughgoing idiot just because she's acting idiotically – she surely acts in different ways in other situations, just like you do.

The critical point here is also a practical point: putting down other people makes respecting others difficult. You need to sustain a level of respect for others in order to be able to consider behaviours objectively and act appropriately assertive.

The alternative to putting down others is to accept them as FHBs – fallible human beings – who may act in objectionable ways (to you). When you consider others as FHBs, you can appropriately condemn the behaviour but not the person. This acceptance is critical in helping you to keep a level head and master your angry feelings.

Accepting other people is the other side of the coin to accepting yourself. You can eventually accept yourself because you're essentially applying the same philosophy to everyone.

Accepting yourself

Sometimes, people default to unhealthy anger because they have a fragile sense of their own worth. If someone treats you poorly, insults you or seems to hold a negative opinion of you, you may be reminded of how low an opinion you have of yourself. In order to protect your self-worth, you may attack the other person. Think of the rationale as: 'If I can put you down, then I can avoid putting myself down.'

By believing that you're an unrateable, complex, ever-changing, fallible human, you may see that you can never be less worthwhile, even when people treat you poorly. In Chapter 14, we offer more guidance on self-acceptance.

Developing high frustration tolerance

Frustration occurs most often when something or someone gets in the way of you achieving your specific goals and aims. The more important your goal is to you, the more angry or annoyed you're likely to feel when something blocks your attempts to reach that goal.

People who frequently experience unhealthy anger tend to have a low tolerance for frustration. Their low threshold for tolerating hassle, mishaps or obstruction from others is echoed in statements like these:

> 'I can't stand it!'

> 'It's intolerable!'

> 'I just can't take it anymore!'

Increasing your tolerance for frustration helps you to experience appropriate levels of healthy annoyance in response to goal obstruction. Having a *high frustration tolerance* (HFT) makes you more effective at solving problems. So, your anger doesn't get in the way of you seeing possible solutions to every-day hassles and setbacks. High frustration tolerance is present in statements such as:

> 'This is an uncomfortable situation but I can stand the discomfort!'

> 'This event is hard to bear but I can bear it – some difficult things are worth tolerating.'

> 'Even if I *feel* like I can't take it anymore, chances are that I can.'

To increase your tolerance for frustration, ask yourself these kinds of questions when life pulls a fast one on you:

> 'Is this situation really terrible or is it just highly inconvenient?'

> 'Is it true that I can't stand this situation or is it more true that I don't like this situation?'

> 'Is this situation truly unbearable or is it really just very difficult to bear?'

Being less extreme in your judgement of negative events can help you to have less extreme emotional responses, such as unhealthy anger.

Most of what you think is intolerable isn't as bad as it seems. Many things are difficult to tolerate but are tolerable, hard to bear but bearable, unpleasant and inconvenient – but you *can* stand them!

Doing your ABCs

Practise writing down your unhealthy angry thoughts on paper and replacing them with healthier thoughts. Refer to Chapter 3 to see how to use an ABC form to tackle toxic thoughts and replace them with realistic renderings, pertinent preferences, additional acceptances, self-acceptance and high frustration tolerance.

To underscore the point, imagine getting stuck in traffic on your way to the airport and then missing your flight. Deeply annoying! However, you getting angry and screaming at the traffic isn't going to make the cars move any faster. Of course, becoming healthily annoyed about the traffic doesn't change the situation either. But your healthy anger is less likely to cause you such extreme discomfort and is more likely to help you create a contingency plan. Rather than using up your energy swearing and bashing your mobile against the dashboard, you can focus your efforts on phoning the airline and trying to get yourself bumped on to the next available flight.

Pondering the pros and cons of your temper

Believing that you're *right* to be angry and steadfastly sticking to this perception is one of the more common obstacles to conquering unhealthy anger.

You certainly have the *right* to feel angry. You may even *be right* to be angry, in the sense of objecting to something you don't like. However, you may feel better and behave more constructively if you have *healthy* anger rather than *unhealthy* anger.

To commit more fully to changing your anger, review the costs and benefits of your current anger, and of a healthier alternative. Refer to Chapter 8 for some pointers on completing a cost–benefit analysis, which can help you to facilitate this change.

Imparting Your Indignation in a Healthy Way

Expressing your feelings readily when they occur can be a good antidote to bouts of unhealthy anger. On the other hand, bottling up your feelings can mean that you allow your emotions to fester until they bubble up to the surface and you explode.

People who talk openly and appropriately about their emotional responses to events are less prone to unhealthy feelings like anger and depression. The following sections offer tips and techniques to improve your communication skills and to deal with dissatisfaction in a healthy manner.

Asserting yourself effectively

Assertion involves standing up for yourself, voicing your opinions and feelings, and firmly ensuring that your basic rights are considered. Assertion differs from aggression, in that it doesn't involve violence, intimidation or disregard for the rights of others.

Using assertion rather than aggression is more effective in getting you what you want. When you're being assertive, you're still in control of your behaviour, but when you're unhealthily enraged much of your behaviour is impulsive. People with unhealthy anger frequently regret their fury-fuelled actions later on once the red mist has cleared.

People are likely to respond to your wishes when you're being assertive simply because you're making yourself clear – not because they're afraid of your anger.

Often, your aggression is about winning an argument and getting the other person to back down and agree that you're right. Assertion is not about winning per se. Rather, assertion is about getting your point across but not insisting that the other person agrees with you or backs down.

If you have a tendency to get angry, and become verbally or physically aggressive quickly, give yourself time out and go and count to ten (or as high as you need to feel calmer). You can then consider your next thinking and behavioural steps. Removing yourself from an inflammatory situation is often a sensible first step in adopting healthy assertion.

Assertion is a skill that you can practise. Many people with anger problems benefit from breaking down assertion into the following steps:

1. **Get the other person's attention.** For example, if you want to make a complaint in a shop, wait until you have the shop assistant's attention rather than shouting at them when they're busy with another task. If you want to talk to your partner about a specific issue, ask for some of her time.

2. **Be in the right place.** The best time to assert yourself may depend on where you are when you get irked. If your boss makes a comment that undermines you during a board meeting, you're probably best to bring it up with her a bit later in less public surroundings.

3. **Be clear in your head about what you want to say.** If you're new to assertion, but more familiar with the shouting and screaming thing, give yourself time to really think about what you want to get across.

4. **Stick to your point and be respectful.** Don't resort to name-calling or hurling insults.

5. **Take responsibility for your feelings of annoyance.** Don't blame the other person for *making* you feel angry. Use statements like 'I feel angry when you turn up an hour late for our appointments', or 'I felt let down and angry that you didn't invite me to your wedding reception'.

Assertion doesn't always work. Simply because you make the superlative effort to stop yelling your lungs out and to stop battering other people about the head, doesn't mean that you're always going to get what you want. No, siree! In fact, some people may even meet your assertion with their own aggression. So, strive to maintain your healthy anger and to behave assertively, even when other people don't. Remind yourself that other people have the right to choose to behave badly and that you have the right to remove yourself from them rather than responding in kind.

Before you assert yourself, decide whether the situation's really worth your time and energy. Ask yourself whether the problem merits you being assertive. Is the issue more trouble than it's worth? If you're a former unhealthy anger junkie, you're probably not used to just letting things go. You can practise deciding when asserting yourself is in your best interests and when you're wiser to simply not respond at all.

Coping with criticism

Criticism isn't always intended to anger or undermine the receiver. Well-delivered specific criticism can provide useful information and need not cause offence. Most people like to hear positive feedback – it's the negative stuff that really gets under your skin.

People who demand perfection from themselves, or expect approval from significant others, can often take criticism badly. They tend to take criticism overly seriously and personally. They often assume that any form of negative comment means that they're less than worthy. If you're this sort of person, a comment from your boss such as 'I'm not entirely happy with this report you've written' gets translated in your head as something like this:

> *My boss thinks my report is rubbish = All my reports are rubbish = I'm rubbish at my job = I'm rubbish*

You may even become unhealthily angry in an attempt to defend your self-worth, and launch a counteroffensive on the person you feel has attacked you.

You can take the sting out of criticism by keeping these points in mind:

✔ Criticism can help you to improve your work performance and your relationships.

✔ You can assess criticism, decide how much of it you agree with, and reject the rest.

✔ Criticism is something pretty much everyone experiences from time to time. You cannot reasonably expect to always avoid being criticised.

If someone criticises you in a global way – for example, your sister calls you an incompetent loser – try asking her to be more specific: 'In what specific ways am I an incompetent loser?' Asking questions can make the criticism more useful to you. Or, if the person cannot be more specific, your question can disarm her. The following section discusses disarming in greater detail.

Using the disarming technique

Okay, not all the criticism that you get is well-intended. Sometimes, another person may bombard you with a load of negative remarks or insults. What are your options? You *can* get unhealthily angry and shout at or otherwise attack your antagonist. Or, you can keep your annoyance in the healthy camp and try non-defensively disarming your critic. The disarming technique works on the following principles:

✔ Look for a grain of truth in what the other person is saying and agreeing with her on that specific point

✔ Show your critic some empathy

✔ Ask your critic for more information about her point of criticism.

✔ Express your own point of view as 'I feel' statements

For example, Heidi's friend criticises her for being late to meet her for coffee. She says angrily: 'You're always late, Heidi. You're just so disorganised!' Heidi would usually be defensive and hostile about criticism, resulting in many past arguments. Instead, this time Heidi uses the disarming technique and replies, 'You're right! I'm not the most organised person in the world' (partial agreement). 'Are you feeling really annoyed?' (empathy/asking for more information). This takes the heat from her friend's anger, who then goes on to say how frustrated she's feeling in general.

Using the disarming technique, you come out on top by keeping your cool. You also gain the satisfaction of having managed a critical comment well. Who knows – you may even *improve* your relationship with your critic.

Acting Assertively in the Workplace

Keeping your cool at work is an important issue for many people. After all, you spend a lot of your waking hours at work and you probably really need a regular income. Sometimes unhealthy anger can lead to unnecessary work life strife or even put your job in jeopardy.

Maintaining good relationships with your colleagues and managers can make working life a lot more pleasant. Work environments are often a trouble spot for people with a history of unhealthy anger. If you think about it, work typically involves encountering criticism, dealing with authority, coping with stressful deadlines, living up to achievement expectations and collaborating with others on projects. If you have fragile self-esteem or a fundamental intolerance of other people's poor behaviour, you'll potentially be going off like a firecracker.

The same attitudes and strategies associated with healthy anger (previously outlined in this chapter) apply to the workplace. However, we offer you some additional specific pointers to help you remain healthily assertive whilst you work:

- ✔ **Desire, but don't demand, success.** Success in your job is an understandable goal to have (see Chapter 8 for more on goals and goal-setting). However, when you strive for a degree of professional success but resist insisting that *you have to get it*, you can safeguard your mental health and avoid unhealthy anger. Unfortunately success is never guaranteed, even with hard work and dedication, so keep your high standards by all means, but be sure to build in a margin for error and failures.

- ✔ **Set realistic performance standards.** Yes, aiming high is fine but you also need to allow for the possibility of failing to meet those standards from time to time. Being a humble human equipped with mere human ability and stamina may mean that you sometimes fall short of your professional performance standards.

- ✔ **Be a team player.** No person's an island. At work, try to share the load with your colleagues when appropriate. Working with others is a skill and it may take practice to develop. You might not agree with everything fellow team members suggest or with the way they do things. But if you avoid working with others for these reasons, you deprive yourself of the chance to grow. Developing confidence in your ability to disagree with others respectfully and offer your own ideas politely will make you less prone to bouts of unhealthy anger.

- ✔ **Make allowances for other people's personal interaction style.** Simply because you're working hard to overcome unhealthy anger doesn't unfortunately mean that all your work mates are doing the same. Some people will be rude; sometimes your boss may speak to you in a less than courteous manner. Rather than letting other people's rudeness throw you into a rage (or eat you up inside), stick to your own standards of courteous communication. You don't have to condone poor behaviour from others but you do need to remember that how they behave is their choice. Resist sinking to the same level and instead rise above it.

✔ **Differentiate between professional and personal comments.** When someone at work makes a negative comment about an aspect of your performance, they don't necessarily mean anything unpleasant about you as a *person*. Even if the comment is tactlessly delivered, you've got a choice about whether or not to feel personally attacked. Try to differentiate clearly between remarks about your work-related performance and those about your character. This may help to diffuse a situation because you're not misinterpreting other people's intentions as deliberately malicious.

If someone at work does level a personal criticism at you, think first and respond later. The other person is probably behaving unprofessionally and you don't have to respond in kind. Give yourself time to cool down before taking any action.

✔ **Strike a work–life balance.** Sometimes tempers fray in the workplace because people are overworked; they may be pressurised into putting in long hours, for example. If you have your own business, you may find it difficult to justify taking much time off. Striking a balance between working life and home life is very important. Not making time for yourself outside of work can leave you burnt out and short of patience. Build in time to recharge your batteries and enjoy yourself.

You're a person *first* and an employee *second* (or even third, fourth or fifth . . . depending on your personal priorities). Over-identifying with your work role can make it harder to keep your perspective (and your cool) when things go awry. No matter how important your work role is to you, bear in mind that you're a whole person – there's more to you than what you do for a living.

Putting your point across positively

Despite your newly cultivated Zen-like ability to take work disagreements in your stride, sometimes issues do need to be addressed. Try using the tips in the following sections to help eliminate unnecessary strife and ensure that you stay in the healthy anger camp – no matter what!

Assessing what you aim to achieve

Before a confrontation, however minor, decide what you aim to achieve. Whether this means requesting a pay rise, time off, more resources or providing an explanation of some kind – assess precisely what you hope to achieve. You stand a better chance of clear, calm communication and of actually getting what you want when you're clear in advance about *what* that is. Also think of acceptable compromises to your ultimate aim before initiating discussion with the other person. In your attempts to rid yourself of unhealthy anger – forewarned is forearmed.

Taking time to think

Give yourself time to think of how best to get your point across. Consider appropriate time and place. Clearly decide on what it is you want to communicate in advance. Write some bullet points on paper to refer to if you think that'll help you stay focused. In some circumstances, it pays to prepare yourself for a negative response and devise ways of dealing with it. Having some definite ideas on how you'll respond to not getting your way or being misunderstood can help you stick to assertion rather than falling into old aggressive patterns.

Leaving well enough alone

At work, as in other areas of your life, there comes a point when further discussion just isn't likely to pay off. In work situations, an endgame often exists that you just need to accept. For example, no funding may actually be available to meet certain requests, deadlines may be immoveable, working hours non-negotiable, and so on. If you continue to push the point with your bosses or co-workers, you may just create extra stress for yourself or rupture your working relationships.

Promoting a professional image

Behaving professionally can help to eliminate confrontation at work and increase your overall confidence. People who take a professional attitude towards work, whatever their occupation, are more likely to remain calm in crisis. They also remember to deal with anger-triggering situations assertively and without flying off the handle. Here are some basic rules of communication that facilitate smooth running in the workplace:

- Keep your head up and maintain good posture
- Make good eye contact with fellow workers and managers
- Speak clearly, audibly and take your time
- Ask questions directly and request support in a straightforward manner when you need it
- Sit centrally in meetings rather than on the fringes
- Strike a balance between offering your ideas and opinions and listening attentively to those of others

Remaining professional

You can also improve your chances of remaining in control of your feelings at work by adhering to the principles of professional conduct. Bear these tips in mind:

- **Be punctual.** Being consistently late is irksome for your boss and those who rely on you being around to do their own jobs. You probably don't like others being late, so make an effort to practise what you preach.
- **Be prepared.** Ensure that you have everything you need to do your job and have put in any preparation needed for certain projects.

✔ **Dress accordingly.** Wearing the garb expected of you in the workplace contributes to looking professional.

✔ **Be polite.** Treat others as you'd like to be treated. Be consistently courteous with your work mates even if you arrive in a bad mood. People feel secure around people who are pretty predictable in terms of politeness.

✔ **Keep home and work life separate.** You're only human, so you're likely to be affected by home troubles when at work occasionally. But airing your 'dirty laundry' (so to speak) at work is likely to bring you other difficulties that you just don't need. You're paid to do your job and that's what your boss and clients will tend to expect of you. If personal problems are clouding your ability to work effectively, consider time off and/or speak about the situation to the relevant person at work.

Dealing with Difficulties in Overcoming Anger

Even if you know that your anger responses are causing you problems in your life, you may still be reluctant to let go of your anger. Sometimes, people are reluctant to break free from unhealthy anger and related behaviours because they can't see an alternative, and think that they may end up being passive or getting walked over instead.

However, if you develop your assertion skills, you may well be more inclined to let go of your anger. Nevertheless, here are some common obstacles to getting rid of unhealthy anger and some suggestions to help you take on healthy anger instead:

✔ **You lack empathy and understanding of the impact your unhealthy anger responses have on those near to you.** When you're not angry, ask your loved ones how they feel about your anger. Try to remember times when you've been on the receiving end of aggressive or intimidating behaviour and how it affected you. Use feedback about your anger, and your own experiences of aggression from others, to help you change how you express feelings of annoyance in the future.

✔ **Letting go of your anger means that you're weak.** You may consider yourself an angry person, and you may like it that way. You may think that if you don't continue to be angry, other people may discover that you're weak, a pushover or someone they can mess with. Work to realise that people who're assertive – firm but fair – tend to earn respect. You don't need to be angry to be strong.

✔ **You think that your unhealthy anger helps you to control other people and encourages them to respect you.** If you're very aggressive, people who are important in your life, such as your children or your partner, may go out of their way to avoid incurring your wrath. Don't mistake fear and dislike for respect. You may control the people in your life by your anger, but their compliance is likely borne of fear and loathing, not from genuine regard for you. When you behave respectfully and assertively, people are likely to respond out of a genuine regard for your feelings rather than out of fear.

✔ **Your unhealthy anger makes you feel powerful.** Although some people find the intensity of their unhealthy anger pretty uncomfortable and even scary, others feel invigorated by the rush of their fury. Unhealthy anger is based on putting down another person. Unhealthy anger often means that you're stepping on another person's rights, or abusing or intimidating somebody else. If you enjoy these aspects of your anger, you probably hold a low opinion of yourself generally. Look for other ways to experience your personal power without undermining those around you.

✔ **Your anger is self-righteous.** You may be clinging stubbornly to your anger because you think it's justified. You may be refusing to admit that you could be wrong or that the other person could be right. Rarely are confrontations as cut and dried as one party being utterly in the right and the other utterly in the wrong. Remind yourself that being wrong is okay. It isn't a sign of weakness or inferiority. Allow yourself to admit that you may be wrong and that the other person may have a good point.

Feeling a bit sceptical? Test out your predictions about adopting healthy anger and behaving in an assertive rather than an aggressive manner. You can use the blank behavioural experiment sheet in Chapter 4. (See Chapter 4 for more help on conducting behavioural experiments.)

Body benefits for bridling your anger

Being angry, especially feeling frequently hostile towards other people and the world, is bad for you. Scientific research shows an association between hostility and raised blood pressure, which can lead to heart problems. Take the pressure off your mind, your interactions with other people and your heart by controlling – rather than being controlled by – your anger.

Part IV
Looking Backwards and Moving Forwards

The 5th Wave   By Rich Tennant

"My hunch, Mr. Pesko, is that you're still making mountains out of mole hills."

In this part . . .

Putting your present problems into context based on your past experiences is central to CBT, and this part helps you to do just that. You'll also find information on how to consolidate new ways of thinking, as well as tips about making productive behavioural changes stick. We'll help you to overcome common obstacles to positive change and show you how to get and best use professional help.

Chapter 16

Taking a Fresh Look at Your Past

. . . .

In This Chapter

▶ Putting your current problems into context

▶ Identifying your core beliefs

▶ Dealing with early experiences

▶ Developing alternative beliefs

. . . .

*Y*our past experiences have an effect on how you think and function now. Sometimes, you may endure bad experiences and be able to make some good things happen from them. At other times, you may be wounded by unpleasant events and carry that injury with you into your present and future.

This chapter encourages you to examine openly whether your past experiences have led you to develop *core beliefs* that may be causing your current emotional difficulties.

People are sometimes surprised to find out that CBT considers the past an important aspect of understanding one's problems. Unlike traditional Freudian psychoanalysis, which focuses intensively on childhood relationships and experiences, CBT specifically investigates past experiences in order to see how these early events may still be affecting people in their *present* lives.

Exploring How Your Past Can Influence Your Present

We don't know what your childhood and early adulthood were like, but many people share relatively common past experiences. The following examples highlight various aspects of past experience that may resonate with your life history. Rather than focusing on the differences between these examples and your own experiences, use the examples to identify similar things that have happened to you in your own life.

- Sybil grew up with parents who fought a lot. She learnt to be very quiet and to keep out of the way so that her parents' anger wouldn't be directed at her. She always tried to be a very good girl and no trouble to anyone.

- Rashid had critical parents. The demands Rashid's parents made of him to be a 'high achiever' made it clear to him that he would get their love and approval only when he did well in sports and at school.

- Beth had a violent father who would frequently beat her and other family members when he was in a bad mood. At other times, her father was very loving and funny. Beth could never predict accurately what mood her father would be in when he came through the front door.

- Milo's relationships have never lasted for very long. Most of the women he's dated have been unfaithful to him. Milo's partners often complain that he's too insecure and suspicious of their friendships with members of the opposite sex.

- Mahesh lost his oldest son and the family business in a fire five years ago. His wife has been depressed since the fire, and their marriage seems to be falling apart. Recently, his teenage daughter has been in trouble with the police. No one seems to offer Mahesh support. He feels dogged by bad luck.

Many other different kinds of difficult experiences can contribute to the development of negative core beliefs:

- Death of loved ones
- Growing up with neglectful, critical or abusive parents or siblings
- Divorce
- Being bullied at school
- Being abandoned by a parent or significant other
- Undergoing a trauma, such as rape, life-threatening illness, accidents or witnessing violent attacks on other people

These are just some examples of the types of event that can have a profound effect on mental health generally. Negative events that contribute to the way you think about yourself, other people and the world often occur in childhood or early adult life. However, events occurring at any stage of your life can have a significant impact on the way you think about the world.

Identifying Your Core Beliefs

Your *core beliefs* are ideas or philosophies that you hold very strongly and very deeply. These ideas are usually developed in childhood or early in adult life. Core beliefs aren't always negative. Good experiences of life and of other people generally lead to the development of healthy ideas about yourself, other people and the world. In this chapter we deal with negative core beliefs because these are the types of belief that cause people's emotional problems.

Sometimes, the negative core beliefs that are formed during childhood can be reinforced by later experiences, which seem to confirm their validity.

For example, one of Beth's core beliefs is 'I'm bad'. She develops this belief to make sense of her father beating her for no real or obvious reason. Later, Beth has a few experiences of being punished unreasonably by teachers at school, which reinforce her belief in her 'badness'.

Core beliefs are characteristically global and absolute, like Beth's 'I'm bad'. People hold core beliefs to be 100 per cent true under all conditions. You often form your core beliefs when you're a child to help you make sense of your childhood experiences, and so you may never evaluate whether your core beliefs are the best way to make sense of your adult experiences. As an adult, you may continue to act, think and feel as though the core beliefs of your childhood are still 100 per cent true.

Your core beliefs are called 'core' because they're your deeply held ideas and they're at the very centre of your belief system. Core beliefs give rise to rules, demands or assumptions, which in turn produce *automatic thoughts* (thoughts that just pop into your head when you're confronted with a situation). You can think of these three layers of beliefs as a dartboard with core beliefs as the bull's-eye. Figure 16-1 shows the interrelationship between the three layers, and shows the assumptions and automatic thoughts that surround Beth's core belief that she's bad.

Another way of describing a core belief is as a lens or filter, through which you interpret all the information you receive from other people and the world around you.

Figure 16-1:
The core
beliefs
dartboard
and Beth's
dartboard,
showing the
three layers
of beliefs.

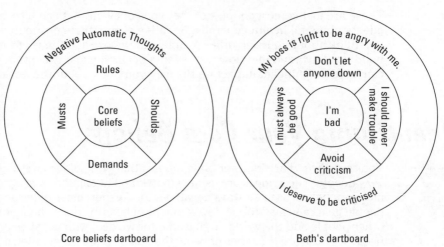

Core beliefs dartboard   Beth's dartboard

Introducing the three camps of core beliefs

Core beliefs fall into three main camps: beliefs about yourself, beliefs about other people, and beliefs about the world.

Beliefs about yourself

Unhelpful negative core beliefs about yourself often have their roots in damaging early experiences. Being bullied or ostracised at school, or experiencing neglect, abuse or harsh criticism from caregivers, teachers or siblings can inform the way in which you understand yourself.

For example, Beth's experiences of physical abuse led her to form the core belief 'I'm bad'.

Beliefs about other people

Negative core beliefs about others often develop as a result of traumatic incidents involving other people. A traumatic incident can mean personal harm inflicted on you by another person or witnessing harm being done to others. Negative core beliefs can also develop from repeated negative experiences with other people, such as teachers and parents.

For example, because Beth's father was violent and abusive towards her but also could be funny when he wanted to be, she developed a core belief that 'people are dangerous and unpredictable'.

Beliefs about the world

People who've experienced trauma, lived with severe deprivation or survived in harmful, insecure, unpredictable environments are prone to forming negative core beliefs about life and the world.

Beth holds a core belief – that 'the world is full of bad things' – which she developed as a result of her early home situation and events at school later on.

Sometimes, core beliefs from all three camps are taught to you explicitly as a child. Your parents or caregivers may have given you *their* core beliefs. For example, you may have been taught that 'life's cruel and unfair' before you have any experiences that lead you to form such a belief yourself.

Seeing how your core beliefs interact

Identifying core beliefs about yourself can help you to understand why you keep having the same problems. However, if you can also get to know your fundamental beliefs about other people and the world, you can build a fuller picture of why some situations distress you. For example, Beth may find being yelled at by her boss depressing because it fits with her core belief 'I'm bad', but the experience also seems to confirm her belief that people are unpredictable and aggressive.

Like many people, you may hold core beliefs that you're unlovable, unworthy or inadequate – these beliefs are about your basic worth, goodness or value. Or perhaps you hold beliefs about your capability to look after yourself or to cope with adversity – these beliefs are about how helpless or powerful you are in relation to other people and the world.

Mahesh, for example, may believe 'I'm helpless' because he's experienced tragedy and a lot of bad luck. He may also hold beliefs that 'the world is against me' and 'other people are uncaring'. Looking at these three beliefs together, you can see why Mahesh is feeling depressed.

Detecting Your Core Beliefs

Because core beliefs are held deeply, you may not think of them or 'hear' them as clear statements in your head. You're probably much more aware of your negative automatic thoughts or your rules than you are of your core beliefs (see Figure 16-1).

The following sections show you some methods you can use to really get to the root of your belief system.

Following a downward arrow

One technique to help you pinpoint your problematic core beliefs is the *downward arrow* method, which involves you identifying a situation that causes you to have an unhealthy negative emotion, such as depression or guilt. (For more on healthy and unhealthy negative emotions, check out Chapter 6.)

After you've identified a situation that brings up negative emotions, ask yourself what the situation means or says about you. Your first answer is probably your *negative automatic thought* (NAT). Keep asking yourself what your previous answer means or says about you until you reach a global, absolute statement, such as 'other people are dangerous' or 'I'm bad' in Beth's case.

For example, when Rashid uses the downward arrow method to examine his feelings about failing a university entrance exam, he has the negative automatic thought:

NAT: 'I'll never get into a good university.'

What does this NAT mean about me?

'I've disappointed my parents again.'

What does disappointing my parents mean about me?

'Every time I try to do well at something, I fail.'

What does failing mean about me?

'I'm a failure.' (Rashid's core belief)

 You can use the same downward arrow technique to get to your core beliefs about other people and the world. Just keep asking yourself what your NAT *means about others or the world*. Ultimately, you can end up with a conclusive statement that is your core belief. The following is an example of how to do this, using the situation of getting a parking ticket:

NAT: 'These kinds of things are always happening to me.'

What does this mean about the world?

'Bad things are always just around the corner.'

What does this mean about the world?

'The world is full of tragedy and hardship.'

What does this mean about the world?

'Life is against me.' (Core belief)

Picking up clues from your dreaming and screaming

Imagine your worst nightmare. Think of dream scenarios that wake you up screaming. Somewhere in these terrifying scenarios may be one or more of your core beliefs. Some examples of core beliefs that can show themselves in dreams and nightmares include:

- ✔ Drying up while speaking publicly
- ✔ Being rejected by your partner for another person
- ✔ Being criticised in front of work colleagues
- ✔ Getting lost in a foreign country
- ✔ Hurting someone's feelings
- ✔ Doing something thoughtless and being confronted about it
- ✔ Letting down someone important in your life
- ✔ Being controlled by another person
- ✔ Being at someone else's mercy

Look for the similarities between your nightmare scenarios and situations that upset you in real life. Ask yourself what a dreaded dream situation may mean about yourself, about other people or about the world. Keep considering what each of your answers means about yourself, others or the world until you reach a core belief.

Tracking themes

Another way of journeying to the core of your core beliefs is to look for themes in your automatic thoughts. A good way of doing this is by reviewing your completed ABC forms (which we describe in Chapter 3).

For example, if you find that you often have thoughts related to failure, getting things wrong or being less capable than other people, you may have a core belief of 'I'm inadequate' or 'I'm incompetent'.

Filling in the blanks

Another method of eliciting your core beliefs is simply to fill in the blanks. Take a piece of paper, write the following, and fill in the blanks:

I am _____

Other people are _____

The world is _____

This method requires you to take almost a wild guess about what your core beliefs are. Ultimately, you're in a better position than anyone else to take a guess, so the exercise is worth a shot.

You can review written work that you've done, which is a good technique for discovering your core beliefs. Going over what you've written again enables you to refine, tweak or alter your beliefs. Be sure to use language that represents how you truly speak to yourself. Core beliefs are very idiosyncratic. However you choose to articulate them is entirely up to you. The same is true of the healthy alternative beliefs you develop (see the 'Developing Alternatives to Your Core Beliefs' section, later in this chapter). Make sure that you put alternative beliefs into language that reflects the way that you speak to yourself.

Understanding the Impact of Core Beliefs

Core beliefs are your fundamental and enduring ways of perceiving and making sense of yourself, the world and other people. Your core beliefs have been around since early in your life. These core beliefs are so typically engrained and unconscious that you're probably not aware of their impact on your emotions and behaviours.

Spotting when you are acting according to old rules and beliefs

People tend to behave according to the beliefs they hold about themselves, others and the world. To evaluate whether your core beliefs are unhealthy, you need to pay attention to your corresponding behaviours. Unhealthy core beliefs typically lead to problematic behaviours.

For example, Milo believes that he's unlovable and that other people cannot be trusted. Therefore, he tends to be passive with his girlfriends, to seek reassurance that they're not about to leave him, and to become suspicious and jealous of their interactions with other men. Often, Milo's girlfriends get fed up with his jealousy and insecurity and end the relationship.

Because Milo operates according to his core belief about being unlovable, he behaves in ways that actually tend to drive his partners away from him. Milo doesn't yet see that his core belief, and corresponding insecurity, is what causes problems in his relationships. Instead, Milo views each time a partner leaves him for someone else as further evidence that his core belief of 'I'm unlovable' is true.

Sybil believes that she mustn't draw attention to herself because one of her core beliefs is 'other people are likely to turn on me'. Therefore, she's quiet in social situations and is reluctant to assert herself. Her avoidant, self-effacing behaviour means that she doesn't often get what she wants, which feeds her core belief 'I'm unimportant'.

Sybil acts in accordance with her core belief that other people are likely to turn on her and, subsequently, deprives herself of the opportunity to see that this is not always going to happen. If Sybil and Milo identify their negative core beliefs, they can begin to develop healthier new beliefs and behaviours that can yield better results. We look more closely at how to develop new, more positive core beliefs later in this chapter.

Understanding that unhealthy core beliefs make you prejudiced

When you begin to examine your core beliefs, it may seem to you that everything in your life is conspiring to make your unhealthy core belief ring true. More than likely, your core belief is leading you to take a prejudiced view of all your experiences. Unhealthy beliefs, such as 'I'm unlovable' and 'other people are dangerous', distort the way in which you process information. Negative information that supports your unhealthy belief is let in. Positive information that contradicts the negative stuff is either rejected, or twisted to mean something negative in keeping with your unhealthy belief.

The prejudice model in Figure 16-2 shows you how your unhealthy core beliefs can reject positive events that may *contradict* them. At the same time, your core beliefs can collect negative events that may *support* their validity. Your unhealthy core beliefs can also lead you to distort positive events into negative events so that they continue to make your beliefs seem true.

Negative information fits in with negative belief

Figure 16-2:
The preju-
dice model
illustrates
how you
sometimes
distort
positive
information
to fit in with
your nega-
tive core
beliefs.

Positive information ignored or dismissed

Positive information distorted to fit in with negative belief

For example, here's how Beth's core belief 'I'm bad' causes her to prejudice her experiences:

✔ **Negative experience:** Beth's boss is angry about a missed deadline, affirming her belief that 'I'm bad'.

✔ **Positive experience:** Beth's boss is happy about the quality of her report, which Beth distorts as 'he's happy about this report only because all my other work is such rubbish', further affirming her belief that 'I'm bad'.

Beth also ignores smaller *positive* events that don't support her belief that she's bad, such as:

✔ People seem to like her at work.

✔ Co-workers tell her that she's conscientious at work.

✔ Her friends telephone her and invite her out.

However, Beth is quick to take notice of smaller *negative* events that do seem to match up with her belief that she's bad, for example:

✔ Someone pushes her rudely on a busy train.

✔ Her boyfriend shouts at her during an argument.

✔ A work colleague doesn't smile at her when she enters the office.

Beth's core belief of 'I'm bad' acts as a filter through which all her experiences are interpreted. It basically stops her from re-evaluating herself as anything other than bad; it makes her prejudiced against herself. This is why identifying negative core beliefs and targeting them for change is so important!

Making a Formulation of Your Beliefs

When you've identified your core beliefs using the techniques outlined in the previous sections, you can use the form in Figure 16-3 to make a formulation of your beliefs and rules. Filling out this form gives you an 'at a glance' reference of what your negative core beliefs are and how they lead you to act in unhelpful ways. The form is a handy reminder of the beliefs you need to target for change and why.

Follow these steps to fill out the form:

1. **Relevant Early/Past Experiences. In this box, write down any significant past events that you think may have contributed to the development of your specific negative core beliefs.**

   For example, Beth records:

   - Father was physically abusive and had unpredictable mood swings

   - Father told me that I was bad

   - I received severe and unreasonable punishment from teachers

2. **Core ('Unconditional') Unhelpful Beliefs. Write your identified core beliefs about yourself, other people and the world in this box.**

   Beth records her beliefs like this:

   - I am bad

   - Other people are unpredictable and dangerous

   - The world is full of bad things

The word 'unconditional' is used on this form to remind you that core beliefs are those beliefs that you hold to be 100 per cent true, 100 per cent of the time, and under any conditions.

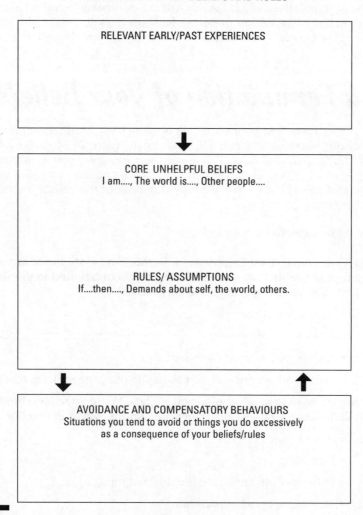

FORMULATION OF MY BELIEFS AND RULES

RELEVANT EARLY/PAST EXPERIENCES

CORE UNHELPFUL BELIEFS
I am...., The world is...., Other people....

RULES/ ASSUMPTIONS
If....then...., Demands about self, the world, others.

AVOIDANCE AND COMPENSATORY BEHAVIOURS
Situations you tend to avoid or things you do excessively
as a consequence of your beliefs/rules

WHAT I'VE GOT GOING FOR ME
List your personal strengths and assets

Figure 16-3:
Make a for-
mulation of
your beliefs
with the
help of this
form.

3. **Rules/'Conditional' Beliefs. In this box write down the rules or demands you place on yourself, other people and the world *because of* your core negative beliefs.**

   Beth writes:

   - I must be 'good' at all times (demand on self).

   - *If* I am criticised *then* it means that I'm a bad person (conditional rule).

   - Other people must not find fault with me or think badly of me (demand on others).

   - The world must not conspire to remind me of how bad I am by throwing negative experiences my way (demand on the world).

4. **Avoidance and Compensatory Behaviours. Use this box to record how you try to avoid triggering your negative core beliefs, or unhelpful things you do to try to cope with your negative core beliefs when they're triggered.**

   Beth records:

   - Being a perfectionist at work in order to avoid any criticism

   - Avoiding confrontation and thereby not asserting myself at work or with friends

   - Over-apologising when I do get criticised or make a small mistake

   - Always assuming that other people's opinions are 'right' and that my own opinions are 'wrong'

   - Being timid in social situations to avoid being noticed

   - Not trusting others and assuming that they're ultimately going to hurt me somehow

5. **What I've got going for me. Write down positive things about yourself that fly in the face of your negative core beliefs.**

   Beth writes:

   - My work colleagues seem to like me.

   - I am very conscientious at work and this has been commented on by my boss and by colleagues.

   - I have some good friends who are trustworthy.

   - There have been some good things that have happened to me, such as finishing college and getting a good job.

   - I am generally hardworking and honest.

   - I care about other people's feelings and opinions.

Information you write down in this box is important because it can be used to help you develop more balanced and helpful alternative core beliefs. (We explain more about how to construct healthy core beliefs in the following sections.)

Limiting the Damage: Being Aware of Core Beliefs

To reduce the negative impact of your unhelpful core beliefs, try to get better at spotting the beliefs being activated. Step back and consider a more unbiased explanation for events rather than getting swept along by the beliefs.

One way of improving your awareness of your core beliefs is to develop a *core belief flashcard*. This written-down statement includes the following:

- ✔ What your core belief is.
- ✔ How your core belief affects the way you interpret events.
- ✔ How you tend to act when the core belief is triggered.
- ✔ What a more unbiased interpretation of events is likely to be.
- ✔ What alternative behaviour may be more productive.

For example, Sybil wrote the following core belief flashcard:

> *When my core belief of 'I'm unimportant' is triggered, I'm probably taking something personally and wanting to withdraw. Instead, I can remember that most people don't hold this view of me, and then I can stay engaged in the social situation.*

Carry your flashcard around with you and review it often, even several times a day. Use your flashcard, especially when you notice that your core belief has *been* triggered, or just before you enter a situation where you know that your old core belief is *likely* to be triggered.

Developing Alternatives to Your Core Beliefs

When you've put your finger on your core beliefs and identified those that are negative and unhealthy, you're in a position to develop healthier alternative beliefs.

Your new core belief doesn't need to be the extreme opposite of your old belief. Changing an extreme belief such as 'I'm unlovable' to 'I'm lovable' may be too difficult when you're just starting out. Instead, cut yourself some slack and realise that simply by beginning to understand that an unhealthy core belief is not 100 per cent true all of the time is enough. Here are some examples:

- ✔ Beth's alternative to her unhealthy belief 'I'm bad' is 'there are good things about me'.

- ✔ Rashid replaces his unhealthy belief 'I'm a failure' with 'I succeed at some things'.

- ✔ Mahesh chooses the alternative 'good things do happen in the world' to replace his old belief 'the world's against me'.

- ✔ Sybil replaces her belief 'other people will turn against me' with the healthier belief 'many people can be kind'.

- ✔ Milo substitutes his old core belief 'I'm unlovable' with the more accurate belief 'some people do like me, and some people will love me'.

Generating alternatives for your unhealthy and absolute core beliefs is not about positive thinking or platitudes, but is about generating less absolute, more accurate, more realistic opinions about yourself, other people and the world around you.

Revisiting history

Many people can look back over their lives and get a fairly clear picture of where their core beliefs have come from. Sometimes, though, the source of core beliefs is not so clear.

Although most core beliefs arise from your early experiences, you can still form deep entrenched ideas about yourself, life and other people when you're older. For example, Mahesh develops his core beliefs about the world being against him following a string of bad luck and tragic events during his adult years.

Revisit your history with a view to coming up with some reasons behind the ways that you think and behave in the present. Be compassionate with yourself, but recognise that you're the only one who can retrain your brain into updated and healthier ways of understanding your experiences.

Replacing old meanings with new meanings

Experiences that you had earlier on in life were given a meaning by you at the time. As an adult, you're in the fortunate position of being able to reassess the meanings you originally gave certain events and to assign more sophisticated meanings where appropriate.

For example, Beth forms the belief 'I'm bad' based on the information she had when her father was abusing her. She was young and worked on various assumptions, including:

- Daddy tells me that I've been bad, and this must be true.
- You get punished when you're bad.
- I must've done something bad to deserve this treatment.

Now that she's no longer a child and recognises that she has this core belief, Beth can choose to look at her father's abuse and assign different meanings to his treatment of her:

- My father had an anger problem that had nothing to do with me.
- No child should be punished so severely, no matter how disobedient they've been.
- My father was wrong to beat me, and I didn't deserve to be beaten.
- My father did a bad thing by beating me and his bad behaviour doesn't mean that I am bad.

Use the three-column old meaning/new meaning worksheet in Appendix B to review past events that contributed to the development of your core beliefs and reinterpret them now as an older, wiser person.

The sheet has three headings. Fill them in as follows:

1. **In the first column, 'Event', record what actually happened.**

2. **Under 'Old Meaning' in the second column, record what you believe the event means about you.**

   This is your unhealthy core belief.

3. **In the 'New Meaning' third column, record a healthier and more accurate meaning for the event.**

   This is the new belief that you want to strengthen.

Table 16-1 shows an example of Beth's worksheet.

Table 16-1	Beth's Old Meaning– New Meaning Worksheet	
Event	*Old Meaning*	*New Meaning*
My Dad yelling, telling me I was bad when I was little.	I must be bad for him to say this so often.	I was much too young and afraid to be 'bad'. It was my father's anger that was the problem.

Incorporating new beliefs into your life

Constructing newer, healthier, more accurate core beliefs is one thing, but beginning to live by them is another. Before your new beliefs are really stuck in your head and heart, you need to act *as if* they're already there. For Beth, this may mean her forcing herself to face up to criticism from her boss and making appropriate adjustments to her work without berating herself. In short, she needs to act *as if* she truly believes that there are good things about herself, even in the face of negative feedback. She needs to operate under the assumption that her boss's anger is a reasonable (or possibly an unreasonable) response to an aspect of her work, rather than proof of her intrinsic badness.

In Chapter 17, we suggest several techniques for strengthening new alternative beliefs.

Starting from scratch

We won't tell you that changing your core beliefs is easy, because that simply isn't true. In fact, erasing your old belief systems is so difficult that we think the best way of dealing with them is to make alternative healthy beliefs stronger so that they can do battle with your unhealthy beliefs.

Think of your old beliefs as well-trodden paths through an overgrown field. You can walk quickly and easily down these paths, as they've been worn down from years of use. Developing new, alternative beliefs is like making new paths through the field. At first, the new paths are awkward and uncomfortable to walk on, because you need to break down the undergrowth.

You may be tempted to walk along the old paths because they're easier and more well-known, but with practice, your new paths can become familiar and natural to walk along. Similarly, with regular practice, thinking and acting along the lines of your alternative beliefs can become stronger and more automatic, even when the going gets tough!

Thinking about what you'd teach a child

When you're challenging your negative core beliefs, try to think about what you'd tell a child. Act as your own parent by reinstructing yourself to endorse healthy ways of viewing others, yourself and the world.

Ask yourself what types of belief you'd teach a child. Would you encourage him to grab hold of the negative core beliefs that you may hold about yourself, or would you want him to think of himself in a more positive and accepting way? Would you wish for him to think of other people as evil, untrustworthy, dangerous and more powerful than himself? Or would you rather he had a more balanced view of people, such as variable but basically okay, generally trustworthy and reliable? Would you want him to believe that he can stand up for himself?

Considering what you'd want a friend to believe

When challenging your core beliefs, think about having a friend like Mahesh, Beth, Rashid, Milo or Sybil. What advice would you give them? Would you say 'Yes, Rashid, you're a failure'? 'I agree, Mahesh – life's against you'? 'Beth, you're bad'? 'Sybil, no one ever thought you were important anyway'?

Or would you be quietly horrified to spout these unhealthy and damaging beliefs? We assume the latter.

If you wouldn't want your dear friends to believe such things, why believe them yourself? Talk to yourself like you would to your best friend when your negative core beliefs are activated.

Shaping your world

When you start to adopt healthy core beliefs, it can feel as if you're going against the grain because in fact that is what you're trying to do. Your old, negative core beliefs are familiar, deeply entrenched and 'feel' like they must be true. New, healthy beliefs can 'feel' false and unnatural at first. Remind yourself that just because you've believed something for a long time doesn't make it true. People believed the earth was flat for a long time but that old belief doesn't change the fact that the world is round!

Some things are true, regardless of whether you believe them. Other things will never be true, no matter how fervently you believe them.

Chapter 17

Moving New Beliefs from Your Head to Your Heart

*A*fter you've identified your unhelpful patterns of thinking and developed more helpful attitudes (see Chapters 2, 3, 14 and 16), you need to reinforce your new thoughts and beliefs. The process of reinforcing new beliefs is like trying to give up a bad habit and develop a good habit in its place. You need to work at making your new, healthy ways of thinking second nature, at the same time as eroding your old ways of thinking. This chapter describes some simple exercises to help you develop and nurture your new beliefs.

In many ways, *integrating* your new method of thinking with your mind, emotions and actions is *the* critical process in CBT. A parrot can repeat rational philosophies, but i doesn't understand or *believe* what it's saying. The real work in CBT is turning intellectual understanding into something you that know in your gut to be true.

Defining the Beliefs You Want to Strengthen

Many people who work at changing their attitudes and beliefs complain: 'I know what I *should* think, but I don't believe it!' When you begin to adopt a new way of thinking, you may *know* that something makes sense but you may not *feel* that the new belief is true.

When you're in a state of *cognitive dissonance* you know that your old way of thinking isn't 100 per cent right, but you aren't yet convinced of the alternative. Being in a state of cognitive dissonance can be uncomfortable because things don't feel quite right. However, this feeling is a good sign that things are changing.

In CBT, we often call this disconnection between thinking and truly believing the *head-to-heart problem*. Basically, you know that an argument is true in your head, but you don't feel it in your heart. For example, if you've spent many years believing that you're less worthy than others or that you need the approval of other people in order to approve of yourself, you may have great difficulty *internalising* (believing in your gut) an alternative belief. You may find that the idea that you have as much basic human worth as the next person, or that approval from others is a bonus but not a necessity, difficult to buy.

Your alternative beliefs are likely to be about three key areas:

✔ Yourself

✔ Other people

✔ The world

Alternative beliefs may take the following formats:

✔ A *flexible preference*, instead of a rigid demand or rule, such as 'I'd very much prefer to be loved by my parents, but there's no reason they absolutely *have* to love me.'

✔ An *alternative assumption*, which is basically an if/then statement, such as '*If* I don't get an A in my test, *then* that won't be the end of the world. I can still move on in my academic career.'

✔ A *global belief*, which expresses a positive healthy general truth, such as 'I'm basically okay' rather than 'I'm worthless', or 'The world's a place with some safe and some dangerous parts' instead of 'The world's a dangerous place'.

When you do experience the head-to-heart problem, we recommend acting *as if* you really do hold the new belief to be true – we explain how to do this in the following section.

One of your main aims in CBT, after you've developed a more helpful alternative belief, is to increase how strongly you endorse your new belief or raise your *strength of conviction* (SOC). You can rate how much you believe in an alternative healthy philosophy on a 0–100 percentage scale, 0 representing a total lack of conviction and 100 representing an absolute conviction.

Acting As If You Already Believe

You don't need to believe your new philosophy entirely in order to start changing your behaviour. Starting out, it's enough to *know* in your head that your new belief makes sense and then *act* according to your new belief or philosophy. If you consistently do the 'acting as if' technique, which we explain here, your conviction in your new way of thinking is likely to grow over time.

You can use the 'acting as if' technique to consolidate any new way of thinking, in pretty much any situation. Ask yourself the following questions:

✔ How would I behave if I truly considered my new belief to be true?

✔ How would I overcome situational challenges to my new belief if I truly considered it to be true and helpful?

✔ What sort of behaviour would I expect to see in other people who truly endorse this new belief?

You can make a list of your answers to the above questions and refer to it before, after and even during an experience of using the 'acting as if' technique. For example, if you're dealing with social anxiety and trying to get to grips with self-acceptance beliefs, use the 'acting as if' techniques that follow, and ask yourself similar kinds of questions, such as:

✔ **Act consistently with the new belief:** If I truly believed that I was as worthy as anyone else, how would I behave in a social situation?

Be specific about how you'd enter a room, the conversation you may initiate, and what your body language would be like.

✔ **Troubleshoot for challenges to your new belief:** If I truly believed that I was as worthy as anyone else, how would I react to any social hiccups?

Again, be specific about how you may handle lulls in conversation and moments of social awkwardness.

✔ **Observe other people.** Does anyone else in the social situation seem to be acting as if they truly endorse the belief that I'm trying to adopt?

If so, note how the person acts and how they handle awkward silences and normal breaks in conversation. Imitate their behaviour.

When you act in accordance with a new way of thinking or a specific belief, you reinforce the truth of that belief. The more you experience a belief *in action*, the more you can appreciate its beneficial effects on your emotions. In essence, you're rewiring your brain to think in a more helpful and realistic way. Give this technique a try, even if you think that it's wishful thinking or seems silly. Actions do speak louder than words. So if a new belief makes sense to you, follow it up with action.

Building a Portfolio of Arguments

When an old belief rears its ugly head, try to have on hand some strong arguments to support your new belief. Your old beliefs or thinking habits have probably been with you a long time, and they can be tough to shift. You can expect to argue with yourself about the truth and benefit of your new thinking several times before the new stuff well and truly replaces the old.

Your portfolio of arguments can consist of a collection of several arguments against your old way of thinking and several arguments in support of your new way of thinking. You can refer to your portfolio anytime that you feel conviction in your new belief is beginning to wane. Get yourself a small notebook to use as your portfolio of arguments. The following sections help to guide you towards developing sound rationales in support of helpful beliefs and in contradiction of unhelpful beliefs.

Generating arguments against an unhelpful belief

To successfully combat unhealthy beliefs, try the following exercise. At the top of a sheet of paper, write down an old, unhelpful belief you want to weaken. For example, you may write: 'I have to get approval from significant others, such as my boss. Without approval, I'm worthless.' Then, consider the following questions to highlight the unhelpful nature of your belief:

- ✔ **Is the belief untrue or inconsistent with reality?** Try to find evidence that your belief isn't factually accurate (or at least not 100 per cent accurate for 100 per cent of the time). For example, you don't *have* to get approval from your boss: the universe permits otherwise, and you can survive without such approval. Furthermore, you cannot be defined as worthless on the strength of this experience, because you're much too complex to be defined.

  REMEMBER

  Considering why a certain belief is *understandable* can help you to explain why you hold a particular belief to be true. For example, 'It's understandable that I think I'm stupid because my father often told me I was when I was young, but that was really due to his impatience and his own difficult childhood. So, it follows that I believe myself to be stupid because of my childhood experiences, and not because there's any real truth in the idea that I'm stupid. Therefore, the belief that I'm stupid is consistent with my upbringing but inconsistent with reality.'

✔ **Is the belief rigid?** Consider whether your belief is flexible enough to allow you to adapt to reality. For example, the idea that you *must* get approval or that you *need* approval in order to think well of yourself, is overly rigid. It is entirely possible that you will fail to get approval from significant others at some stage in your life. Unless you have a flexible belief about getting approval, you're destined to think badly of yourself whenever approval isn't forthcoming. Replace the word *must* with *prefer* in this instance, and turn your demand for approval into a flexible preference for approval.

✔ **Is the belief extreme?** Consider whether your unhelpful belief is extreme. For example, equating being disliked by one person with worthlessness is an extreme conclusion. It's rather like concluding that being late for one appointment means that you'll always be late for every appointment you have for the rest of your life. The conclusion that you draw from one or more experiences is far too extreme to accurately reflect reality.

✔ **Is the belief illogical?** Consider whether your belief actually makes sense. You may want approval from your boss, but logically she doesn't *have* to approve of you. Not getting approval from someone significant doesn't logically lead to you being less worthy. Rather, not getting approval shows that you've failed to get approval on this occasion, from this specific person.

✔ **Is the belief unhelpful?** Consider how your belief may or may not be helping you. For example, if you worry about whether your boss is approving of you, you'll probably be anxious at work much of the time. You may feel depressed if your boss treats you with indifference or visibly disapproves of your work. You're less likely to say no to unreasonable requests or to put your opinions forward. You may actually be less effective at work because you're so focused on making a good impression. You may even assume that your boss is disapproving of you when actually this isn't the case. So, is worrying about your boss's approval helpful? Clearly not!

Running through the preceding list of questions is definitely an exercise that involves putting pen to paper or fingertips to keyboard. Try to pick out your unhelpful beliefs and to formulate helpful alternatives, then generate as many watertight arguments against your old belief and in support of your new belief as you can. Try to fill up one side of A4 paper for each belief you target.

You can include in your portfolio evidence gathered from other CBT techniques you use to tackle your problems, such as ABC forms (Chapter 3) and behavioural experiments (Chapter 4). You can use any positive results observed from living according to new healthy beliefs as arguments to support the truth and benefits of these new beliefs.

Generating arguments to support your helpful alternative belief

The guidelines for generating sound arguments to support alternative, more helpful ways of thinking about yourself, other people and the world, are similar to those suggested in the preceding section, 'Generating arguments against an unhelpful belief'.

On a sheet of paper, write down a helpful alternative belief that you want to use to replace a negative, unhealthy view you hold. For example, a helpful alternative belief regarding approval at work may be: 'I want approval from significant others, such as my boss, but I don't *need* it. If I don't get approval, I still have worth as a person.'

Next, develop arguments to support your alternative belief. Ask yourself the following questions to ensure that your helpful alternative belief is strong and effective:

- ✔ **Is the belief true and consistent with reality?** For example, you really can want approval and fail to get it sometimes. Just because you want something very much doesn't mean to say you'll get it. Lots of people don't get approval from their bosses, but it doesn't mean they're lesser people.

- ✔ **Is the belief flexible?** Consider whether your belief allows you to adapt to reality. For example, the idea that you *prefer* to get approval but that it isn't a dire necessity for either survival or self-esteem, allows for the possibility of not getting approval from time to time. You don't have to form any extreme conclusions about your overall worth in the face of occasions of disapproval.

- ✔ **Is the belief balanced?** Consider whether your helpful belief is balanced and non-extreme. For example, 'Not being liked by my boss is unfortunate but it's not proof of whether I'm worthwhile as a person.' This balanced and flexible belief recognises that disapproval from your boss is undesirable and may mean that you need to reassess your work performance. However, this recognition doesn't hurl you into depression based on the unbalanced belief that you're unworthy for failing to please your boss on this occasion.

- ✔ **Is the belief logical and sensible?** Show how your alternative belief follows logically from the facts, or from your preferences. It follows logically that your boss's disapproval about one aspect of your work is undesirable and may mean that you need to work harder or differently. It does not follow logically that because of her disapproval you're an overall bad or worthless person.

✔ **Is the belief helpful?** When you accept that you want approval from your boss but that you don't *have* to get it, you can be less anxious about the possibility of incurring your boss's disapproval or failing to make a particular impression. You also stand a better chance of making a good impression at work when you prefer, but are not desperate for, approval. You can be more focused on the job that you're doing and less preoccupied by what your boss may be thinking about you.

Imagine you're about to go into court to present to the jury arguments in defence of your new belief. Develop as many good arguments that support your new belief as you can. Most people find that listing lots of ways in which the new belief is helpful makes the most impact. Try to generate enough arguments to fill one side of A4 paper for each individual belief.

Review your rational portfolio regularly, not just when your unhealthy belief is triggered. Doing so helps you reaffirm your commitment to thinking in healthy ways.

Understanding That Practice Makes Imperfect

Despite your best efforts, you may continue to think in rigid and extreme ways and experience unhealthy emotions from time to time. Why? Well, – oh yes, we say it again – you're only human.

Practising your new, healthy ways of thinking and putting them to regular use minimises your chances of relapse. However, you're never going to become a perfectly healthy thinker – humans seem to have a tendency to develop thinking errors and you need a high degree of diligence to resist unhelpful and unhealthy thinking.

Be wary of having a perfectionist attitude about your thinking. You're setting yourself up to fail if you expect that you can always be healthy in thought, emotion and behaviour. Give yourself permission to make mistakes with your new thinking, and use any setbacks as opportunities to discover more about your beliefs.

Dealing with your doubts and reservations

You must give full range to your scepticism when you're changing your beliefs. If you try to sweep your doubts under the carpet, those doubts can re-emerge when you least expect it – usually when you're in a stressful situation. Consider Sylvester's experience:

> Sylvester, or Sly for short, believes that other people must like him and goes out of his way to put people at ease in social situations. Sly takes great care to never hurt anyone's feelings and puts pressure on himself to be a good host. Not surprisingly, Sly's often worn out by his efforts. Because Sly's work involves managing other staff, he also feels anxious much of the time. Sly also worries about confrontation and what his staff members think of him when he disciplines them.

> After having some CBT, Sly concludes that his beliefs need to change if he's ever going to overcome his anxiety and feelings of panic at work. Sly formulates a healthy alternative belief: 'I want to be liked by others, but I don't always *have* to be liked. Being disliked is tolerable and doesn't mean I'm an unlikeable person.'

> Sly can see how this new belief makes good sense and can help him feel less anxious about confronting staff members or being not-so-super-entertaining in social situations. But deep inside, Sly feels stirrings of doubt. Still, Sly denies his reservations about the new belief and ignores niggling uncertainty. One day, when Sly's confronting a staff member about persistent lateness, his underlying doubts rear up. Sly resorts to his old belief because he hasn't dealt with his doubts effectively. Sly ends up letting his worker off the hook and feeling angry with himself for not dealing with the matter properly.

Had Sly faced up to his misgivings about allowing himself to be disliked, he may have given himself a chance to resolve his feeling. Sly may then have been more prepared to deal with the stressful situation without resorting to his old belief and avoidant behaviour.

Zigging and zagging through the zigzag technique

Use the zigzag technique to strengthen your belief in a new, healthy alternative belief or attitude. The zigzag technique involves playing devil's advocate with yourself. The more you argue the case in favour of a healthy belief and challenge your own attacks on it, the more deeply you can come to believe in it. Figure 17-1 shows a completed zigzag form based on Sly's example.

HEALTHY BELIEF

I want to be liked by other people but I don't *always have* to be liked. It's tolerable to be disliked and it doesn't mean that I'm an unlikable person.

Rate conviction in Healthy Belief _40_ %

THE **ZIG-ZAG** FORM

ATTACK

Yeah but, if *LOTS* of people don't like me it's awful! I can't stand that.

DEFENCE

Lots of people not liking me would be *unfortunate* but not the worst thing in the world. Trying to get everyone to like me makes me really clumsy and anxious socially.

ATTACK

But lots of people not liking me *must* mean there's something wrong with me. It proves I'm unlikable.

DEFENCE

First of all, I'm more likely to *assume* lots of people don't like me and I don't actually know that it's true. I simply can't be everyone's cup of tea. *I* like some people more than others and it doesn't mean there's something wrong with them.

Rate conviction in Healthy Belief _75_ %

Figure 17-1:
Sly's completed zigzag form.

You can find a blank zigzag form in Appendix B. To go through the zigzag technique, do the following steps:

1. **Write down in the top left-hand box of the zigzag form a belief that you want to strengthen.**

   On the form, rate how strongly you endorse this belief, from 0 to 100 per cent conviction.

   Be sure that the belief's consistent with reality or true, logical and helpful to you. See the 'Generating arguments to support your helpful alternative belief' section earlier in this chapter for more on testing your healthy belief.

2. **In the next box down, write your doubts, reservations or challenges about the healthy belief.**

   Really let yourself attack the belief, using all the unhealthy arguments that come to mind.

3. **In the next box, dispute your attack and redefend the healthy belief.**

   Focus on defending the healthy belief. Don't become sidetracked by any points raised in your attack from Step 2.

4. **Repeat Steps 2 and 3 until you exhaust all your attacks on the healthy belief.**

   Be sure to use up all your doubts and reservations about choosing to really go for the new, healthy alternative way of thinking. Use as many forms as you need and be sure to stop on a defence of the belief you want to establish rather than on an attack.

5. **Re-rate, from 0 to 100 per cent, how strongly you endorse the healthy belief after going through all your doubts.**

If your conviction in the healthy belief hasn't increased or has increased only slightly, revisit the previous instructions on how to use the zigzag form. Or, if you have a CBT therapist, discuss the form with her and see whether she can spot where you zigged when you should have zagged.

Putting your new beliefs to the test

Doing pen-and-paper exercises is great – they really can help you to move your new beliefs from your head to your heart.

However, the best way to make your new ways of thinking more automatic is to put them to the test. Putting them to the test means going into familiar situations where your old attitudes are typically triggered, and acting according to your new way of thinking.

So, our friend Sly from earlier in the chapter may choose to do the following to test his new beliefs:

✔ Sly confronts his member of staff about her lateness in a forthright manner. Sly bears the discomfort of upsetting her and remembers that being disliked by one worker doesn't prove that he's an unlikeable person.

✔ Sly throws a party and resists the urge to make himself busy entertaining everyone and playing the host.

✔ Sly works less hard in work and social situations at putting everyone at ease and trying to be super-likeable mister nice guy.

If you're really, really serious about making your new beliefs stick, you can *seek out* situations in which to test them. On top of using your new beliefs and their knock-on new behaviours in everyday situations, try setting difficult tests for yourself. Sit down and think about it: if you were still operating under your old beliefs, what situations would really freak you out? Go there. Doing so will 'up the ante' with regard to endorsing your new beliefs.

Coping with everyday situations, such as Sly's previous example, are very useful, and they're often enough to move your new belief from your head to your heart. But if you really want to put your new beliefs under strain, with a view to making them even stronger, put yourself into out-of-the-ordinary situations. For example, try deliberately doing something ridiculous in public or being purposefully rude and aloof. See if you can remain resolute in your new belief such as 'disapproval does not mean unworthiness' in the face of your most feared outcomes. We think you can! This is a tried and tested CBT tool for overcoming all sorts of problems, such as social anxiety. (Refer to Chapter 14 for more guidance on developing *self-acceptance* and Chapter 24 for more on devising *shame attacking* exercises.)

Here are some tests that Sly (or we could now call him 'Braveheart') may set up for himself:

✔ Go into shops and deliberately be impolite by not saying 'thank you' and not smiling at the shop assistant. This test requires Sly to bear the discomfort of possibly leaving the shop assistant unhappy after making a poor impression.

✔ Say good morning to staff without smiling and allow them to form the impression that he's 'in a bad mood'.

✔ Mooch about, deliberately trying to look moody and aloof in a social setting.

✔ Make a complaint about faulty goods he's purchased from a local shop where the staff know him.

✔ Bump into someone on public transport and don't apologise.

You may think that Sly's setting himself up to be utterly friendless as a result of this wretched belief change lark. On the contrary. Sly has friends. Sly still has a reputation of being a generally kind and affable bloke. What Sly doesn't have now is a debilitating belief that he has to please all the people all the time. Rather, Sly can come to truly believe that he can tolerate the discomfort of upsetting people occasionally and that being disliked by one or more people is part of being human. That's life. That's the way it goes sometimes. Sly can believe in his heart that he's a fallible human, just like everyone else, that he's capable of being liked and disliked, but basically he's okay.

Nurturing Your New Beliefs

As you continue to live with your alternative helpful beliefs, gather evidence that supports your new beliefs. Becoming more aware of evidence from yourself, other people and the world around you that supports your new, more helpful way of thinking, is one of the keys to strengthening your beliefs and keeping them strong.

A *positive data log* is a record of evidence you collect that shows the benefits of holding your new belief. The positive data log helps you overcome the biased, prejudiced way in which you keep unhelpful beliefs well-fed, by soaking up evidence that fits with them and discounting or distorting evidence that doesn't fit. Using a positive data log boosts the available data that fit your new belief and helps you to retrain yourself to take in the positive.

Your positive data log is simply a record of positive results arising from acting in accordance with a healthy new belief and evidence that contradicts your old, unhealthy belief. You can use any type of notebook to record your evidence. Follow these steps:

1. **Write your new belief at the top of a page.**

2. **Record evidence that your new belief is helpful to you; include changes in your emotions and behaviour.**

3. **Record positive reactions that you get from others when you act in accordance with new beliefs.**

4. **Record any experiences that contradict your old belief.**

   Be specific and include even the smallest details that encourage you to doubt your old way of thinking. For example, even a newspaper vendor making small talk when you buy your paper can be used as evidence against a belief that you're unlikeable.

5. **Make sure that you record every bit of information in support of your new belief and in contradiction to your old belief.**

   Fill up the whole notebook if you can.

If you still have trouble believing that an old, unhelpful belief is true, start by collecting evidence on a daily basis that your old belief isn't 100 per cent true, 100 per cent of the time. Collecting this sort of evidence can help you steadily erode how true the belief seems.

In your positive data log, you can list the benefits of operating under your new belief, including all the ways in which your fears about doing so have been disproved.

For example, Sly might record the following observations:

✔ His staff members still seem to generally like being managed by him, despite the fact that he disciplines them when needed.

✔ Being less gregarious at parties doesn't stop others from having a good time or from engaging with him.

✔ His anxiety and panic about the possibility of being disliked have reduced in response to his belief change.

Your positive data log can not only remind you of the good results you've reaped from changing your unhealthy beliefs to healthy ones, but also help you be *compassionate* with yourself when you relapse to your unhealthy beliefs and corresponding behaviours. Use your positive data log to chart your progress, so when you *do* fall back you can assure yourself that your setback need be only temporary. After all, practice makes imperfect.

Many people add to their positive data log for months or even years. Keeping the log provides them with a useful antidote to the natural tendency to be overly self-critical.

Be sure to refer to your positive data log often, even daily, or several times each day when you're bedding down new beliefs. Keep it in your desk or handbag or wherever you're most likely to be able to access it during the day. As a general rule, you can't look at your positive data log too often!

Chapter 18

Heading for a Healthier and Happier Life

*T*he way that you think influences the way that you feel and behave. How you behave also influences the way you end up feeling and thinking . . . and round and round the cycle goes.

So, how you *live* from day to day has an effect on your overall mood. In this chapter, we look at what makes a lifestyle *healthy*. Developing a healthy lifestyle can contribute enormously to keeping you in tip-top physical and psychological condition.

We use the term 'healthy' to mean looking after your physical self, which includes exercise, sleep, sex, your eating habits, and keeping your living environment a pleasant place to be. Psychological health is about doing things that give you a sense of enjoyment and achievement, holding helpful and balanced attitudes toward life, and building satisfying relationships.

Being in tip-top psychological and emotional health also involves revisiting your values. Taking a thorough look at what is *really* most important to you, and making time in your busy schedule to reflect your values through regular action, greatly contributes to an overall sense of well-being.

Make looking after yourself a priority rather than an afterthought. An ounce of prevention really is worth a pound of cure.

Planning to Prevent Relapse

Once you start to recover from your problems, your next step is to devise a plan to prevent a resurgence of symptoms – to ensure that you don't suffer a *relapse*. A relapse basically means that you return to your original state of mind. An important part of your relapse prevention plan is nurturing yourself and guarding against falling back into old, unhelpful lifestyle habits, such as working too late, eating unhealthily, drinking too much caffeine and alcohol, or isolating yourself. Chapter 20 deals with relapse prevention in depth. The following sections in this chapter provide some pointers on how you can make your life fuller and how to take better care of yourself.

Filling In the Gaps

When you start to recover from some types of emotional problem, such as depression, anxiety or obsessions, you may find that you have a considerable amount of spare time available to you, which previously your symptoms took up. Indeed, you may be astounded to find out just how much energy, attention and time common psychological difficulties can actually consume.

Finding constructive and enjoyable things to do to fill in the gaps where your symptoms once were is important. Keeping yourself occupied with pursuits that are meaningful to you (and reflect your core values and priorities) gives you a sense of well-being and leaves less opportunity for your symptoms to re-emerge.

Choosing absorbing activities

Activities that you used to enjoy may take a back seat while you wrestle with your problems. However, maybe you can think of some new activities that interest you and that you may like to try. The following are a few pointers to help you generate ideas about what activities and hobbies you can begin building into your life:

- Make a list of things you used to do and would like to start doing again.
- Make a separate list of new activities that you'd like to try.
- Try to create a balance between activities that do and don't involve physical exercise.
- Include everyday activities like cooking, reading, DIY and keeping up social contacts. These activities are often neglected when you're overwhelmed by symptoms.
- Choose to focus on around five activities to revive or pursue, depending on how full your life is with work and family commitments.

In case you're still at a loss as to what you want to do, here's some ideas – but remember that this list is by no means exhaustive: antiques, art appreciation, astronomy, baking, chess, dance, drama, dressmaking, enamelling, fishing, football, gardening, golf, interior decorating, kick boxing, languages, motoring, painting, pets Rhena has a cat called Jack, who's transformed her life! And since the first publication of this book she's also acquired a West Highland terrier called Powder Puff, who's the most adorable and consuming creature . . . everyone agrees . . . possibly even Jack), quizzes, tennis, voluntary work, wine-tasting, writing . . .

Pets are great companions. But they also require some considerable work and commitment (especially dogs, no matter how small). Before you decide to get a pet, do some research to determine the best pet for your living environment, work routine and financial situation. Otherwise you may find yourself lumbered with an animal that's far more high maintenance than you initially expected.

Don't just think about it! Decide *when* you're going to begin doing your chosen activities. If you don't give yourself a concrete start date, forgetting about things or putting them off can be all too easy.

Matchmaking your pursuits

You know yourself better than anyone else, so you're the best person to judge which hobbies can bring you the most satisfaction. Try to match your recreational pursuits to your character. If you know that you love paying attention to detail, you may enjoy needlework or making jewellery. Extreme sports may appeal to you if you've always been good at physical activities and like adrenalin rushes. Conversely, if you've never been very musical, taking up an instrument may not be the best choice for you.

We recommend that you stretch yourself by trying things that you haven't done before. Who knows – you may end up really liking the new activities. However, if you choose pursuits that are too far removed from your fundamental personality or natural abilities, you might lose heart and abandon them.

Putting personal pampering into practice

Oh, the joys of a good massage, a hot foamy bath or a trip to the opera (okay, we understand that not everyone feels the same about opera). You can't overcome your problems without a significant degree of personal effort. Congratulate yourself for your hard work, and treat yourself to a few nice things.

Take care of yourself on a day-to-day basis, and look out for times when you deserve a few extra special treats. Friday nights are a good time to regularly treat yourself after a long week at work.

Your treats don't have to be expensive. You can do many small things – such as putting some cut flowers in a vase, making your living space smell nice, playing pleasant music, watching a favourite film or television programme – which are free or inexpensive.

Consider pampering yourself as part of your *relapse-prevention plan* (see Chapter 20 for more on relapse prevention). Even doing little things like using nice bath oils or eating a special meal once a week can remind you to value yourself and to treat yourself with loving care.

Overhauling Your Lifestyle

We suggest that you take a close look at the way you currently live and decide on the things that are good and the things that are not so good for you. Be sure to consider the following key areas:

- **Regular and healthy eating.** The principle is relatively simple: have three meals and a couple of healthy snacks a day, with plenty of fruit, vegetables and wholegrain foods. Minimise your consumption of sugar and simple carbohydrates, like white bread, and don't overdo the saturated fat. Have what you fancy in moderation. If you think you need extra help with healthy eating, talk to your doctor, who can refer you to a dietician.

  Try keeping a record of everything you eat, for a week. Identify where you can make positive changes towards eating more regularly and more healthily. If you find that your actions don't match with your good intentions, use the Tic-Toc technique (which we discuss in Chapter 19) to tackle the thoughts and attitudes that can get in the way of healthy eating.

- **Regular exercise.** Ample evidence suggests that exercise is very beneficial for both your mental and physical health. Aim for at least three sessions of physical exercise, lasting 20–30 minutes each, per week (five sessions is ideal, but you may need to build up to it). Consult your doctor if you haven't exercised regularly for some time.

- **Leisure pursuits.** Include activities that bring you pleasure or satisfaction and aren't attached to your job or home life. Remind yourself of what you used to do and of what you've been meaning to do, when choosing activities and hobbies.

- **Social contact.** Get to know new people or reinvigorate your existing relationships. Sometimes relationships suffer as a result of psychological illness. See the 'Getting intimate' section later in this chapter which talks about intimacy and communication.

- **Vitally-absorbing interests.** Get involved with causes you feel are important, such as recycling or animal rights campaigns. Even small, everyday actions like smiling at a shopkeeper, holding the door for a stranger, forgiving an indiscretion or picking up a bit of litter can help you recognise that you're contributing to the kind of world you'd like to live in.

✔ **Resource management.** This catch-all may involve you drawing up a budget, getting an accountant, developing a system to deal with your household bills efficiently, renegotiating your working hours, earmarking time for relaxation, arranging some babysitting or hiring a cleaner.

Ideally, you can create a nice balance between the different aspects of your life so that none is neglected.

Everyone needs delineated time for the replenishment of psychological and physical energy *as well* as for getting things done. Be aware of both – because you can't have one without the other.

Look at the things you do on a daily or weekly basis, and decide what you're doing *too much of*, such as drinking in the pub, working late or eating fast food. Try to replace some of these activities with others that you're doing too little of, such as getting exercise, spending time with your family, cooking tasty, healthy meals or studying.

Walking the walk

The best-laid plans of mice and men are apt to go astray. And how.

You're really serious about making positive changes to your lifestyle; however, just thinking about it and setting out plans aren't enough – although they *are* a great first step. The next step is to *do it!* Actions speak louder than words, so act on your intentions sooner rather than later.

Keeping your body moving

We cannot emphasise enough the multiple benefits of you taking regular exercise. It's so good for you, in so many ways. If you don't believe us, try it out! Exercise a few times each week and see if you don't end up feeling better – we defy you to contradict us.

You can exercise in ways that don't involve going to the gym. Gardening, walking, cycling, dancing and housework all give your body a workout. Find out which activities suit your interests, schedule and current level of fitness – *and do them!*

Be careful that you're exercising for the right reasons, such as to enjoy yourself, de-stress and keep physically and mentally healthy. Check that you're not exercising obsessively. The following are unhealthy motivations for taking exercise:

✔ **To keep your weight lower than is medically recommended.** People who suffer from eating disorders often exercise fanatically.

✔ **To improve your looks.** People with body dysmorphic disorder (BDD) sometimes use exercise to compensate for imagined defects in their physical appearance (Chapter 13 has more about this psychological problem). Also, if you have a very poor body image or an eating disorder (see Chapter 11), you may exercise in an attempt to make yourself more physically acceptable to yourself and others.

✔ **To punish yourself.** People with feelings of shame and low self-worth may exercise to excess as a means of self-harming.

Ask your physician to work out your *body mass index* or 'BMI', which gives you a weight range that is normal for your age and height.

Using your head

Perhaps your emotional problems get in the way of your work or study. Maybe your difficulties interfere with you making progress in your career or changing jobs – after all, many people with psychological problems also experience work and education difficulties.

Start to set goals for how you'd like your work or academic life to develop. Build a realistic plan of action for reaching your professional or educational goals by following these steps:

1. **Start your plan by considering where you'd like to be and what you need to do in terms of study and training to get there.**

2. **Break your ultimate goal down into smaller, bite-sized chunks.** You may need to gather references, build a portfolio, write a CV or apply for a loan or grant to fund your studies.

3. **Investigate facilities for learning.** Use the Internet to look for specific courses, contact universities and colleges for a prospectus, see a careers advisor or visit an employment agency.

4. **Build your study or training plan into your life with a view to keeping a balance between study, work, social and leisure activities.**

5. **Set a realistic timeframe to achieve your goal.** Pushing yourself to get there too fast is likely to cause you stress, impair your enjoyment of the journey to your goal, or even lead you to abandon your goal all together.

Go out and study just for the sake of it. Developing a new skill or exploring a new subject area can be highly rewarding for you, whether or not the studying is applicable directly to your work. Adult education classes and intensive workshops can be a great way for you to explore new topics – and for you to meet new people, which can be beneficial if your social life has suffered during your illness.

Getting involved

Think about the kind of world you want to live in and how you can contribute towards creating it. You can get involved with anti-litter campaigns, local building-restoration projects, charities, or whatever you feel is important. You can usually choose how much time to devote to these pursuits.

Becoming spiritual

Sometimes people with specific disorders, such as obsessive-compulsive disorder (OCD) or extreme guilt, can find that their religion or spiritual beliefs get mixed up with their problems. Re-establishing a healthy understanding of your faith can be an important aspect of your recovery. Resuming your usual manner of worship – be it meditation, attending mass or going to a synagogue – can help you to reintegrate with your religious beliefs or your community. You might also find that discussing your recent problems with a religious leader or a member of your congregation is helpful.

Talking the talk

Emotional problems can have a detrimental effect on your personal relationships. Sometimes, your symptoms can be so all-consuming that you have little space to show interest in what others around you are feeling and doing. Therefore, you may need to do some work to rebuild your existing relationships when you feel better.

When your symptoms subside, you may want to give more of your attention to the other people in your life. This may involve playing with your kids, talking to your partner about how your problems have affected your relationship (without blaming yourself, of course) or renewing contact with friends and extended family.

People in your life are likely to be aware of how troubled you've been and they may notice recent positive changes in you. Let them talk about the changes they've noticed within you. Listening to other people's experiences of your problems can help to reinforce the idea that the other people in your life care about you. Improving your relationships and simply spending time in the company of other people can help you keep your symptoms at bay. You can also involve others in your relapse-prevention plan, if appropriate.

A supportive relationship with a significant other can help you to stay healthy. This relationship doesn't need to be a romantic one – platonic relationships are important as well. Research has shown that having a network of social contacts, as well as having someone you're able to confide in, helps to reduce your emotional problems in general.

It's never too late for you to make friends. Even if your problems have led you to isolate yourself, now's the time to go out and meet people. Be patient and give yourself the time and opportunity to start forming good relationships. Go to where the people are! Join some clubs or classes.

Six steps for talking and listening

Good relationships are sustained by thoughtfulness, effort and time. Many of the changes in your relationships may occur naturally because as you become less preoccupied with your problems you're more able to focus on the world around you.

Effective communication is the cornerstone of good relationships. Bear in mind that you can communicate not only with what you say, but also with how you *listen*. Your body language can also convey a message to others. Things like eye contact and physical contact are also means of getting the message across. A simple hug can really mean a lot.

Try the following six steps to improve your communication skills:

1. When you have something important to discuss with someone, find a mutually good time to do so. Make sure that you both have ample time to talk and listen to each other.

2. Use 'I feel' statements, such as '*I feel* disappointed that you came home late', rather than blaming language, such as '*You* made me so angry'.

3. If you want to give negative feedback to someone about his behaviour, keep it clear, brief and specific. Remember to also give positive feedback about the behaviour you want to reinforce, for example thank your partner for calling to say he'll be late.

4. After you've given positive or negative feedback, ask the person how he feels and what he thinks about what you've said.

5. Don't fall into the trap of thinking that a right or true way of doing things exists. Accept that different people value different things. Seek compromises when appropriate. Listen to the other person's point of view.

6. Be prepared to accept negative feedback and criticism from others. Look for points that you agree with in what the other person is saying. Give the other person a chance to air his views before you get defensive or counteractive. Give yourself time to assess the feedback you receive.

Getting intimate

Your specific problems may lead you to avoid intimate relationships with other people. You may have been too preoccupied by your problems to be able to form or maintain intimate relationships. If you want to be close to others, you've got to get your head round the concept of letting others into your life. Allowing yourself to trust others enough to share at least some of your personal history can make you feel closer to your listeners. Intimacy is a give-and-take affair – ideally, the balance is roughly equal.

If you think you're incapable of getting truly close to someone else, you're probably wrong. Give other people – and yourself – a chance to be honest with each other. Reciprocally-enhancing relationships usually evolve naturally, but you need to be open to the possibilities of intimate relationships for this evolution to happen.

Sex and other animals

Your interest in sex, regardless of your age or gender, may diminish as a result of your emotional disturbance. Many people dealing with emotional problems can lose interest in sex. When you begin to feel better, getting your sex life back on track may take some time.

Sex drive is a bit like appetite: you don't always realise you're hungry until you start eating.

Sometimes, couples stop having sex regularly but don't ever discuss the change. Often, both partners get into a routine of not being sexually intimate and try to ignore the problem. Some people are too shy to talk about sex or feel guilty for having lost interest in it. Additionally, many people are too embarrassed to discuss their loss of sex drive with their doctor, or indeed friends.

Taking the plunge and talking about changes in your sex drive with your therapist or doctor can be very worthwhile. Your therapist or doctor may offer you useful suggestions and may even tell you that certain medications you've been taking may contribute to your decreased interest in sex.

Loss of interest in sexual activities is a normal side effect of certain experiences. Many psychological disorders, such as depression, post-traumatic stress disorder, obsessional problems, health anxiety, postnatal depression and low self-esteem, can impact your ability to feel aroused. Bereavement, physical illness and stress can also put your sexual desires on the backburner. Fortunately, decreased libido is often temporary.

Talking about sex

'Birds do it, bees do it, even educated fleas do it', but sometimes the issue of sex is like an elephant in a tutu doing the dance of the seven veils in the middle of your bedroom. Both you and your partner can end up studiously ignoring its presence, even though it's right there, begging for your attention.

If you can't bring yourself to broach the topic of sex with your partner as you begin to recover, you can do a few things to help rekindle the flames of desire. Try some of the following:

- **Resume non-sexual physical contact.** Hold hands, stroke your partner's arm or back as you chat, sit closer to each other on the sofa and reintroduce cuddling. Non-sexual contact can help you to get comfortable with touching one another again, and set the scene for a revival of more intimate contact.

- **Kiss.** If you've got into the habit of a quick kiss on the cheek as you leave the house, aim for the mouth instead. Kissing is a powerful form of communication. It also can be highly sensual and enjoyable.

✔ **Create opportunities.** Getting into bed at the same time, before you're both bone tired, and then snuggling up can create a non-threatening reintroduction to sexual relations.

✔ **Take the pressure off.** If you tell yourself that you've *got* to get aroused or you've *got* to have sex tonight, you can work yourself into such a state that all spontaneity is quashed. Try to take the attitude that if it happens, it happens.

✔ **Give yourself a chance to get in the mood.** You don't have to feel very aroused to start getting intimate. Sometimes you may need to have a lot of low-level sexual contact like stroking petting, and kissing before you're ready to go further. Be patient with yourself and try to talk to your partner about how you're feeling. Sometimes, just talking about sex is enough to relax you to let nature take its course.

✔ **Take the onus off orgasm.** Any sexual or close physical contact can be fulfilling. You may not be able to achieve orgasm for some time, so instead enjoy foreplay like you may have done in the early stages of your relationship. For example, kissing is a very powerful form of expression. You can really get your sex life back on track, and you may even be able to make it better than it was before, if you give a lot of attention to the preliminaries.

Whatever turns you on is worth exploring further. Talk to your partner: you may be able to find things that can help you both get more in the mood for lovemaking. Try to be open-minded about your sex life. Just be careful to set your own personal boundaries about what turns you on and what has the opposite effect.

Living in Line with Your Values

Most people enjoy life most when they consistently act in accordance with their personal values. People we see in CBT treatment typically report better mood, improved self-opinion, a general sense of well-being and of 'being true to themselves' – once they've identified and started to act in line with their individual value systems.

By 'values' we mean the things in life that are most important to you: your personal ethics, morals, philosophies, ideals, standards and principles. Sometimes, however, your depression, anxiety, poor self-esteem and other types of emotional problem can relegate your interests and values to the sidelines. Now is the time to rediscover and honour them, in the interest of your continued mental health and happiness.

Because all people are unique individuals, you won't always share the same values. That said, however, people with similar values are generally attracted to one another and end up in the same places. You may find like-minded people at workshops, rallies, charitable events, courses, and so on. So taking a closer look at your personal values can potentially have the additional benefit of enriching your social life.

Getting back in touch with your core values can be difficult if your mind has been clouded with anxieties and dark thoughts for some time. Be patient with yourself and permit yourself time to rediscover what you're all about.

Use the items in this list to help you pinpoint your personal principles:

- Work and career
- Study and skills-based training
- Community involvement
- Neighbourhood watch projects
- Cultural pursuits and identity
- Religion and spirituality
- Sports and other active hobbies
- Nature, animal welfare, wildlife and the environment
- Friendships and friendship groups (book clubs, social clubs and so on)
- Family and home life
- Causes and charities
- Politics
- Travel
- Overall social responsibility
- Art, music and theatre (either observing or participating)
- Reading for pleasure
- Cooking
- Doing crafts like woodwork, knitting or pottery
- Upholding standards for social conduct, such as being polite, friendly and assisting others

This list merely outlines some of the more common areas of value-based activity. Don't be restricted by it! Be creative – think both big and small. Anything you do in honour of your values, minor or major, is equally valid and beneficial (to you and those around you).

For example, one of our colleagues has a strict rule of conduct that she leaves a public toilet in the state she'd like to find it (an often grim task!). Another mutual friend values the services of his local rubbish collectors very highly. He habitually thanks them heartily and always tips them when appropriate.

You may find defining your personal values easier if you reflect on the values of a person you respect and admire. Try following these steps:

1. **Think of someone that you either know very well (like a friend or family member) or you know a lot about (maybe a celebrity or historical figure). Record their name on a sheet of paper.**

2. **Make a list of the values they seem to hold, have openly talked about or demonstrate through their actions. Chances are that you'll realise that you share some basic values with this person.**

3. **Make specific notes about the things your admired person does that support and reflect their personal (and your shared) values.**

4. **Make definite plans to follow this person's example!** Write down things you can do and when you can realistically do them. Use the blank form in Table 18-2, later in this chapter, to help you organise your thoughts. Don't forget the tiny, everyday things that can really have a positive impact on yourself and others.

The purpose of this is to help you remember and recognise what's most important to *you*. Nobody has a monopoly on values, so sharing them is a natural and normal part of life. Just beware of unwittingly adopting other people's values because self-doubt tells you that your own views and opinions can't be trusted. Allow others to provide you with inspiration but make up your own mind about your values.

Reflecting your values through action

Identifying your values can be easier said than done. But you can help yourself become more value aware by asking yourself some basic questions. Consider the following example.

Callum has battled with social anxiety for the past five years (for more on this, see Chapter 9). Though always a sensitive and shy child, Callum's anxiety about what others may think of him came to a head during late adolescence. Adolescence is a common time for people to develop social anxiety. Callum has spent so many years worrying, striving to impress his peers, guessing and trying to influence other people's opinions of him that he's largely forgotten what he *actually* thinks about things *himself*.

Like many people struggling with poor self-esteem and extreme fear of being judged negatively by others, Callum consistently held beliefs like 'others know better than me' and 'my opinions don't carry much weight'. As a result of this way of thinking, Callum's values, interests and opinions have been seriously neglected. Happily, he successfully used CBT to get himself out of the trap of social anxiety.

Here are some of the questions Callum asked himself to help get reacquainted with his forgotten values, opinions and interests:

✔ What were my earlier interests before social anxiety overtook my thinking?

> *I used to be interested in mechanics and vintage cars. I also used to really enjoy sci-fi films and novels. I still have an interest in these two areas today.*

✔ If I put the opinions of others to one side, what might be some of my personal principles and mottos?

> *I believe in living in a socially responsible manner that adds to the community around me.*

> *I believe in 'working to live' rather than 'living to work'.*

> *I believe in supporting the rights of less privileged, vulnerable groups such as the elderly, people with disabilities, those living in poverty and animals.*

✔ What pursuits do I get really passionate about?

> *Supporting charities that aim to improve the lives of children and the elderly.*

> *Being a responsible pet owner.*

> *Supporting sustainable farming and reducing CO_2 emissions. Travelling and enjoying nature. Reading and learning for pleasure.*

> *Being consistently polite and friendly to other people.*

Whether social anxiety, general poor self-esteem, depression or some other problem has over-shadowed your values, you can apply the same questions Callum used to yourself.

Once you've made yourself familiar with your core values, honouring them through deliberate and persistent action makes sense. Doing so is very likely to improve your overall enjoyment and give you a sense of living your life well. In order to turn your good intentions into actions, make a plan.

Callum made some plans to live more consistently with his values. He identified several actions that reflect his principles and interests and scheduled in clear times for carrying them out, as shown in Table 18-1.

Table 18-1	Callum's value-based behaviours form	
Value	*Related Activity*	*Frequency*
Working to live	Booking regular time off	Booking holiday times at the start of each year
Responsible pet ownership	Taking my dog for a long walk	Thrice weekly
Supporting vulnerable groups	Donating to charities	Monthly
Reducing CO_2 emissions	Walking to work	Daily
Being polite to others	Saying 'thank you', smiling at those I meet	Daily
Reading and learning for pleasure	Reading novels	Twice weekly

Use the blank form provided in Table 18-2 to schedule in your own value-based behaviours.

Table 18-2	My value-based behaviours form	
Value	*Related Activity*	*Frequency*

Wanting to be accepted and feel part of a larger social group is human nature. However, bear in mind that, whilst the thoughts and views of people around you are important, they aren't more important than your own. Nor is it necessary to base your self-image solely on the way others seem to think about you.

You can reject other people's judgements of you entirely or in part, or accept them if you think they're accurate. At the end of the day, you know yourself better than anyone else does.

Staying focused on what's most important

Unearthing your basic broad values can help you to remember what things in your life are most important to you on a day-to-day basis. Sometimes the pressures of modern living can skew your idea of what matters. For example, being at a work meeting may seem more important than attending your nephew's school play. However later, when he's excitedly telling you how he remembered all his lines, you may regret having put work demands first.

You can't always do what's fundamentally most important to you without incurring unwanted consequences, of course. However, if you scrutinise things more closely, you'll probably find several opportunities to honour the important things in life rather than blindly responding to external pressures from work, and so on.

Reshuffling priorities

Knowing your personal values really well also helps you to prioritise daily duties more effectively. In general, your priorities will be compatible with and mirror your intrinsic value system.

Review your work in the previous sections of this chapter and make a numbered list of your personal priorities. Keep your list handy and refer to it regularly as a reminder of how you ideally want to live your life.

Priorities shift and shuffle according to what's actually going on in your life. For example, putting work first (for a time) if you need extra money to pay off debts is normal and constructive. Or you may carve out extra time for your elderly relative during his convalescence from an operation. Remind yourself, however, that changes in your fundamental priorities are usually temporary; reshuffle them once a crisis has passed.

Chapter 19

Overcoming Obstacles to Progress

* *

In This Chapter

▶ Getting to know the feelings that bind you

▶ Taking a progressive attitude

▶ Avoiding getting stuck on the road to recovery

* *

*H*uman beings have a keen way of blocking their progress and sabotaging their goals. Maybe you obstruct your progress without even being aware that you're doing it. Or perhaps you're conscious that you're sabotaging yourself with faulty thinking. Whatever the case, this chapter explores common obstacles that get in the way of positive change, and suggests some tips for overcoming blocks to progress.

Tackling Emotions That Get in the Way of Change

As if having an emotional problem isn't enough, you may be giving yourself an extra helping of discomfort and distress as a result of some of the meanings you attach to your original problems. Some of the feelings that you may experience about your primary emotional problems, such as shame, guilt or even pride, can result in *progress paralysis*.

Shifting shame

When people feel ashamed of their problems, they usually believe that their symptoms are a sign that they're weak, flawed or defective. If you feel ashamed, you're less likely to seek help, because you worry that other people may judge you harshly for having a psychological problem, such as depression or an addiction (see Chapters 12 and 10, respectively), or perhaps they may think that you're silly for having other types of problems, such as anxiety or social phobia. You may worry that anyone you tell about your problem will be horrified by some of your thoughts or actions, and reject you. If you suffer from obsessive-compulsive disorder (OCD), which is typified by unpleasant and unwelcome thoughts or ideas, you may worry that other people won't understand you. People with OCD frequently assume that no one else in the world experiences the kind of upsetting thoughts that they do. In fact, everyone has intrusive and upsetting thoughts from time to time. In Chapter 13, we talk about some of the intrusive thoughts that are common in OCD.

You may be too ashamed to even admit to yourself that you have a problem. Blaming the problem on external events or other people is often a result of shame. Shame is really corrosive to change because it can:

 ✔ Make you isolate yourself, which can lower your mood even further.

 ✔ Lead you to deny the problem. And you can't work on problem-solving if you're unwilling to acknowledge that the problem exists in the first place.

 ✔ Result in you blaming other people and events for your problems, robbing you of your personal power for change.

 ✔ Make you overestimate your symptoms as 'abnormal', 'weird' or 'unacceptable'.

 ✔ Lead you to overestimate the harsh degree by which others judge you for having the problem.

 ✔ Stop you from seeking out more information that can help to make you realise that your problem isn't so unusual.

 ✔ Prevent you from getting appropriate psychological help, or the right medication.

Fight back against shame by refusing to hide your problems from yourself. Seek out information to make some of your experiences seem more normal. Practise self-acceptance beliefs like the ones we outline in Chapter 14. Take responsibility for overcoming your emotional problems – but resist blaming yourself for your symptoms.

Getting rid of guilt

Guilt is an unhealthy negative emotion that's particularly notorious for blocking positive change. You may be telling yourself guilt-provoking things like the following:

 ✔ 'I'm causing my family a lot of bother through my problems.'

 ✔ 'Other people in the world are so much worse off than me. I've no right to feel depressed.'

 ✔ 'I should be more productive. Instead, I'm just a waste of space.'

Guilt sabotages your chances of taking positive action. Guilty thoughts, such as the preceding examples, can lead you to put yourself down further, thereby making yourself more depressed. Your depression leads you to see the future as hopeless and saps your motivation. (Have a peek at Chapter 6 for more information about unhealthy negative emotions and how they work against you.)

Even if the thoughts that are making you feel guilty about your depression, anxiety or other emotional problem hold some truth, try to accept yourself as someone who's *unwell*. For example, your diminished ability to be productive is a side effect of depression, not an indication that you're a bad or selfish person.

Shame and guilt grow in the dark. Hiding your problems, and your feelings *about* your problems, from other people tends to make things worse over time. Talking about your obsessions, depression, addiction or other problems gives you the chance to share your fears and discomfort with someone else, who may be far more understanding than you imagine.

Putting aside pride

Having too much pride can get in the way of your progress. Sometimes, pride is a sort of compensatory strategy for feelings of shame. Your pride may protect you from the shame that you think you'd experience if you were to accept that the methods you've used thus far to overcome your problems have been less than ideal. The following are common pride-based attitudes that may be stopping you from making positive changes:

- ✓ **'It's absurd to say that I can help myself – if I could make myself better, I'd have done it ages ago!'** Actually, people very rarely know how best to help themselves out of emotional problems. Often, you need to read some self-help books or have techniques explained to you before you really understand how to implement specific techniques, and why these methods work.

- ✓ **'I'm an intelligent person and I should be able to work out this stuff on my own!'** Maybe you *can* work out how to help yourself overcome emotional problems without any help whatsoever. But remember: even the most intelligent people need to see specialists for advice from time to time. For example, you may be very bright but you still need to take your car to a mechanic to be fixed.

- ✓ **'I like to think of myself as strong. Admitting to having these problems shows me up as weak.'** Getting a bout of flu doesn't make you a weak person – and neither does a bout of depression or anxiety. For example, refusing to seek medical treatment for an infected wound is foolish, not an example of strength.

Swallow your pride and be ready to seek advice and help. Recognising and accepting that you have a problem and that you need to get guidance on how to deal with it, takes strength, not weakness.

Seeking support

After you begin to get over your shame, guilt and pride, you can start to look for help in earnest. The help you seek may take the form of reading a self-help book like this one, approaching a therapist, talking things over with a friend (who could even support you using this book) or looking through some online resources. Some people find that self-help techniques are enough. But if you think you need more support, be sure to get help sooner rather than later. Putting off seeking professional help when you need it only prolongs your discomfort. Don't wait until your problem has advanced to the stage where your relationships, employment situation or daily functioning are suffering before you take positive action. (In Chapter 21 we explain how to seek professional help.)

Trying a little tenderness

Shame and guilt involve kicking yourself – and really putting the boot in – when you're already feeling down. Kicking someone in an attempt to get them back on their feet just doesn't make sense.

You haven't *chosen* your problems, although you may accept that you're stuck in a pattern that's making your problems worse. Take other contributing factors into account when you think about how your problems may have started.

You can take responsibility for overcoming your emotional disturbances and you can be compassionate with yourself in the process. Being kind to yourself when you're working hard to get better makes sense, particularly if you consider that a lot of the work involves making yourself uncomfortable in the short term. Surely you deserve to give yourself a little encouragement during exposures and behavioural experiments, rather than piling on the self-criticism.

Try being your own best friend instead of your own worst critic for a while, and see whether this helps you to make some positive strides. (Have a look at Chapter 14 for more tips on how to treat yourself with compassion.)

Book now to avoid disappointment

Many people with emotional problems wait months or even years before sharing them with anyone else. For example, people with OCD put up with their symptoms for an average of ten years before they seek professional help – they may even keep their problems secret from their friends and family. People with depression and other anxiety problems can also wait for months or years before talking about their problems with another person.

The most common reason for keeping problems under wraps is shame. Thinking that you need to keep problems a secret is quite tragic, because you end up suffering in silence needlessly. You can refer to the list of professional resources we supply in Appendix A. Exploring your options *now* can assure you that your symptoms are common and that you have nothing to be ashamed of. Get yourself on the road to recovery now to avoid feeling disappointed that you didn't get help sooner, and you can start to begin reclaiming enjoyment from life.

Adopting Positive Principles That Promote Progress

Some of the attitudes you hold probably aren't going to do you any favours as you try to overcome your emotional problems. Fortunately, you can swap your unhelpful attitudes for alternative beliefs that can give you a leg-up on the ladder to better emotional health.

Understanding that simple doesn't mean easy

Most of the steps to overcoming psychological problems with CBT are relatively simple. CBT isn't rocket science – in fact, many of the principles and recommendations may seem like common sense. However, CBT may be sense, but it ain't that common – if it was, fewer people would be suffering with emotional problems.

Even if CBT is as simple as ABC, the actual application of CBT principles is far from easy. Using CBT to help yourself requires a lot of personal *effort*, *diligence*, *repetition* and *determination*.

Because CBT seems so simple, some people get frustrated when they discover that they're not getting well fast or easily enough for their liking. If you want to make CBT work for *you*, take the attitude that getting better doesn't have to be easy. Your health is worth working for.

Being optimistic about getting better

One of the biggest blocks preventing you from getting better is refusing to believe that change is possible. Be on the lookout for negative predictions that you may be making about your ability to get better. Challenge any thoughts you have which resemble the following:

- ✔ 'Other people get better, but they're not as messed up as me.'
- ✔ 'I'll never change – I've been like this for too long.'
- ✔ 'This CBT stuff will never work for someone as useless as me.'

If these thoughts sound familiar, check out the 'Trying a little tenderness' section earlier in this chapter, which covers how to be a little kinder to yourself. Would you encourage a friend to believe such thoughts, or would you urge her to challenge her thinking? Try to give yourself the kind of good advice that you'd give another person with your type of problem.

Look for evidence that you *can* make changes. Remind yourself of other things you've done in the past that were difficult and required lots of effort to overcome. If you don't give a new treatment method a fair shot, then how can you possibly *know* it can't work?

Don't fall into the trap of deciding that your problems are so special and unusual that you can't be helped by conventional methods like CBT. Sometimes, people can be quite defensive about their emotional problems because they believe that they're part of what makes them unique. You'll still be a unique person when you've recovered from your problems – you'll just be happier. Clinging to the idea that no one can possibly understand or assist you can become a self-fulfilling prophecy. You may hold rigidly to the idea of being a hopeless case because it protects you from getting your hopes up and being dis-appointed. Take the risk of possible disappointment for the chance of success.

Staying focused on your goals

If you want to continue making healthy progress, occasionally you need to renew your commitment to your goals. You may find that you stop dead in your tracks because you've forgotten what the point is. Or perhaps you find yourself feeling ambivalent about getting over your problems. After all, stay-ing anxious, depressed or angry may seem easier than changing.

Remind yourself regularly of your goals and the benefits of striving to achieve these goals. You can use the cost–benefit analysis (CBA) form to reaffirm the benefits of making goal-directed changes. In Chapter 8, we describe the CBA form and give you some more information about setting goals. Turn to Appendix B for a blank version of the CBA form.

Always try to set goals that are within your grasp, and you can establish shorter-term goals along the way. For example, if your goal is to move from being largely housebound to being able to travel freely, set a goal of being able to go to a particular shop to buy something specific. You can then concentrate on the steps needed to reach that particular smaller goal, before moving on to tackle larger goals.

Persevering and repeating

We often hear people say that they tried a technique or experiment once but that it didn't make them feel better. The reason for this lack of success is that once is very rarely enough. When you work at changing ingrained patterns of thinking and behaving, you're likely to have to try out new alternatives many times before you appreciate any beneficial change. You need to give yourself plenty of opportunity to get used to the new thought or behaviour. Also, you can expect new ways of thinking and behaving to feel very unnatural at first.

Think of your core beliefs and old ways of behaving as automatic responses, just like using your right hand to apply your lipstick. If you break your right arm, and are unable to use it for a while, you have to use your left hand to do so. Imagine that your new healthy beliefs and behaviours are represented by your left hand. Each time you go to use your new beliefs, they feel awkward and don't seem to work very well. Every morning when you reach for your lipstick with your broken right arm, you have to remind yourself to struggle with using your left arm instead. You find it difficult to make a good outline of your lips and on some occasions look almost clown-like. However, over time you get better and better at using your left hand to apply make-up, until one day your automatic response is to reach for the lipstick with your left hand.

People can retrain themselves into using new patterns of behaviour all the time. Think about people who are giving up smoking or changing their diets. Even moving house and altering your route to work are examples of behavioural retraining. You can retrain your thinking as well as your behaviour – perseverance and repetition apply to both.

Tackling Task-Interfering Thoughts

The 'Tic-Toc' technique is a simple yet effective way of unblocking obstacles to change. The technique gives you a helping hand toward achieving your goals.

TICs are *task interfering cognitions*, the thoughts, attitudes and beliefs that get in the way of your progress. You need to respond with *TOCs* – *task orienting cognitions*, which are constructive alternatives to TICs. The list of unhelpful attitudes (sand traps) in the nearby sidebar is helpful for getting some ideas about task interfering cognitions.

Fill out the Tic-Toc sheet by following these steps:

1. **Identify the goal or task you want to focus on.**

2. **In the left column (TICs), list your thoughts, attitudes and beliefs that get in the way of you achieving your aim.**

3. **In the right column (TOCs) put responses to each of your TICs that will help you achieve your goal or task.**

You can find a blank Tic-Toc form in Appendix B. Use it whenever you notice that you're not pursuing a goal or carrying out a self-helping task. Table 19-1 is an example of a Tic-Toc sheet.

Table 19-1	**Example of a Tic-Toc sheet**
Goal or task: Setting time aside and filling out my university application forms.	
Task Interfering Cognitions (TICs)	*Task Orienting Cognitions (TOCs)*
1. If I start I'll get too stressed.	1. Doing this is a hassle, but if I take it one step at a time I'll cope.
2. It's too complicated; I'm bound to get it wrong.	2. If I read the guide carefully I'll probably do a good enough job.
3. I'm bound to be rejected.	3. I've got a good chance and I'll really regret it if I miss the deadline.
4. There's no point in trying, I always end up putting it off.	4. I have put it off but it's not inevitable that I'll keep doing it, especially if I start now!

Sidestepping sand traps

Along the path to better mental health, you're sure to encounter obstacles. The following are popular reasons for abandoning your goals or not getting started with pursuing goals in the first place:

✔ **Fearing change.** Despite feeling really miserable, you may be afraid of what'll happen if you take steps to change. You may have been depressed or anxious for so long that you can't really imagine doing anything else. Perhaps some of the people in your life are helping you to live with your problems, and you fear that by getting better you may lose those people. However, getting yourself well gives you a chance to build more fulfilling relationships and to develop your independence.

✔ **Having low-frustration tolerance.** When the going gets tough, the tough go home to bed, right? No! You may be tempted to go to bed, but you just wake up every morning with the same old problems. The only way to increase your tolerance to frustration in all its forms is to grit your teeth and stick with it. However uncomfortable you may be while working on changing yourself, the effort is almost certainly a lot less painful than staying unwell for the rest of your life.

✔ **Being passive.** Maybe if you wait long enough someone else will get better for you! Perhaps a miracle will happen to change your life, or a magic button will appear for you to push! Hey presto! – and you're fixed. Maybe, but don't hold your breath waiting. Take responsibility for doing the work needed to get you feeling better.

✔ **Having a fear of being bossed around.** Some people have a very strong sense of autonomy and they can be sensitive to other people trying to influence or coerce them. If you're one of these people, you may think that your therapist, or somebody close to you, is trying to take over when they suggest you try new strategies. Try to be open-minded to what professionals and people who care about you suggest. Deciding to give someone else's ideas a try is up to you. No one else can really control you or your decisions.

✔ **Being fatalistic.** Perhaps your motto is: 'This is the way I am and how I'm destined to be for all time.' Being convinced that your moods are governed by forces beyond your control, such as chemicals, hormones, biology, the past, fate or God, means that you're prone to surrender yourself to your symptoms. Why not put your theories to the test by making a real effort to rewrite your supposed destiny? You never know: Your original assumptions may be wrong!

✔ **Love is the drug that I'm thinking of . . .** You may be convinced that love is the only true path to happiness. You may be unable to imagine that you can have a satisfying life by learning to cope with your problems on your own. You may think that you will remain unhappy and emotionally disturbed until your special someone rides in on a steed to rescue you from this crazy mixed-up world. Love is a real bonus to human existence, make no mistake. However, the healthiest relationships are those where both parties are self-sufficient and enjoy the companionship of one another without being overly dependant.

✔ **Waiting to feel motivated.** A lot of people make the mistake of waiting to feel like doing something before they get started. The problem with waiting for inspiration, or motivation, is that you may hang about for far too long. Often, action precedes motivation. When overcoming emotional disturbance, you often need to do an experiment (check out Chapter 4) or you can stick to an activity schedule (in Chapter 12), even when doing so is the last thing that you feel like doing. Positive action is the best remedy for overcoming the feelings of lethargy and hopelessness.

Chapter 20

Psychological Gardening: Maintaining Your CBT Gains

. . . .

In This Chapter

▶ Taking care of the fruits of your hard work

▶ Avoiding potential relapse and overcoming actual relapse

▶ Sowing the seeds of love (and compassion)

. . . .

*L*ooking after the positive changes you've made is a major part of helping you stay emotionally healthy. You can nurture your belief and behaviour changes every day. The process is a bit like watering a plant to keep it thriving. The more care you take of yourself both generally and specifically – for example, by practising your new ways of thinking and acting – the more you reduce the chances of returning to your old problematic ways.

This chapter provides tips and advice that can help you avoid relapses and manage setbacks if they do occur.

Knowing Your Weeds from Your Flowers

Think of your life as a garden. Unhealthy, rigid ways of thinking and corresponding behaviours like avoidance, rituals, safety strategies, perfectionism and trying too hard to please (to name but a few) are the weeds in your garden. The flowers consist of your healthy, flexible thinking, such as accepting yourself and others, accepting uncertainty and allowing yourself to be fallible, and your healthy behaviours, such as assertion, communication, problem-solving and exposure (see Chapters 4 and 13 for more about exposure and response prevention).

No garden's ever weed-free. Planting desirable plants isn't enough. You need to continuously water and feed the flowers, and uproot the weeds to keep your garden healthy. If you tend your garden regularly, the weeds don't get a chance to take hold because there you are with your trowel, digging 'em out at the first sign of sprouting. Depending on the virulence of your weeds, you may need to use some weedkiller from time to time in the form of appropriately prescribed medication. So, *know thy garden*.

After you've identified your unhealthy behaviours and thinking tendencies, and bedded down some healthy alternatives, you can keep a better look out for emerging weeds and keep an eye on the health of your flowers.

To differentiate your weeds from your flowers, ask yourself the following questions:

- ✔ **What areas do I most need to keep working at in order to maintain my CBT gains?** The areas you identify are those where weeds are most likely to first take root.

- ✔ **What CBT strategies aid me most in overcoming my emotional problems?** Think about the new attitudes you've adopted towards yourself, the world and other people. These areas are your tender, new flowers – their delicate shoots need your attention.

- ✔ **What are the most useful techniques that I've applied to overcoming my emotional problems?** Think about the new ways of behaving that you've adopted (daffodils) and the old ways of behaving that you've dropped (thistles). Stick to your new, healthy behaviours and be vigilant against slipping back into your former unhealthy patterns of behaviour. Use an activity schedule to help you carry out beneficial routines and behaviours (jump to Chapter 12 for more about activity scheduling).

Write down the answers to the preceding questions so that you can look at them often to remind yourself of where to put in the hoe.

Working on Weeds

This section deals with weed-related topics and offers you some suggestions on how to stop them from taking over your garden, anticipating where they're likely to grow, and how to manage those that keep coming back.

Nipping weeds in the bud

Out of the corner of your eye, you see a weed sticking up its insidious little head. You may be tempted to ignore it. Maybe it'll go away or whither and die on its own. Unfortunately, weeds seldom eliminate themselves. Rather, they tend to spread and smother your burgeoning bluebells. Assume that any weed you identify needs savage and prompt killing.

A common reason for ignoring resurging problems is shame (which we talk about in Chapter 19). If you feel ashamed that your problems are recurring, you may try to deny it, and avoid seeking help from professionals or support from friends or family. You may be less likely to make a personal effort to whack down the problems in the way you did the first time.

Setbacks are a normal part of development. Human beings have emotional and psychological problems just as readily as physical problems. You don't have to be ashamed of your psychological problems, any more than you should be ashamed of an allergy or a heart condition.

Another common reason for people ignoring the reappearance of psycho-logical problems is *catastrophising* or assuming the worst (head to Chapter 2 for more info on thinking errors). Many people jump to the conclusion that a setback equals a return to square one – but this certainly doesn't have to be the case. You can take the view that a problem you conquered once is at a fundamental disadvantage when it tries to take hold again. This is because you know your enemy. Use what you already know about recognising and arresting your old thinking and behaviour to help you pluck that weed before it gets too far above the ground.

Some emotional and psychological problems are more tenacious than others, for example bipolar disorder, obsessive-compulsive disorder (OCD) and eating disorders. Just because a problem's tenacious, it doesn't mean that it has to take over your life, or even cause you too much interference in it. However, you can expect to meet tenacious problems again. Keep up with treatment strategies even when your original problems are no longer in evidence; doing so will help prevent a relapse.

For example, if you have a history of depression, you may notice that weeds are popping up when you do some of the following:

- Begin to think in a pessimistic way about your future and your ability to cope with daily hassles.
- Ruminate on past failures and on how poor your mood is.
- Lose interest in seeing your family and friends.
- Have difficulty getting out of bed in the morning, and want to sleep more during the day instead of doing chores or taking exercise.

If you spot these stinging nettles making their way into your otherwise floral existence, try some of these techniques:

- ✔ Challenge your pessimistic thinking bias, and remind yourself that your thoughts are not accurate descriptions of reality but symptoms of your depression. (See Chapter 2 for more on thinking errors.)

- ✔ Interrupt the rumination process by using task-concentration and mindfulness techniques. (We explain these in Chapter 5.)

- ✔ Continue to meet with family and friends, despite your decreased interest, on the basis that doing so makes you feel better rather than worse.

- ✔ Force yourself out of bed in the morning and keep an activity schedule. (Have a read of Chapter 12 for more on activity schedules.)

Whatever your specific problems, follow the preceding example: write down your descriptions of anticipated weeds and some specific weed-killing solutions to have at hand.

Don't ignore signs that your problems are trying to get their roots down. Be vigilant. But also be confident in your ability to use the strategies that worked before and in your ability to use them time and again, whenever you need to.

Spotting where weeds may grow

To prevent relapse, become aware of where your weeds are most likely to take root.

Most people, regardless of their specific psychological problems, find themselves most vulnerable to setbacks when they're run down or under stress. If you're overtired and under a lot of environmental stress, such as dealing with work deadlines, financial worries, bereavement or family/relationship difficulties, you tend to be more prone to physical maladies, such as colds, flu and episodes of eczema. Psychological problems are no different from physical ones in this regard: they get you when you're depleted and at a low ebb.

You may notice that some problems, like OCD, anxiety and depression, are more evident when you're recovering from a physical illness. Recognising this common human experience can help you to combat any shame that you may feel, and to de-catastrophise a return of your symptoms.

Compile a list of situations and environmental factors that are likely to give your weeds scope to take on triffid-like power. For example, you may be able to pinpoint *environment triggers* for your depression, such as the following:

✔ Seasonal change, especially during autumn, when the days get shorter and the weather becomes colder.

✔ Sleep deprivation, due to work commitments, young children, illness or any other reason.

✔ Lack of exercise and physical activity.

✔ Day-to-day hassles piling up at once, such as the boiler breaking down in the same week that the washing machine explodes and a few extra bills arrive.

✔ Reduced opportunity for positive social interaction with friends and family.

You can also identify *interpersonal* triggers for your depression, such as the following:

✔ Tired and tetchy partner.

✔ Disagreements with your partner, children, parents or extended family.

✔ Critical or demanding boss.

✔ Disagreeable work colleagues.

Compile a list of high-risk situations for yourself, including situations that are most likely to fire up your unhealthy core beliefs (we explain core beliefs in Chapter 16), and situations that put you under strain. Creating such a list helps you to have a clear idea of when you're most vulnerable to relapse and identify which psychological soil is the most fertile for weed growth.

Dealing with recurrent weeds

Some weeds just seem to keep coming back. You may think you're rid of them, only to open your garden door to a scene from *Little Shop of Horrors* ('Feed me, Seymour!').

Some unhealthy beliefs are harder to erode than others. *Core beliefs* (refer to Chapter 16) are those that typically you've held to be true for a very long time – most of your life even. These beliefs will keep trying to take root and may be particularly resistant to your attempts to kill them off. Certain unhealthy behaviours, such as addictions and rituals associated with eating disorders or OCD, for example, can be very stubborn.

The best way to deal with these recurrent weeds is to not become complacent. Keep reinforcing your alternative beliefs. Keep up with activities that fill the gaps left by your addictions or preoccupation with food. Keep doing exposure and response-prevention activities (refer to Chapter 13) to combat your OCD. Trust that over time and with persistence, your new ways of thinking and acting will get stronger.

Are you unwittingly feeding your weeds? Avoidance is a major weed fertiliser. You may have developed a healthy belief, such as 'I want to be liked by people, but I don't have to be. Not being liked by some people doesn't mean that I'm unlikeable.' And yet, if you still avoid social situations, self-expression and confrontation, you're giving your old belief that 'I must be liked by everyone or it means that I am an unlikeable person!', the opportunity to germinate.

Check out your reasons for avoiding certain situations and experiences. Are you not going to a party because you don't want to, or because you want to avoid the possibility of others judging you negatively in some way? Are you not visiting a farm because it doesn't interest you, or because you want to avoid contamination from pesticides?

When you spot a recurrent, mulish weed in your garden, dig it out from the root. You can kill off weeds entirely by getting the roots, *and* the shoots, out of the soil. Try not to make half-hearted efforts at challenging your faulty thinking. Dispute your thinking errors (Chapter 2) and push yourself back into challenging situations using your healthy coping strategies (we cover thinking errors in Chapter 2, and we talk about coping strategies in Chapters 4, 13 and 16.)

Tending Your Flowers

Knowing when you're most prone to the symptoms of your original problems re-sprouting is one thing. But knowing how to troubleshoot problems and prevent weeds from growing back is another thing altogether.

The techniques, behavioural exercises and experiments that helped you to overcome your problems in the first place will probably work again. So, go back to basics. Keep challenging your negative thinking and thinking errors. Keep exposing yourself to your feared situations. If your life is in turmoil due to inevitable things like moving house, work difficulties or ill health, try to keep to your normal routine as much as possible.

Above all, even when things are going well, water your pansies! *Psychological watering* involves keeping up with your new ways of thinking and behaving, by giving yourself plenty of opportunity to consistently practise and test your new ways of living. As we mention in Chapter 16, healthy, alternative beliefs take time to become habitual. Be patient with yourself and keep doing healthy things, even when you're symptom-free.

Developing a plan for times of crisis is another good idea. Here are some examples of what you may wish to include in your plan to overcome a possible relapse:

✔ Consider seeing your GP or psychiatrist to determine whether you need to go on medication for a while.

✔ Talk about your feelings to someone you trust. Pick a person who you can rely on to be supportive. Seek the help of a professional if talking to a friend or family member isn't enough.

✔ Review your efforts from previous CBT work and re-use the exercises that were most effective.

✔ Keep your lifestyle healthy and active.

Planting new varieties

Digging out a weed (unhealthy belief and behaviour) is important, but you also need to plant a flower (healthy belief and behaviour) in its place. For example, if you notice that an old belief like 'I have to get my boss's approval, otherwise it proves that I'm unworthy' resurging, dispute the belief with arguments about the logic, helpfulness and truth of the belief. (Chapter 16 has more about disputing unhealthy beliefs.)

You also need to plant a healthy belief, such as 'I want my boss's approval, but I don't have to get approval in order to be a worthwhile person'. You can strengthen the new belief by gathering arguments for the logic, helpfulness and truth of the alternative healthy belief.

To strengthen new beliefs and behaviours further, you can devise situations that you know are likely to trigger your old unhealthy beliefs, and work at endorsing and acting according to your new beliefs instead. For example, deliberately seek your boss's feedback on a piece of work that you know is not your best. Resist your old behaviours that arise from the unhealthy belief that 'I must get my boss's approval', such as over-apologising or making excuses. Instead, accept yourself for producing a less than good piece of work and take note of constructive criticism (refer to Chapter 14 for more about self-acceptance, and head to Chapter 16 for more techniques to strengthen new beliefs).

You can dig out unhealthy behavioural weeds and plant behavioural flowers in their place. For example, you may note that you drink more alcohol in the evenings as your mood lowers with the shortening days. You know that the onset of winter gets you down because you spend more time in the house. You can make the choice to stop drinking more than one glass of wine in the evening and start going to a local dance class or some other activity instead. You can also make a list of activities to do indoors, which will keep you occupied during the winter evenings.

Plant flowers in place of weeds, and tend those flowers to keep them hardy. Your weeds will have greater difficulty growing again where healthy flowers are thriving.

A happy gardener's checklist

Here are some points to help you prevent and overcome relapse. Use this checklist to stop your marigolds getting choked by bindweed.

✔ **Stay calm.** Remember that setbacks are normal. Everyone has ups and downs.

✔ **Make use of setbacks.** Your setbacks can show you the things that make you feel worse as well as what you can do to improve your situation. Look for preventive measures that you may have used to get better, but that you may have let slide when your symptoms reduced.

✔ **Identify triggers.** A setback can give you extra information about your vulnerable areas. Use this information to plan how to deal with predictable setbacks in the future.

✔ **Use what you have learned from CBT.** Sometimes you think that a setback means that you're never going to get fully well, or that CBT hasn't worked for you. But if the stuff you did worked once, then chances are the same stuff can work again. Stick with it; you've nothing to lose by trying.

✔ **Put things into perspective.** Unfortunately, the more you've improved your emotional health, the worse black patches will seem in contrast. Review your improvement and try to see this contrast in a positive way – as evidence of how far you've come.

✔ **Be compassionate with yourself.** People often get down on themselves about setbacks. No one's to blame. You can help yourself get back on track by seeing a setback as a problem to overcome, rather than a stick with which to beat yourself.

✔ **Remember your gains.** Nothing can take your gains away from you. Even if your gains seem to have vanished, they can come back. You can take action to make this happen more quickly.

✔ **Face your fears.** Don't let yourself avoid whatever triggered your setback. You can devise further exposure exercises (refer to Chapters 13 and 17) to help you deal with the trigger more effectively next time it happens.

✔ **Set realistic goals.** Occasionally, you may experience a setback because you bite off more than you can chew. Keep your exercises challenging but not overwhelming. Break bigger goals into smaller, mini-goals.

✔ **Hang on!** Even if you aren't able to get over a setback immediately, don't give up hope. With time and effort, you can overcome the setback. Don't hesitate to get appropriate support from friends and professionals if you think you need to. Remind yourself of times in the past when you felt as despairing and hopeless as you do now. Remind yourself of how you got out of the slump – and use the same strategies now.

Happy gardening!

Being a compassionate gardener

What do you do if one of your precious plants isn't doing so well? If you notice that you've got blight on your prize rose, do you deprive it of food and water, or do you try to treat the disease? It's better not to abuse or neglect the plants in your garden for failing to thrive because – if you do, they may only wilt further. You probably don't blame the plant for ill-health, so why should you blame yourself when you relapse?

Yes, take responsibility for anything that you may be doing that's self-defeating. And yes, accept responsibility for taking charge of your thinking, and ultimately, for engineering your own recovery. But, also take a compassionate view of yourself and your problems. Some of your unhealthy tendencies may have taken root partly due to childhood and early adulthood experiences. Others may have some biological underpinnings. Some of your problems may have arisen from a trauma. You're not alone in having emotional problems. You're part of the human race, and there is no reason to expect more of yourself than you do of others with regard to staying emotionally healthy.

If you take a responsible, compassionate view of setbacks, you will be more able to help yourself get well again.

 You know that 'they' say you should talk to your plants to make them grow? Well, it may sound a bit daft, but maybe there's something in it. Try imagining yourself as a little pot plant on your kitchen windowsill. Talk to yourself encouragingly and lovingly when you notice your leaves drooping. Give yourself the types of messages that nurture rather than deplete you.

How does your garden grow?

Research shows that CBT has a better relapse-prevention rate than medication on its own or other types of therapy. This difference may be because CBT encourages you to become your own therapist. Doing behavioural and written exercises does seem to help people to stay well, and for longer. Try to continue to be an active gardener throughout your life. Left to their own devises, most gardens become over-run with weeds. Think of maintaining the health of your psychological garden as an ongoing project.

Chapter 21

Working with the Professionals

CBT has gained popularity in recent years, due in part to research showing that it's an effective treatment for many common psychological problems. CBT is increasingly becoming the treatment of choice for most mental health problems. Doctors and psychiatrists are referring more people for CBT therapy than ever before. In the UK, more government funding has been allocated to train CBT therapists in order to meet rising demand. These days, you can access CBT treatment in books, on the Internet, in groups and in one-to-one sessions (Appendix A lists websites and organisations that you may want to contact). This chapter helps you determine how to seek further help, how to select a CBT therapist and how to get the most out of your treatment.

Procuring Professional Help

The information in this book may be all you need to overcome your emotional problems. Or, you may consider checking out some of the other self-help books we recommend in Chapter 25, which can give more guidance on specific problems.

Instead of helping yourself, to help you tackle your difficulties you may decide that you want or need additional assistance from a qualified therapist. If you have problems that are severe or difficult to overcome, your doctor may also prescribe medication, or refer you to a psychiatrist for a more specialised assessment of your difficulties. Psychiatrists can usually refer you to a psychotherapist who's qualified to treat your specific problems. Your GP may also be able to suggest a therapist, whether or not you've also been referred to a psychiatrist.

Self-help approaches, such as books like this one, have the advantage of costing little, being easily available – even in the middle of the night and during holidays – and providing enduring advice for years to come. Perhaps most importantly, when you use a self-help book, you know that the person who's making the changes in your life is *you*. A good self-help book can be invaluable, even if you're also seeking professional help. In fact, most CBT therapists recommend a book or two during treatment. Your therapist may collaborate with you, using a book of your choice – such as this one – as a resource. Alternatively, ask your therapist whether she has any suggestions for material you can read to help you get the most from your treatment.

Ask yourself the following questions to determine whether *now* is the right time for you to look for professional help:

- ✔ **How severe are your current problems?** For example, if you have severe depression or if you feel like you can't go on any more, seeking expert help is strongly recommended, as you may be too ill to benefit fully from self-help techniques. By 'severe' we mean that your problem is interfering significantly with your relationships, ability to work or carry on with normal daily activities. If you've experienced uninterrupted symptoms for more than two months, or if you notice that your symptoms are coming back more often, you must seek out professional help.

- ✔ **Have you tried self-help approaches in a consistent and systematic manner for at least two (and ideally six) weeks?** If you feel you're making some progress on your problems, you may not need to work with a professional at this time. However, if you're not satisfied with your rate of progress and still feel bad much of the time, then structured therapy sessions may help you.

Check out how long you need to wait for National Health Service (NHS) treatment in the UK. Putting your name on a waiting list sooner, rather than later, is a good plan if resources are overstretched in your area.

- ✔ **Do your problems interfere with your ability to concentrate and utilise self-help material?** If so, a therapist may well be able to help you digest information and techniques at a pace you can manage.

- ✔ **Do you see the sense in self-help principles but struggle to apply them to your own life?** Most therapists are much more experienced than you in applying psychological principles to specific types of problems. They can suggest more ways to help you move forward and guide you on how best to use the therapeutic techniques described in self-help books.

- ✔ **Have you reached a plateau or obstacle in your self-help programme that you can't overcome on your own?** By working with a trained and experienced therapist, you may develop the ability to overcome barriers and jump-start your treatment. A therapist can often suggest ideas that you may not have tried, which can serve as a motivator to get your treatment moving again.

✔ **Are you ready to share your problems with someone and team up with her on achieving shared goals for therapy?** Therapy is a team effort. Therapists don't 'fix' you. Your treatment still needs lots of input from you.

Thinking about the right therapy for you

Doctors and psychologists often recommend CBT because research evidence supports its effectiveness (refer to Chapter 1). Specifically:

✔ CBT is an active problem-solving approach that helps you develop skills and enables you ultimately to become your own therapist.

✔ CBT focuses on the present, whereas many other therapies focus on personal history. In CBT, you use your childhood experiences to help you and your therapist understand how you may have developed specific beliefs and ways of behaving. However, the focus is on your *current* problems and the ways in which your thinking and acting perpetuate your problems.

✔ CBT emphasises a collaborative relationship in therapy. CBT therapists can help you build skills and they're likely to expect you to carry out assignments in between sessions.

Several newer branches of CBT treatment are now developing that stick to the core principles outlined previously but also incorporate some novel ideas. Some of these include:

✔ **Schema-focused therapy:** This is often used to help people dealing with enduring personality difficulties that interrupt their ability to form healthy relationships.

✔ **Mindfulness-based CBT (MBCBT):** This therapy combines core CBT principles with ideas rooted in Zen Buddhism. It's been proved useful for the treatment of depression and anxiety problems.

✔ **Acceptance and commitment therapy (ACT):** This treatment has proved useful for depression. It emphasises self-acceptance and compassion as you strive to get well. (For more on ACT, see Chapter 12.)

✔ **CBT hypnotherapy:** This therapy enhances CBT with hypnosis. Self-hypnosis can be learnt and may be particularly helpful for those suffering from trauma, phobias or general anxiety disorders.

As with any form of therapy, be sure to research the treatment before you commit to it. Also make sure you find a fully accredited and qualified practitioner.

In addition to CBT, you may come across dozens more therapeutic approaches when you investigate your treatment options. Some of the more common psychotherapies practised today include:

- **Transactional analysis:** Focuses on the internal relationship between the parent, adult and childlike aspects of human personalities.

- **Person-centred therapy:** Emphasises the therapist displaying warmth, empathy and genuineness towards the client, but without directing the client.

- **Psychodynamic therapy:** Focuses on the client expressing feelings derived from early experiences, as these feelings arise during the ongoing relationship between client and therapist.

- **Systemic therapy:** Commonly used with families and couples, this emphasises the idea that emotional problems are the product of a dysfunctional system, for example a family or relationship.

- **Interpersonal therapy (IPT):** Focuses on changes in life roles, grief and disputes with significant others. IPT is another proven treatment for depression and some eating disorders.

Meeting the experts

Lots of mental health professionals are able to provide general counselling and support. If you specifically want CBT, don't hesitate to say so. Many psychiatrists, psychologists and nurses have had some training in CBT, but check out the extent of their training and experience. Ideally, choose someone who's had specialist training in CBT. *Specialist training* means that the therapist has obtained a degree, diploma or Master's qualification in CBT from a university or recognised training institute.

Ask your therapist if she's accredited with either the UKCP (United Kingdom Council for Psychotherapy) or BABCP (British Association for Behavioural and Cognitive Psychotherapies), if you live in the UK (contact details for these organisations are listed in Appendix A). You can also ask your therapist to tell you where and when she studied, and if you're sceptical, you can check this information out with the relevant educational bodies. Some therapists have their certificates, which outline their qualifications, on display. If you're referred to a therapist by a psychiatrist, the psychiatrist may be able to give you more details about your therapist's credentials, or to verify the information that a therapist gives you.

In the UK, anyone can call themselves a counsellor or psychotherapist, regardless of whether they have any professional training. A therapist with a recognised professional qualification will not be offended if you ask about their relevant training. You have every right to satisfy your desire to know about your therapist's background and training, because this is *your* treatment. If you know that you want CBT as part of your treatment, you must ask about the CBT specifics of your therapist's training and experience.

In case you're a bit flummoxed by the range of different professionals offering help, here's a little breakdown of them:

- *Psychiatrists* are medical doctors who specialise in psychological problems. They can prescribe medication and typically are more knowledgeable than family doctors about the drugs used to treat psychiatric illness. Not all psychiatrists are trained in CBT, although many can refer you to a CBT therapist who they're familiar with.

- *Clinical psychologists* have usually studied a broad range of therapies and have basic training in how to apply therapeutic principles to specific problems. Many can offer CBT but may not have specialist training.

- *Counselling psychologists* have been trained in basic counselling and different types of psychotherapy. Like clinical psychologists, most counselling psychologists have no specialist training in CBT, but they may offer it as part of the techniques they use.

- *Nurse therapists* are originally trained in psychiatric nursing. They have a more in-depth understanding of psychological processes and disorders than general nurses. Psychiatric nurses in the UK may have undergone further training to specialise in CBT.

- *Counsellors* are usually trained in listening and helping skills. They may hold a certificate in basic counselling, or be more specialised in certain problem areas, such as addiction. They do not always have a psychology degree, or in-depth knowledge of psychological problems. Often, counsellors will not be specialised in a specific psychotherapeutic orientation like CBT.

- *Psychotherapists* have normally specialised in a specific school of therapy, for example CBT or person-centred therapy. The level of training and experience, however, can vary widely.

You have the right to ask your therapist or other mental health professional (such as community-based nurses, social workers and occupational therapists) how much experience they have of using CBT and to what level they've trained. You can also ask them how much experience they have of dealing with your specific problems, such as depression, panic disorder or obsessive-compulsive disorder (OCD). If you're not satisfied with the answers you receive, take the matter further. In most cases, you can request a referral to another therapist either through your GP or psychiatrist.

Tracking Down the Right CBT Therapist for You

After you've decided to search specifically for a therapist with CBT training, you may have a bewildering number of questions to ask both yourself and potential therapists. This section poses, and helps you begin to answer, these questions.

Asking yourself the right questions

Sifting through directories of CBT therapists can be quite a daunting prospect. You may feel like there's a lot you want to find out about but aren't sure exactly how to ask for the information.

To help locate and select the best CBT therapist for you, consider the following questions:

- ✔ **Where can I find a CBT-trained therapist?** Begin by asking for recommendations from your doctor, psychiatrist or friends. Many practitioners are listed in the telephone directory, although you may need to call them to find out more about their backgrounds. Additionally, you can look on websites (see Appendix A) for accredited CBT therapists. *Accredited therapists* have usually reached a recognised level of training and experience. In the UK, therapists are accredited by the BABCP or the UKCP (or both). In the US, therapists are licensed by the state in which they practise.

- ✔ **How much can I afford to pay?** In the UK, CBT is sometimes available on the NHS, but you'll probably be placed on a waiting list first. Your GP is your best first port of call. Unfortunately, relatively few GP surgeries offer CBT treatment on site. You do have a right to appropriate treatment through the NHS. If your doctor recommends you for CBT, then technically the NHS needs to provide it for you. If you've done some background research on your specific problems and have articles outlining CBT as the recommended treatment, you can show these to your doctor and request a referral.

  Fees for private CBT vary from practitioner to practitioner, depending on location, training and experience. In general, the more experienced and highly trained the therapist, the higher the fees. But, shopping around can save you money. Some practitioners have a limited number of lower-fee sessions for people on low incomes. Sometimes, trainee CBT therapists offer a reduced rate. Many trainees are very competent and provide good-quality service. However, before beginning therapy with a trainee, find out who she reports to, her arrangements for consulting, and who monitors her professional supervision. Then, you know who to talk to if you have any concerns or complaints about the treatment your trainee therapist provides.

✔ **Would I prefer a male or female practitioner?** When you're selecting a therapist, try to be open-minded about their gender. However, some people, perhaps because they have issues with sexual abuse or relationships, may prefer either a male or a female therapist. If you feel the gender of your therapist impairs your ability to discuss your problems openly, raise your concerns with them or your doctor, who should then refer you to another therapist.

You may also wish to have therapy with someone who's from the same cultural background as you are. Ask your doctor if they can recommend a local service that may be able to offer culturally specific counselling.

✔ **Does the therapist have the appropriate background or training?** If you have a specific problem, such as panic attacks, addiction or OCD, you're best looking for a therapist with experience in treating your specific disorder. If you find a practitioner who you like but who doesn't have experience in your disorder, ask whether they're prepared to find out more about your problem. If not, find another therapist.

✔ **How many sessions do I need?** Estimating the number of therapy sessions you may need is difficult. In general, CBT is briefer than psychoanalysis or psychodynamic therapy, which typically involves regular sessions for a year or more. Unless your problem is very specific, such as snake phobia, we suggest initially trying six sessions and then reviewing the treatment progress with your therapist.

A common estimate for CBT is between 8 and 20 sessions. You'll normally start off with weekly sessions and build in bigger gaps as you progress. However, for complex and longstanding problems, CBT can last two years or more, with multiple sessions per week. Ask your therapist to give you a rough idea of how many sessions she believes you need after her initial assessment of your problems.

Your therapist can also regularly review your treatment with you, which may help give you a clearer sense of how many more sessions you need.

Ultimately, you – not your therapist – must determine how long you choose to stick with CBT treatment.

✔ **Can I take along my copy of *CBT For Dummies* or another self-help book?** As we mention earlier, CBT therapists often suggest self-help material and can usually help you work through a self-help book. If you've been using a book that you find useful, take it along to your first sessions. Your therapist may already be familiar with the resource; if not, she may be prepared to read through it.

Fighting your fears about seeking specialist help

We often comment to each other about how strange our jobs are. We like what we do very much, but the reality is that for most people therapy is an unfamiliar experience. Most people don't sit in front of a stranger and tell her about personal problems. Being apprehensive about starting therapy is entirely natural, and you may have some common worries about seeking help, such as the following:

✔ **What if working with a professional doesn't help me?** Treatment may not have an immediate effect. However, if you're committed to getting better, the treatment will probably have at least some benefit. Proceeding down the professional path may seem like a big risk, but you're very likely to be glad you took it.

✔ **What if talking about my problems makes them worse?** Good therapy, and/or the right medication, very rarely worsens problems. Sometimes, you may feel a temporary increase in discomfort while on the road to long-term recovery. We discuss this more in Chapters 7 and 9.

✔ **What if I'm too embarrassed to tell my therapist what's really bothering me?** Tell your therapist if you're feeling embarrassed or ashamed. She may well be able to put your mind at rest by explaining that many of your feelings are normal. You don't have to divulge all to your therapist straightaway (although doing so may be the most efficient route), and you can take some time to build trust between the two of you.

✔ **What if my therapist thinks I'm mad and wants to keep me in hospital?** Your therapist or psychiatrist is not going to think that you're mad or judge you negatively for being disturbed. She will frequently see patients with your type of problems. People are assessed to be hospitalised against their will only in extreme circumstances. If you're a danger to yourself or to others, if you're actively suicidal or are neglecting yourself badly, you may be detained in hospital – but this would be to keep you safe, not to punish you. Most areas in the UK now have home treatment teams so that regular visiting is available to support people in their own homes, so they don't need to go to hospital.

✔ **What if my therapist passes on my private information to social services or my employer?** The information that you share with any mental health professional is confidential and will not be given to family members or employers without your explicit (usually written) consent. An exception to this is when very clear risks to yourself or others – including children – are identified.

Only in very extreme and relatively rare circumstances do therapists ask social services to assess the impact of a mental health problem on a patient's family or children. In all but the most extreme circumstances, your therapist can tell you of her intention to involve any outside agencies.

If you have any of the above worries, voice them with your doctor or therapist. Worrying is normal, and any mental health professional with even the smallest amount of therapy experience can be sensitive to your concerns and discomfort. If they're not sensitive to your needs, consider seeking help from somebody else.

Speaking to the specialists

Make the most of your initial phone contact with possible therapists by asking whatever questions are on your mind. Once you make an assessment appointment with a therapist, you may want to list a few things that you want to discuss during your first meeting.

Although CBT therapists vary as to how much they're prepared to discuss over the phone before your first meeting, the following questions are reasonable after you identify a potential therapist:

✔ How much do you charge [if the therapist is a private practitioner]?

✔ How long are your sessions?

✔ Do you charge a cancellation fee?

✔ Do you have any experience of treating my particular kind of problems?

✔ Are sessions booked in a fixed time slot each week, or can they vary?

✔ Where do you practise? Do you have a waiting room?

✔ Can I tape-record our sessions?

If you're comfortable with the answers you receive from phoning your therapist, seek out answers to the following more detailed questions during your first meeting:

✔ Can you explain your theory about what's maintaining my problems?

✔ What sort of things do you think I need to do to overcome my problems?

✔ How many sessions do you estimate that I need?

✔ What do you expect of me in therapy – and what can I expect from you?

✔ Can you recommend any reading or self-help materials to me?

Making the Most of CBT

So what can you expect from your CBT therapist? As a general rule, a lot! Most likely, you'll end up feeling that you're working hard both during and between sessions.

Discussing issues during sessions

When you meet with your CBT therapist, expect extensive two-way discussion, as well as some challenging questions from her. Topics for collaboration may include the following:

- ✔ **Treatment goals:** CBT is goal-focused. Your therapist is likely to ask you about your therapeutic goals early in treatment. If your goals aren't realistic, your therapist will discuss this with you.

- ✔ **Specific problems, causes and solutions:** A skilled CBT therapist can share her ideas about what's perpetuating your problems, and invite you to work with her on what can help you in the long run. You can also expect your therapist to agree *with you* to a treatment strategy, which is likely to include homework assignments.

Although you may, on occasion, feel awkward with your therapist, she's speaking from a place of sound, clinical experience, and knows that some behavioural exercises, although they can be uncomfortable for you in the short term, can get you better in the long term.

Expect your sessions to be focused. Your therapist may interrupt and refocus you if you stray off the point, and do not address the actual issues that brought you to treatment. Additionally, a good CBT therapist may pull you up if you avoid working on your problem areas.

Overall, your CBT therapist is likely to be pretty human. Your CBT therapist shouldn't give the impression that she considers herself above you, or fundamentally different from you, simply because you're the patient and she's the professional. Most skilled CBT therapists acknowledge that they're the experts on CBT, and possibly on particular psychological problems, but that *you* know *yourself* best. Therefore, they may ask you a lot of questions about your experiences, thoughts and feelings, rather than telling you what you experience, think and feel.

Just as you can expect your CBT therapist to be open and honest during sessions, you can get even more from your sessions by being open about your own doubts and reservations. Although doubt is wholly natural, be prepared to reconsider your reluctant feelings about change.

Even if you know intellectually that a new way of thinking or acting is better, you may still have a gut reservation. For example, we often see clients who realise that their perfectionism is highly toxic but still fear that they may perform badly if they give it up. In these cases, we often have to help people see that being more flexible doesn't mean dropping their ideal standards. You can strive for excellence without demanding perfection.

Hallmarks of a good CBT therapist

CBT practitioners exhibit some fairly predictable behaviours in session. You can use the following list of attitudes, actions and interactions to help you determine whether you're actually receiving CBT treatment, and to assess the standard of your therapy. In general, good CBT therapists:

✔ Help you define problems and ask about your goals and expectations for therapy.

✔ Explain a bit about CBT at your first meeting and invite you to ask questions.

✔ Use scales and measures, such as a *depression inventory* (see Chapter 12), to help monitor your progress.

✔ Evaluate your problems based on the CBT model and explain this process to you so that you can do it yourself in the future.

✔ Ask questions to elicit your thoughts and help you evaluate them.

✔ Are active in sessions, educating you about CBT and its perspective on your problems, asking questions, writing things down and suggesting ways to try to improve your problems.

✔ Develop therapy homework exercises with you, to be carried out between sessions.

✔ Review your homework. If you haven't done it, a thorough therapist can discuss the obstacles that stopped you doing so.

✔ Regularly review your progress and reassess your goals with you.

✔ Invite feedback about therapy generally, and openly listen to any constructive criticism you give.

✔ Invite you to voice any doubts, reservations and fears you have about aspects of your CBT.

✔ Challenge your unhelpful beliefs and behaviours and help you to do the same on your own.

✔ Encourage you to be independent and to take personal responsibility for your mental health.

✔ Answer most of your questions, and tell you why if they don't or can't answer others.

✔ Refer you to another professional if you require additional or alternative help.

✔ Receive regular clinical supervision (in which they have their work listened to or have discussion with other therapists) to improve their practise. Don't be afraid to ask about this: It's important!

Okay, so this list is rather long, but we recommend consulting it if you have any doubts about your CBT therapist. Don't hesitate to take this list to your therapist and ask her to clarify her position on any or all of these points. Even though you may be seeing an experienced or qualified CBT practitioner, attitudes and styles of therapeutic delivery can vary dramatically. Like many therapists, we're always pleased when clients suggest ways in which we can make sessions more helpful.

Being active between sessions

CBT is in part educational, so your therapist may use a whiteboard, pen and paper, and various printed forms in your treatment. At some stage, your therapist may give you an ABC form or a thought record sheet (which we explain in Chapter 3).

Some of your homework will be written and some will be behavioural – whatever form it takes, however, you can expect your therapist to give you a solid rationale for any intervention they use or homework they suggest. Your therapist is also likely to give you handouts and reading matter.

Being ready to engage actively in therapy is a major key to your success, so if you're asked to do an exposure assignment or behavioural experiment that you don't feel ready to take on , say so, and suggest an alternative. You may want to address any ambivalence about therapy using a cost–benefit analysis: weigh up the costs and benefits of carrying on as you are versus trying out new ways of thinking and behaving.

In order to make your CBT experience successful, do your homework! We find that whether a client completes therapy assignments or not is the single best predictor of success. CBT involves retraining your attention, changing your behavioural patterns and adopting new ways of thinking. Breaking old patterns and replacing them with new ones takes practice and repetition.

Consider therapy as a temporary experiment. Give your therapist's advice a shot and see what happens. You can always return to your old ways or try out a new strategy if you think your therapy isn't working.

Part V
The Part of Tens

In this part . . .

*T*his Part of Tens is a source of vital CBT information. You'll find ten fundamental pointers toward living in an upbeat and enjoyable way, ten books to benefit your library, and ten self-esteem boosters that don't work and alternatives that do.

Chapter 22

Ten Healthy Attitudes for Living

....

In This Chapter

▶ Taking responsibility for your feelings

▶ Philosophising rationally

▶ Enhancing your psychological health

▶ Staying interested

....

A s we discuss many times in this book, the attitudes you hold about yourself, other people and the world greatly affect your ability to respond successfully to negative life events. Even in the absence of unusual or difficult circumstances, your core philosophies influence your overall experience of life. People who hold rational philosophies are generally less prone to emotional disturbances, such as anxiety and depression, and are more readily able to solve problems.

This chapter offers ten rational philosophical standpoints that are good for your psychological health. Read them, re-read them, think them through and test out acting upon them to see for yourself.

Assuming Emotional Responsibility: You Feel the Way You Think

Bad or unfortunate things, such as splitting up from a partner, being made redundant or having a car accident, can happen to anyone. You may reasonably have negative feelings in response to such events. Experiencing extreme sadness or annoyance in the face of misfortune is wholly understandable.

In some instances, bad things occur through no fault of your own. In other cases, you may have some personal responsibility. We don't suggest that you blame yourself for every bad thing that comes your way. However, try to assess a given situation and determine whether you have any *legitimate responsibility* for its development and look for a resolution.

Even if you're not personally responsible for a negative event, you can still take responsibility for your emotional and behavioural *responses* to the event. People who deny their part in creating their own emotional problems in the face of negative events don't recognise how their thoughts and actions can make a bad situation worse. They hand over their personal power to make things better by waiting passively for someone or something to step into the breach.

When you hold an attitude of personal responsibility for your feelings and actions, you're more able to find creative solutions, and your belief in your ability to cope with adversity is heightened. You empower yourself by focusing on your ability to influence the way you feel even if you can't control events.

On a cheerier note, when good things happen, you can also assess the extent to which they're a result of your own efforts – and then give yourself credit where due. You can appreciate good fortune without sabotaging your positive feelings with worries that your luck may run out.

Thinking Flexibly

Making demands and commands – thinking in terms of 'must', 'should' and 'have to' – about yourself, other people and the world around you has a fundamental problem: such thinking limits your flexibility to adapt to reality. The human capacity to adapt creatively to what's going on is one of the hallmarks of the species' success. However, humans are fallible, and the world continues to be an imperfect place. Insisting 'It shouldn't be this way!' can leave you irate, depressed or anxious and much less able to focus on how to cope with and adapt to reality.

Although circumstances may well be *desirable*, *preferable* and even *better* if the situation were different, they don't *have* to be a particular way. Accepting reality and striving to improve it where wise and achievable can help you save your energy for creative thought and action. See Chapter 2 for more on demands, and Chapter 14 for more on developing realistic attitudes towards yourself.

Valuing Your Individuality

You can express your individuality in many ways, such as in your dress sense, musical tastes, political opinions or choice of career. Yet perhaps you're hesitant to express your individuality openly because you fear the reaction of others. People who develop the ability to value their idiosyncrasies and to express them *respectfully* tend to be well-adjusted and content. Accepting that you're an individual and have the right to live your life, just as other people have the right to live theirs, is a pretty good recipe for happiness.

As social animals, humans like to feel part of a group or social structure, and tend to be happier when interacting meaningfully with other humans. However, the ability to go against group mentality when it's at odds with your own personal views or values is a tremendous skill. You can be both socially integrated and true to your values by accepting yourself as an individual and by being a selective non-conformist. Check out Chapter 14 for more on accepting yourself.

Accepting That Life Can Be Unfair

Sometimes, life's just plain unfair. Sometimes, people treat you unjustly and nothing gets done to put the balance right. Bad things happen to the nicest of people, and people who don't seem to have done a deserving thing in their lives get a winning ticket. On top of being unfair, life's unpredictable and uncertain a great deal of the time. And really, that's just the way life is.

What can you do? You can whine and moan and make yourself thoroughly miserable about the lamentable state of the world. Or you can accept things and get on with the business of living. No matter how much you insist that the world should be fair and you should be given certainty about how things are going to pan out, you ain't going to get it.

Life's unfair to pretty much *everyone* from time to time – in which case, perhaps things aren't as desperately unfair as you thought. If you can accept the cold, hard reality of injustice and uncertainty, you're far more likely to be able to bounce back when life slaps you in the face with a wet fish. You're also likely to be less anxious about making decisions and taking risks. You can still strive to play fair yourself, but if you accept that unfairness exists you may be less outraged and less horrified if and when justice simply doesn't prevail.

Understanding That Approval from Others Isn't Necessary

Receiving approval from someone important to you is nice. Getting a bit of praise from a boss or a friend can feel good. But if you believe that you *need* the approval of significant others or, indeed, everyone you meet, then you probably spend a lot of time feeling unhappy and unsure of yourself. Many people get depressed because they believe they're only as good as the opinions others hold of them. These people can't feel good about themselves unless they get positive feedback or reassurance from others.

Accept yourself, independent of overt approval from other people in your life. Having a *preference* for being liked, appreciated and approved of by others – but not believing that you *need* approval – means that your self-opinion can be stable and you can weather disapproval. You may still behave in ways that are more likely to generate approval than disapproval, but you can also assert yourself without fear. You can consider praise and compliments a bonus rather than something you must cling to and work over-hard to maintain.

If you hold the belief that you *need* rather than *desire* approval, you may pay emotionally for it somewhere along the line. You're likely to feel anxious about whether approval's forthcoming – and when you get approval you may worry about losing it. If you fail to get obvious approval or – horror of all horrors – someone criticises you, you're likely to put yourself down and make yourself depressed. Refer to Chapter 9 for more on combating anxiety, and Chapter 12 for tackling depression.

You cannot please all the people all the time – and if that's what you try to do, you're almost certainly going to be overly passive. If you can take the view that disapproval isn't the end of the world, intolerable and an indication that you're less than worthy, you can enjoy approval when you get it and still accept yourself when you don't.

Realising Love's Desirable, Not Essential

Some people would rather be in any relationship – even an unsatisfying or abusive one – than in no relationship at all. This need may stem from a belief that they can't cope with feelings of loneliness or get through life in general if they're alone. Other people consider themselves worthy or lovable only when they're reassured by being in a relationship.

Romantic relationships *can* enhance your enjoyment of life, but they're not essential for you to enjoy life. Holding this attitude can help you to feel good about yourself when you're not part of a couple and may lead you to make more discerning partner choices in future since you will choose, rather than be compelled, to be with someone. Believing that your basic lovability is relatively constant, regardless of whether a significant other actively loves you, can help you to feel secure *within* a relationship and secure within yourself *outside* of a relationship.

People who strongly *prefer* having a partner and yet believe that they can survive a break up tend to experience little romantic jealousy. Jealousy can be a big obstacle to relationship satisfaction – jealous people tend to believe that they *must* keep their partner and end up focusing on signs (real or imagined) of infidelity or waning interest rather than on the pleasure of the relationship. Jealousy's turned many a relationship sour. A jealous partner can end up alienating the other person through constant reassurance-seeking or monitoring, leaving both members of the couple feeling that mutual trust doesn't exist between them.

Preferring instead of *demanding* to have a relationship helps you to retain your independence and individuality. Then when you *are* in a relationship, you're less likely to fall into the trap of trying to be the perfect partner – which means you can continue to attend to your own interests while being able to negotiate compromises when appropriate. You'll also be able to call a halt to destructive relationships when evidence suggests that there's no way forward.

Tolerating Short-Term Discomfort

Healthy, robust and successful people are often able to tolerate temporary discomfort in the pursuit of longer-term goals. They practise self-denial and delay gratification when doing so is in their long-term interests. These people are the ones who are able to eat healthily, exercise regularly, save money, be romantically faithful, study effectively, and so on.

You *can* experience intense pleasure in the present and the future, but often some degree of pain and effort *today* are necessary to win you greater pleasure *tomorrow*. This will be true for many of the achievements you've already made in life. Putting up with temporary discomfort is also going to be crucial in *reducing* painful feelings of anxiety and depression. See Chapters 9, 12 and 13 for more on overcoming these problems.

Enacting Enlightened Self-Interest

Enlightened self-interest is about putting yourself first most of the time and one, two or a small handful of selected others a very close second. Enlightened self-interest is about looking after your own needs and interests while also being mindful of the needs of your loved ones and other people living on the planet.

So why put yourself first? When you reach a certain age, you need to look after yourself because nobody else is going to do so for you. If you can keep yourself healthy and content, you're better able to turn your attention to caring for the people in your life that you love.

Many people make the mistake of always suppressing their own needs and end up tired, unhappy or ill. People may think they're doing the right thing by putting others first all the time, but in fact they're left with very little to give.

Of course you *will* experience times when putting someone else's needs before your own and making personal sacrifices is a good choice. For example, parents frequently put the welfare of their children before their own. But you must still make space for your own pursuits too.

If you're starting to get concerned that 'self-interest' translates to 'selfish beast', stop! To clarify: self-interest involves taking responsibility for looking after yourself because you understand that you're worth taking care of. Self-interest means being able to care for others very deeply. When you're self-interested, you're able to meet your own needs and take a keen interest in the welfare of other people in the world around you. You can also determine when you're going to put yourself *second* for a period of time because some-one else's need is greater than your own – which is where the 'enlightened' part comes into play.

Selfishness is not – we stress, *not!* – the same animal as self-interest. Ultimately, selfish people put their own wants and needs first, *to the exclusion and detriment of other people.* Selfishness is much less about taking respon-sibility for looking after yourself and much more about demanding that you get what you want, when you want and to hell with everybody else. The two concepts are very different – so don't be scared. Head to Chapter 18 for more on building a lifestyle that promotes taking care of yourself.

Pursuing Interests and Acting Consistently with Your Values

Loads of evidence indicates that people are happier and healthier if they pursue interests and hobbies. Have you let your life become dominated by work or chores at home, and do you spend your evenings sitting in front of the television as a means of recharging? If your answer to this question is 'Yes!', then you're in extremely good, but not optimally healthy, company.

One of the arts of maximising your happiness is to pursue personally mean-ingful goals, such as furthering your education, participating in sport and exercise, developing skills, improving relationships, or acting in ways that contribute to the sort of world you'd like to live in, for example by doing some voluntary work. Try to structure your life to ensure that you have some time for personally meaningful pursuits. Check that the things you do in life reflect what you believe is important.

As far as we can tell, life isn't a dress rehearsal. Will you really look back and regret missing a bit of TV because you dragged yourself out to spend time on a hobby, to exercise, to enjoy a night out with your friends or to participate in some charity work?

Tolerating Uncertainty

Healthy and productive people tend to be prepared to tolerate a degree of risk and uncertainty. Demanding certainty and guarantees in an uncertain world is a sure-fire recipe for worry and inactivity. Safety (or more accurately, the *illusion* of complete safety) comes at a cost – fewer rewards, less excitement, fewer new experiences.

The fact that you don't know what the future holds is grounds for *calculated risks* and *experiments*, not avoidance, reassurance-seeking or safety precautions. You can make educated decisions and take calculated risks, but if you accept that 100 per cent certainty is exceptionally rare (and, in fact, unnecessary), you can reduce undue anxiety and worry. Risk is inherent to existence. You know that you're mortal and therefore destined to die one day but, in order to remain sane, you keep that knowledge on the outer track of your daily consciousness. You live in an uncertain world every single day of your life. Embrace it, enjoy it and relegate it to your peripheral vision.

Chapter 23

Ten Self-Esteem Boosters That Don't Work

. . . .

In This Chapter

▶ Identifying techniques that are counterproductive to your self-esteem

▶ Substituting healthier self-esteem strategies

. . . .

*Y*ou may be trying to manage your low self-esteem in ways that are counterproductive, particularly in the long term. This chapter highlights ten techniques that don't boost your self-esteem effectively.

'Why focus on where I'm going wrong?' you may ask. Well, using the strategies we describe in this chapter to boost your self-esteem is like trying to dig your way out of a hole. Your first step is to realise you're only digging yourself deeper – so put down that shovel! Only when you stop digging, can you begin to look for other ways to get out of the hole. Fortunately, we include several self-esteem ladders within this book to help you find your way out.

The following ten points describe counterproductive strategies for boosting your self-esteem. We explain why they don't work and suggest more constructive ways of increasing your sense of self-worth.

Putting Others Down

If you measure your self-esteem by comparing yourself with other people and tend to regard yourself as inferior, you may try to boost your worth by putting down other people, whether in your mind, by moaning about them to others or by criticising them directly.

By increasing your sense of other people's inferiority, you may manage to persuade yourself temporarily that you're less inferior. But, you won't change the underlying problem – your attitude towards yourself. Putting down others is tiring, not only for you but also for other people – and doing so does not elicit warm responses from others.

Instead, try respecting your own uniqueness – and that of others. The human race is a species, not a competition. Focus on following your own values and pursuing your own goals. Pay more attention to your own strengths rather than others' weaknesses.

If you feel inferior, re-evaluating your attitude towards yourself is more effective than trying to pull down someone else's self-esteem.

Thinking You're Special

Trying to replace a sense of worthlessness with a feeling of 'specialness' is another common self-defeating technique you can adopt for beating low self-esteem. Look out for times when you tell yourself 'If I'm not different, I'm nothing' or 'Being average or normal is like not existing'.

The problem here is that, as far as the universe is concerned, you're not special. No one is. You may be unique, but so is everyone else. In fact, you may well try so hard to avoid the 'horror' of mediocrity that you end up living an unhappy and unfulfilled life. This tendency largely stems from an extreme form of *all or nothing thinking* (which we cover in Chapter 2) and the mistaken idea that you need to reduce low self-esteem by wildly overcompensating.

Rather than trying to assert that you're special, focus your attention in a more constructive direction. Challenge the idea that you need to be 'special' in order to feel okay about yourself. Accept yourself as a normal, ordinary, worthwhile individual, just like everyone else.

Trying to Get Everyone to Like You

Substituting your dislike of yourself by trying to win the approval of other people is a recipe for anxiety. You can end up feeling anxious about not achieving your goal of being liked by someone or a group. If you do achieve your goal and win approval, you're likely to become anxious about losing your prize.

The real pity is that your imagined 'need' for approval may not help you give off the attractive, self-assured air you'd so dearly like. Believing that you need to be liked in order to like yourself can leave you in a desperate position. Allowing people to walk all over you in an attempt to win their approval has a pretty negative impact on your self-esteem, for fairly obvious reasons.

Rather than attempting to win approval, strive for respect. If you respect yourself, you give off an air of being comfortable in your own skin. People with true self-respect are those often most respected by others. You don't have to be a slave to this principle, but seeking respect can help you assert yourself more readily.

Placing Yourself above Criticism

Placing yourself above criticism is a classic tactic if you believe that being criticised reveals you to be inadequate, useless or a failure. Perfectionism, covering up your weaknesses and defensiveness are the inevitable result. You try to be flawless so that other people can't criticise you. However, you end up being unduly harsh with yourself for your shortcomings and errors. You may even believe that you can knock yourself into shape by criticising yourself, unwittingly lowering your self-image further.

Instead, try to accept your human fallibility without condemning yourself. Mistakes and flaws are an unavoidable aspect of being human, no matter how hard you try to change things. Don't be ashamed of your shortcomings – everyone else has flaws too. Do you think people really lose respect for you if they find out you're only human? They probably don't. Chances are, they'll be relieved and feel more able to relax in your company. Their respect for you may even grow, because they can accept you, warts and all.

Reveal an imperfection and check out the response you get. Try accepting yourself non-defensively in the face of criticism. If someone criticises you, try asking them for more information. Most people find owning up to their human fallibility a far more productive strategy than striving to be perfect.

Choosing perfection as your goal is setting yourself up to fail because *no one* is capable of being perfect. The more you fail to reach your unrealistic goal, the more you put yourself down. Don't be tempted to try harder to be perfect. Instead, try harder to accept your imperfection.

Avoiding Failure, Disapproval, Rejection and Other Animals

You may find that you avoid situations, places or people that trigger your tendency to put yourself down. This approach is very much a way of papering over the cracks. Your underlying attitude towards yourself remains the problem. By avoiding potential failure, you don't change your attitude: you simply postpone setting off your insecurity for a while.

A long-lasting, elegant solution to overcoming poor self-esteem is for you to uncover, examine and change any unhelpful attitudes you may have developed towards yourself. Then, you can deliberately seek out the things you've been avoiding, while practising your new self-accepting attitude (head to Chapter 14 for more).

Avoiding Your Emotions

You may try to block out certain emotions because you regard them as a sign of weakness. Although you may try to persuade yourself that you're strong because you can control your emotions, your relationships and psychological health are likely to suffer.

Having a wide range of emotions is part of what makes you human. Try as you might, avoiding these emotions is difficult – and unhealthy. You may end up feeling isolated, cold and aloof in your relationships, which can rob you of much richer and more satisfying experiences. Begin to accept your feelings and recognise that this acceptance shows courage, not weakness.

Sometimes, experiencing strong negative emotions is a natural response to adversity, a part of the healing process and a sign of strength in facing up to difficulties.

Attempting to Feel More Significant by Controlling Others

If you try to control others, the underlying assumption is that you need to *prove* your significance by having an effect on other people. The problem is that without this *proof*, you are (in your eyes) insignificant.

Perhaps you immediately offer unsolicited advice or try to convert others to a favourite cause to prove that you are a person of influence? Unfortunately, your lack of respect for others' thoughts, feelings and behaviours may actually be a turn-off to those other people.

Compulsively trying to influence or affect people actually shows you have a lack of control. You also reinforce a negative self-image by acting as if you have to prove something to be worthwhile or significant.

Imagine how you'd interact with people if you didn't have the need to prove your power or influence. You can use this imagining exercise as a guide to new healthier behaviour.

Over-Defending Your Self-Worth

We don't advocate you being a doormat, but the healthy alternative to being passive is to stay calm in the face of minor slights. Constantly defending your self-worth can lead to verbal or physical aggression (have a glance at Chapter 15). Besides, if you're confident in your self-worth, do you really need to guard it so carefully? Insisting that others must show you respect at all times leads to unhealthy anger. Your compulsive outrage at being disrespected can simply drive you to take people to task for minor assaults on your fragile self-esteem.

Respect yourself regardless of whether other people treat you respectfully. Self-respect affords you the ability to assert yourself appropriately when it's *worth* doing so.

Feeling Superior

You may have superior, equal and inferior traits compared with other people, but the idea that you're either an inferior or superior *person* is an overgeneralisation. No one is superior *or* inferior to everyone else in every way. We all have different strengths and weaknesses.

Some people can only feel good about themselves when they convince themselves that they're 'the best'. Many people with this tendency try to demonstrate their superiority by showing off their physical or psychological strength. For example, you may feel driven to impress people with your wit, intellect or other talent. Unfortunately, these solutions are only temporary ones to your underlying feelings of inferiority, which can be your real target for change. At worst, your attempts at superiority serve only to alienate other people and mask your true strengths.

Although the notion of the 'real you' is a bit simplistic, try dropping the superiority. Be as authentic as you can and see how people respond to you.

Blaming Nature or Nurture for Your Problems

Blaming your problems on your past, genetics, hormones, brain chemistry or other people does have the distinct advantage of temporarily alleviating any sense that you're stupid, pathetic or less worthwhile. This blame system stems from the mistaken idea that if you take an appropriate degree of responsibility for your emotional problems, then it means that you're to blame for those problems. Protecting your self-esteem by blaming something or someone else can typically backfire, which makes real change more difficult because you attribute your problems to factors outside of your control.

Half of the people in the Western world experience some kind of significant emotional problem during the course of their lives. So, having an emotional problem simply means you're human.

Use your understanding of your past and your 'make-up' to develop a compassionate, sympathetic perspective towards your current difficulties. Take some personal responsibility for keeping your problems going. Recognising how you may be making your problems worse gives you the power to make changes for the better.

Unhelpful ideas about how to feel good about yourself can stem from childhood messages. Teachers or parents may have told you to 'Be the best', 'Never admit that you're wrong', 'Our family is better than other families', 'Failure is not an option' or 'Big boys don't cry'. Such messages may have been offered to you as words of wisdom, but as an adult you can re-evaluate their truth and helpfulness. You can decide to dump them in favour of updated, self and other acceptance beliefs.

Chapter 24

Ten Ways to Lighten Up

In This Chapter

▶ Discovering the benefits of not taking things too seriously

▶ Finding yourself funny

▶ Getting more enjoyment out of life

▶ Throwing caution to the wind

Sometimes you can make life more arduous than necessary by taking yourself too seriously. If you take yourself *overly* seriously you may well find that you feel hurt, angry and depressed far more frequently than you'd like. Being unduly earnest can prevent you from seeing the funny side of things, lead you to misinterpret innocent comments as criticism and urge you to turn minor misfortune into major disaster. This chapter lists ten ways to lighten up a little, live with life's ups and downs and increase your overall enjoyment of things. Go through the list and pick out the headings that apply most to you.

Accept That You Can – and Will – Make Mistakes

Consider the following attitudes to making mistakes:

> *I'm only human/Of flesh and blood I'm made/I'm only human/Born to make mistakes.*
>
> – The Human League, British band

> *Success isn't permanent, and failure isn't fatal*
>
> – Mike Ditka, American football coach

Success is the ability to go from one failure to another with no loss of enthusiasm.

– Sir Winston Churchill, British prime minister and statesman

Eighty per cent of success is showing up.

– Woody Allen, US comedian and film director

If you take yourself overly seriously, you're likely to consider your mistakes unacceptable. You may also believe that other people may reject you on the basis of your blunders. Moreover, you probably judge yourself harshly when you make a social gaffe or a poor decision.

Everyone gets things wrong and mucks up from time to time. If you try to hide or ignore your mistakes, you can deny yourself the opportunity to develop from them. By acknowledging mistakes, and accepting yourself for making them, you give yourself the chance to do things differently next time. You'll also become more comfortable with making errors in the first place and are likely to spend less time worrying about whether you get things 'right'. Giving yourself permission to get things wrong can encourage you to take the risk of trying things in the first place – even at the risk of error or failure. Try to remember that your own mistakes are generally far more important to *you* than they are to *others*. Most people respect someone who can own up to and take responsibility for his mistakes, poor decisions, mis-demeanours and foot-in-mouth moments. Remember that most of the time mistakes are a small price to pay for rich experiences.

Try Something New

Perhaps you're reluctant to play a different sport, change your usual holiday destination or acquire a new language or skill. Maybe you're even reluctant to try a fresh route to work in case you get lost and look foolish. The fear of looking silly can stop many people dead in their tracks. If you can cope with looking a trifle daft now and again, you'll find it a lot easier to discover novel interests, immerse yourself in new experiences and acquire new skills. Even doing small things like eating different cuisines or going on a one-day medita-tion course (or a course on anything that interests you!) can broaden your horizons.

Doing something foolish doesn't mean you're a fool. It's pretty much impos-sible for you to learn a new language or how to play the piano without making lots of grammatical gaffes or hitting the wrong notes. By giving yourself the opportunity to try new things, you may have a lot of fun in the process, even if you don't become a polyglot or a pianist in the Royal Philharmonic. Lots of things in life are worth doing simply for the sake of it!

Stamp on Shame

Taking yourself too seriously can lead you to experience unnecessary emotional upset. For example, if you need to look as though you're in complete control and composed all the time, you're a prime candidate for experiencing frequent bouts of shame.

Feelings of shame and humiliation are often linked to perceiving that your weaknesses, errors or faults have been exposed and that others will reject you as a result. For example, if you fall over while boarding a train, you may experience intense, unpleasant feelings of shame rather than getting appropriately embarrassed. The shame you experience about somebody seeing you trip up is likely to last longer than simple embarrassment, and cause you far more distress than any physical injuries you may have sustained.

As one of your goals, you can have a go at overcoming your propensity to feel ashamed. Try deliberately exposing yourself to scrutiny using the following four-step technique:

1. **Make yourself conspicuous.** Wear a ridiculous outfit, make animal noises, sing to yourself, wear your underwear on the outside of your normal clothing, ask a really stupid question, or do anything else silly you can think of. Whatever you choose, do it *on purpose* and *in a very public place*. Travelling on public transport provides an excellent opportunity to carry out shame-attacking exercises.

2. **Stay in the situation long enough for your feelings of shame and general discomfort to subside on their own.** Don't hide yourself away in the corner, run away from the public place or remove your clown hat, for example. Stay in the situation until you notice that your uncomfortable feelings are beginning to subside (sometimes this may take ten minutes and other times it may take an hour). The important point is to stick with the exercise for whatever length of time it takes for you to feel *less* embarrassed, ashamed or anxious.

   Don't expect to feel totally calm and happy when you're deliberately doing something ridiculous in public. The idea is for you to see that nothing terrible happens to you when other people look at you as though you're weird.

3. **Hold an attitude of self-acceptance throughout the experience.** This means that you act as if you truly believe that being judged as odd or weird isn't the end of the world. (This just isn't the case, or the world would have ended long ago.) Tell yourself that you can tolerate uncomfortable feelings, which you associate with possible negative evaluation from others. (You can: feelings of shame and embarrassment don't kill people.)

4. **Repeat variations of the exercise often and without long gaps in between.** Doing the exercise once isn't enough. Repetition is the key to making yourself desensitised to scrutiny so that you don't feel shame as a result. Try doing this exercise daily for a week; it's a great way to lessen your distress.

Laugh at Yourself

Many people claim that laughter's the best medicine. This adage may well carry a sizeable grain of truth. Finding the funny angle in an otherwise awkward situation can help remove the sting. Sometimes you can take the horror out of your mistakes and shortcomings by finding them amusing.

If you're able to value yourself as a worthy person *and* recognise your human imperfection, you won't fall into the trap of taking yourself so seriously that you're unable to laugh. Think of people you know who can't take a joke: they're very likely people who take themselves and everything they do far too seriously. Being overly earnest is a bit tragic: anything that happens to you or anything you do that is, in your mind, less than acceptable has a profound impact on your global opinion of yourself. You can glean much more enjoyment out of life and your personal relationships if you can have a giggle at your own expense.

Don't Take Offence So Easily

If you believe that everyone must respect you and that you're only as good as what others think of you, then you're going to get offended if someone fails to appreciate you. You're pretty much destined to take offence much of the time unless you live in an air-conditioned bubble all on your own. In the real world, sometimes people are rude to each other and fail to behave in a thoughtful, respectful manner.

We're not suggesting that you take the stance of a passive victim when others treat you unacceptably. You can respect yourself and have clear boundaries about the type of people you choose to associate with and the type of behaviour you're prepared to tolerate.

Unfortunately, you (like all of us) are not impervious to bad behaviour from other people. However, you don't need to take undue offence to it. You can make your life easier by distinguishing between when, and when not, to bother asserting yourself. For example, if a friend jibes you about a recent screw-up you made, is it really that dire? Or if someone bumps into you on the street without apologising, don't consider it an assault on your personal worth and respectability – you may find it rude and annoying, but do you really need to take offence?

Feeling offended is akin to feeling angry. Anger is tiring and unpleasant. Chances are that if you hold too serious a view of yourself, you're experiencing anger more often than you actually need to (refer to Chapter 15).

Make Good Use of Criticism

Constructive criticism is a vital element of learning. Of course, not all the criticism you receive may be delivered in a skilled or constructive way. Nevertheless, if you can step back from negative feedback long enough to access its validity, you can use it to your advantage. Often, other people can see more clearly than you where you're going 'wrong' – others can have the benefit of an objective viewpoint.

If you believe that you *must* get *everything* right or perfect, and that any indication that you're failing at a task is evidence that you're inadequate, then you can get very disturbed by criticism. Rather than using feedback to evaluate your approach to a specific task, you're likely to use it as a battering tool on your sense of worth. You may become defensive at the first sniff of less-than-positive comments on your performance.

Rather than reacting to critical comments over-sensitively, you can develop more tolerance to such comments so that you find them useful. Try the following techniques:

- ✔ Get rid of your defensive stance. Listen openly to what people are saying about you (head to Chapter 18).

- ✔ Understand that you don't *need* to be right every time. You have the option to behave less than perfectly now and again. Accepting that you can be wrong sometimes means that you can find criticism easier to take.

- ✔ Take time to weigh up the validity of the comments made and then to use any legitimate information offered to aid your development.

Settle into Social Situations

When you have an overly serious attitude towards yourself, you're prone to feeling uncomfortable in social settings. The fear that you may say the wrong thing, offend someone or expose yourself as stupid or boring can lead you to clam up and say little. You may find that you censor much of what you say or rehearse it in your head before you speak. Alternatively, you may try too hard to be witty and entertaining. Either way, you're not relaxing into the occasion and enjoying the interaction. You're probably much more focused on the impression you're making than on what the other people present are actually talking about.

If you fall into this camp, social situations for you are more likely to be something to get through rather than enjoy. You're probably taking more than your fair share of responsibility for the interaction going smoothly. Remember: you're only ever *part* of a social group, even when there are only two of you – the other person or people present also have a part to play in the smooth running of conversation.

To help yourself relax and be 'more yourself' in social settings, try these tips:

- ✔ **Focus your attention away from yourself and on to the other people present.** Really listen to the conversation and observe others.

- ✔ **Say things spontaneously.** Resist the urge to rehearse witty responses in your head before you speak. Take the risk of dropping in comments during the conversation.

- ✔ **Drop your safety behaviours** (refer to Chapter 7 for more on safety behaviours). Avoid sitting on the outside of a group or fiddling with your drink, handbag or phone when conversation lulls. These types of behaviour may distract you from your feelings of social awkwardness but they also stop you from getting used to natural social interaction.

- ✔ **Express yourself until you feel heard.** If you start to say something and are interrupted, try again in a few moments, maybe a little louder.

- ✔ **Reign yourself in.** If you tend to overcompensate for your social discomfort by talking a lot or putting on a bit of a show, give others the chance to fill in the gaps and silences.

- ✔ **Enjoy yourself.** Above all, remind yourself that social gatherings are meant to be fun. Make enjoying the company and conversation of other people your main reason for socialising.

You don't have to provide witty, imaginative or profound contributions to every topic of conversation. Inevitably there will be some subjects that you find more interesting and know more about than others. Acknowledge that having little or nothing to say on some subjects is okay. Don't decide that this means you're dull or uninformed generally!

Encourage Your Creativity to Flow

To act creatively, whether at work or in your personal life, you have to accept the possibility that some of your ideas won't be considered that great. If you've got a suggestion for an advertising campaign at work or a novel way to spice up your sex life, you'll be less inclined to put forward your ideas if you worry too much about them being rejected or going down like a lead balloon.

Creativity is self-generative: if you try out your ideas, they tend to give rise to more ideas. If you constantly suppress them, you may find that the stream of ideas diminishes over time.

Act Adventurously

Breaking your routine can help you to lighten up. Changing a regular pattern can relieve boredom and improve your mood generally. Even the smallest things, such as choosing a different recipe in a cookbook or walking to a place to which you normally drive, can make a significant difference to your mood.

Following a routine in order to avoid unpredictable outcomes is all too easy. Unfortunately, getting stuck in a rut may mean that you miss out on new, exciting experiences. Urging yourself to do things differently or to risk a foray into unknown territory can challenge the demands you hold about having control at all times. Most people like to have some degree of control in their lives and to feel that they have some degree of certainty about what they can expect from life. However, in reality, life is unpredictable and our sense of certainty is largely an illusion.

Accepting your limitations to control events and to be certain about the outcome of events can help you to act more adventurously and live life more fully. Increasing your tolerance for uncertainty and limited control is also likely to help you become more adaptive when life throws unexpected problems your way. (Head to Chapter 9 for more on coping with anxiety.)

Enjoy Yourself: It's Later than You Think

There's no time like the present for chilling out and lightening up. If you never get round to making time for pleasurable or novel activities, you may find that you don't ever do them. Schedule in some time for trying out new things and meeting new people. Stretch yourself beyond your comfort zone and see what the experience brings. People who hold a responsible yet light-hearted attitude to themselves, and life in general, are usually far more pleasant to hang around with. These people give off an air of 'seizing the moment'. Making the most of the present moment can keep you young at heart, even as the years go by.

Chapter 25

Ten Books to Add to Your Library

In This Chapter

▶ Self-help books and therapist manuals

▶ Books for learning more about CBT

▶ Book recommendations for tackling specific kinds of problems using CBT

*N*umerous self-help and professional manuals on CBT are available. We've tried to choose books that reflect the diversity of CBT as an approach, and that can add to your armoury of knowledge and skills in tackling disturbing emotions or behaviours. The books included in this chapter are all ones that we know very well ourselves and have used successfully with our clients over the years (some we have written!). The list is not exhaustive, but these ten suggestions can point you in the right direction when it comes to investigating helpful, sound CBT literature.

Cognitive Behavioural Therapy Workbook For Dummies

This book makes an excellent companion to the one you're currently reading. It includes lots of extra practical exercises to help you put core CBT skills into practice. It can be used for independent self-help or in conjunction with a CBT therapist. Written by Rhena Branch and Rob Willson (Wiley, 2007) this book is a valuable resource both for anyone seeking help overcoming their problems and for trainee CBT therapists alike.

Boosting Self-Esteem For Dummies

No, the title isn't intended to be ironic! This is our latest For Dummies book (Branch and Willson, Wiley, 2009) and we're pretty proud of it, actually. It focuses on helping the reader to understand the underpinnings of poor self-esteem and the ways in which it is maintained. In it we also offer clear CBT-based strategies to improve your relationship with yourself (and others). This is a very useful and informative book for those many people in the world who struggle daily with feelings of low self-worth.

Cognitive Therapy and the Emotional Disorders

Cognitive Therapy and the Emotional Disorders by Aaron T. Beck (Penguin Psychology, 1991) is the founder of cognitive therapy's original text on his research-based approach to emotional problems. Beck's contribution to the field of CBT has been phenomenal, not least because of the emphasis placed on scientifically evaluating CBT treatments. This is an historic book, and a good introduction to the fundamentals of CT.

The Mindful Way Through Depression – Freeing Yourself from Chronic Unhappiness

Mark Williams, John Teasdale, Zindel Segal and Jon Kabat-Zinn (Guilford Press, 2007) are some very influential authors in the field of CBT and psychology in general. Together they have created an excellent manual for treating depression with mindfulness-based CBT strategies. Mindfulness is a part of a new wave in psychological treatment that focuses on what we *do* with our minds rather than the content of our thoughts. Written in an engaging and accessible manner, this book offers a host of techniques to help the reader embark on meditation practices to alleviate depression and anxiety. It also includes a guided meditation CD!

Flow

Billed as 'the classic work on how to achieve happiness' *Flow* by Mihaly Csiksentmihalyi (2002, Rider Press) discusses principles that aid ordinary people in living meaningful and enjoyable lives. The book deals with the phenomenon of 'flow', a state in which an individual becomes wholly involved in a given activity and experiences true enjoyment. There are many interesting concepts in this text that compliment CBT principles. It can be hard going at times (it's quite academic) but is well worth reading.

Overcoming . . .

The *Overcoming . . .* books (published by Robinson Press) are an excellent series that attend to specific kinds of problems. These books are usually written by experts in their field and are frequently recommended by professional therapists. The series includes: *Overcoming Childhood Trauma* by Helen Kennerly; *Overcoming Depression* by Paul Gilbert; *Overcoming Obsessive Compulsive Disorder* by David Veale and Rob Willson; *Overcoming Health Anxiety* by Rob Willson and David Veale; *Overcoming Body Image Problems and BDD* by Rob Willson and David Veale; *Overcoming Social Anxiety and Shyness* by Gillian Buttler; *Overcoming Traumatic Stress* by Claudia Herbert and Ann Wetmore; and *Overcoming Mood Swings* (bipolar affective disorder) by Jan Scott.

Overcoming Anger

Windy Dryden, author of *Overcoming Anger* (Sheldon Press) has written or edited more than 150 books in the areas of counselling and psychotherapy. In a clear and forceful style, Windy shows how we create our anger with our attitudes and beliefs. He goes on to show how thinking rationally helps overcome unhealthy anger and communication with others. This Sheldon series also includes several other self-help books written by Windy Dryden focused on overcoming common emotional disorders such a hurt, envy and shame.

Oxford Guide to Behavioural Experiments in Cognitive Therapy

The *Oxford Guide to Behavioural Experiments in Cognitive Therapy*, edited by James Bennett-Levy, Gillian Butler, Melanie Fennell, Ann Hackman, Martina Mueller, and David Westbrook (Oxford University Press) is like a distilled essence of CBT. Many cognitive behavioural therapists wish that the book had been written years earlier! Focusing on the 'lets find out' element of CBT, the book covers a huge range of psychological problems, and how to test out the negative thoughts related to them.

Reason and Emotion in Psychotherapy

Dr Albert Ellis, the author of *Reason and Emotion in Psychotherapy: A Comprehensive Method for Treating Human Disturbances, Revised and Updated* (Birch Lane Press), is the true founding father of cognitive behavioural therapy. The rational emotive behaviour therapy approach, described in this extensive volume, was the first fully developed cognitive behavioural theory and treatment, dating back to the mid-1950s. This version of Ellis' seminal text gives an insight into the philosophy underpinning the approach and Ellis's phenomenal mind. Anyone interested in how reason and philosophy can be applied to reduce human suffering would do well to read this book.

The Cognitive Behaviour Counselling Primer

This is a concise, readable introduction to the fundamentals of CBT (Rhena Branch and Windy Dryden, PCCS books, 2008). It includes an overview of how CBT has developed over the years and clearly outlines key philosophical CBT foundations. This book is particularly valuable to students of psychology, CBT therapists in training and anyone interested in understanding what CBT is all about.

Appendix A

CBT Resources

• •

*T*his appendix lists organisations in the United Kingdom and the United States that you may want to contact for further help, support, and information.

Organisations in the UK and Europe

Use the contacts here to find a therapist, discover where to browse the Internet and get in touch with organisations that can help with specific issues or problems.

CBT therapists

You can find a qualified CBT (cognitive behavioural therapy) therapist in Britain and Europe through the professional associations we list here. These organisations can also help you find CBT therapists in your area with experience and training specific to your individual problems.

- ✔ **Association for Rational Emotive Behaviour Therapy (AREBT)**, Englewood, Farningham Hill Road, Farningham, Kent DA4 0JR; phone 01322-862158; website www.arebt.org.

- ✔ **British Association of Behavioural and Cognitive Psychotherapies (BABCP)**, BABCP General Office, The Globe Centre, PO Box 9, Accrington, BB5 0XB; phone 01254-875277, fax 01254-239114; email babcp@babcp.com, website www.babcp.org.uk/.

- ✔ **European Association of Behavioural and Cognitive Therapies (EABCT)**, EABCT Office, Maliebaan 50B, 3581 CS Utrecht, The Netherlands; phone +31-30-2543054, fax +31-30-2543037; email eabct@vgct.nl, website www.eabct.com.

Other therapists

Many other types of therapy are available in addition to CBT. If you're looking for another type of therapist, or for information about the psychological treatments recommended for specific disorders, try contacting the organisations we list here. Remember that discussing other treatment options with your GP or psychiatrist, to ensure that you pursue a therapy that has been proven effective for your particular problems, is always a good idea.

- ✔ **National Institute for Health and Clinical Excellence (NICE),** MidCity Place, 71 High Holborn, London, WC1V 6NA; phone 0845-003-7780, fax 0845-003-7784; email `nice@nice.org.uk`, website `www.nice.org.uk/`.

- ✔ **United Kingdom Council for Psychotherapy (UKCP),** 2nd Floor, Edward House, 2 Wakley Street, London, EC1V 7LT; phone 020-7014-9955, fax 020-7014-9977; email `info@ukcp.org.uk`.

Online support

Websites devoted to specific disorders include:

- ✔ **The Mood Gym:** Developing CBT for treatment of depression. `www.moodgym.anu.edu.au`.

- ✔ **The Organization for Bipolar Affective Disorders:** `www.obad.ca`.

Organisations

Literally thousands of organisations devote themselves to helping people with various addictions, conditions and disorders. Some of the best include:

- ✔ **Action on Smoking and Health (ASH),** First Floor, 144–145 Shoreditch High Street, London, E1 6JE; phone 020 -7739-5902, fax 020-7729-4732; website `www.ash.org.uk`.

- ✔ **Alcoholics Anonymous**, PO Box 1, Stonebow House, Stonebow, York, YO1 2NJ; phone 01904-644026/7/8/9.

- ✔ **Anxiety UK (formerly the National Phobics Society)**, Zion Community Resource Centre, 339 Stretford Road, Hulme, Manchester, M15 4ZY; phone 0870-770-0456, fax 0161-227-9862; email `nationalphobic@ btinternet.com`, website `www.phobics-society.org.uk/ contact.php`.

- ✔ **Association of Post-Natal Depression**, 25 Jerdan Place, Fulham, London, SW6; phone 020-7836-0868.

✔ **The British Acupuncture Council (BAcC),** 63 Jeddo Road, London, W12 9HQ; phone 020-8735-0400, fax 020-8735-0404; website www.acupuncture.org.uk.

✔ **Depression Alliance**, PO Box 1022, London, SE1 7GR; phone 020-7721-7672 (recorded information).

✔ **First Steps to Freedom**, 1 Taylor Close, Kenilworth, CV8 2LW; phone 0845-120-2916 (freephone helpline 10 a.m.–10 p.m.); email info@first-steps.org, website www.first-steps.org/.

✔ **Manic Depression Fellowship**, 8–10 High Street, Kingston-Upon-Thames, London, KT1 1EY; phone 020-8974-6550 and 020-8546-0323.

✔ **MIND,** The National Association for Mental Health, Granta House, 15–19 Broadway, Stratford, London, E15 4BQ; phone 020-8519-2122.

✔ **No Panic**, 93 Brands Farm Way, Telford, TF3 2JQ; phone 01952-590005, freephone helpline 0808-808-0545 (10 a.m.–10 p.m.); email ceo@nopanic.org.uk, website www.nopanic.org.uk/.

✔ **OCD Action,** Suite 506–509 Davina House, 137–149 Goswell Road, London, EC1V 7ET; phone 020-7253-5272; website www.ocdaction.org.uk.

✔ **Seasonal Affective Disorder Association (SADA)**, PO Box 989, Steyning, BN44 3HG; website www.sada.org.uk/.

✔ **Triumph over Phobia (TOP) UK**, PO Box 3760, Bath, BA2 3WY; phone 0845-600-9601; email info@triumphoverphobia.org.uk, website www.triumphoverphobia.com.

Organisations in the United States

If you're based in the United States of America, you may find these addresses useful.

✔ **Albert Ellis Institute,** 45 East 65th Street, New York, NY 10021-6593. Tel: 212 535-0822. Fax: 212 249-3582. Web site: www.rebt.org

✔ **American Foundation for Suicide Prevention,** 120 Wall Street, 22nd Floor, New York, NY 1005. Tel: 212 363 3500. Web site: http://www.afsp.org

✔ **American Mental Health Foundation,** 2 East 86th Street, New York, NY 1008

✔ **Anorexia Nervosa and Related Eating Disorders, Inc,** PO Box 5102, Eugene, OR 97405. Tel: 541 344 1144. Web site: www.anred.com

✔ **Anxiety Disorders Association of America,** 8730 Georgia Avenue, Suite 600, Silver Spring, MD 20910. Tel: 240 485-1001. Fax: 240 485-1035. Web site: www.adaa.org

- **Association for the Advancement of Behavior Therapy,** 305 Seventh Ave, New York, NY 10001-6008, USA. Tel: 212 647 1890. Web site: http://server.psyc.vt.edu/aabt/

- **Children and Adults with Attention Deficit Disorders,** 499 Northwest 70th Avenue, Suite 308, Plantation, FL 33317. Tel: 305 587 3700. Web site: www.chadd.org

- **Kidscope, Obsessive-Compulsive Foundation** (children's newsletters), PO Box 70, Milford, CT 06460-0070

- **National Alliance for the Mentally Ill,** 200 N. Glebe Rd., Suite 1015, Arlington, VA 22203-3754. Tel: 800 950 NAMI (800 950 6264)

- **National Anxiety Foundation,** 3135 Custer Drive, Lexington, KY 40517-4001. Tel: 606 272 7166. Web site: http://lexington-on-line.com/naf.ocd.2.html

- **National Association of Anorexia Nervosa and Associated Disorders,** Box 7, Highland Park, IL 60035. Tel: 847 831 3438. Web site: www.healthtouch.com

- **National Attention Deficit Disorder Association,** PO Box 972, Mentor, OH 44061. Tel: 800 487 2282 or 216 350 9595. Web site: www.add.org

- **National Depressive and Manic-Depressive Association,** 730 North Franklin, #501, Chicago, IL 60610. Tel: 800 82N DMDA

- **National Foundation for Depressive Illness,** PO Box 2257, New York, NY 10116. Tel: 800 248 4344

- **National Institute of Mental Health,** 9000 Rockville Pike, Building 10, Room 30–41, Bethesda, MD 20892. Tel: 301 496 3421. Information services: Panic and other anxiety disorders: 800 647 2642. Depression: 800 421 4211

- **National Mental Health Association,** 1201 Prince St, Alexandria, VA 22314-2971. Tel: 703 684 7722

- **National Mental Health Consumers Self-Help Clearinghouse,** 1211 Chestnut St, Philadelphia, PA 19107. Tel: 800 553 4539

- **Obsessive Compulsive Anonymous, Inc. (OCA),** PO Box 215, New Hyde Park, New York 11040. Tel: 516 741 4909. Web site: http://members.aol.com/west24th/index.html

- **Obsessive Compulsive Foundation,** 676 State Street, New Haven, CT 06511. Tel: 203 401 2070. Fax: 203 401 2076. E-mail: info@ocfoundation.org. Web site: www.ocfounadtion.org/

- **Trichotillomania Learning Center,** 303 Potrero, Suite 51, Santa Cruz, CA 95060. Tel: 831 457 1004. Web site: www.trich.org/

Further Reading

If you're interested in finding out more about dealing with the disorders described in Chapter 3 of this book, consult the 'Overcoming' series published by Constable and Robinson. The books in this series are widely available in larger bookstores and over the Internet.

For more information on cognitive behavioural therapy and how to apply it your own life, try the exercises in *Cognitive Behavioural Therapy Workbook For Dummies*. It's written by your faithful authors, published by Wiley and part of the *For Dummies* series (just like this book!).

Appendix B
Forms

. . . .

*I*n this Appendix you can photocopy these blank forms and fill them in, using the instructions provided here and within specific chapters.

The 'Old Meaning–New Meaning' Sheet

The sheet has the three headings. Fill them in as follows:

1. **In the first column, 'Event', record what actually happened.**

2. **Under 'Old Meaning' in the second column, record what you believe the event means about you.**

   This is your unhealthy core belief.

3. **In the 'New Meaning' third column, record a healthier and more accurate meaning for the event.**

   This is the new belief that you want to strengthen.

Head to Chapter 14 for a worked example of the sheet, and for more about reviewing past events.

Event	Old Meaning	New Meaning

The Cost–Benefit Analysis Form

Carry out a *cost–benefit analysis* (CBA) to examine the pros and cons of something can help galvanise your commitment to change. You can use a CBA to examine the advantages and disadvantages of a number of things, such as:

- **Behaviours:** How helpful is this action to you? Does it bring short-term or long-term benefits?

- **Emotions:** How helpful is this feeling? For example, does feeling guilty or angry really help you?

- **Thoughts, attitudes, or beliefs:** Where does thinking this way get you? How does this belief help you?

- **Options for solving a practical problem:** How can this solution work out? Is this really the best possible answer to the problem?

Evaluate the pros and cons:

- In the short-term

- In the long-term

- For yourself

- For other people

Try to write CBA statements in pairs, particularly when you're considering changing the way you feel, act, or think. What are the *advantages* of feeling anxiety? And the *disadvantages*? Write down pairs of statements for what you feel, do, or think *currently,* and for other, healthier alternatives. Head to Chapter 8 for worked examples of the form.

Costs and benefits of:	
Costs (Disadvantages)	*Benefits (Advantages)*

The 'Tic-Toc' Sheet

TICs are *task interfering cognitions*, the thoughts, attitudes, and beliefs that get in the way of your progress. You need to respond with *TOCs – task orienting cognitions*, which are constructive alternatives to TICs. The list of unhelpful attitudes (sand traps) in the nearby sidebar is helpful for getting some ideas about task interfering cognitions.

Fill out the Tic-Toc sheet by following these steps:

1. **Identify the goal or task you want to focus on.**

2. **In the left column (TICs), list your thoughts, attitudes, and beliefs that get in the way of you achieving your aim.**

3. **In the right column (TOCs) put responses to each of your TICs that will help you achieve your goal or task.**

Head to Chapter 19 for more on the Tic-Toc sheet.

Goal or task:	
Task Interfering Cognitions (TICs)	*Task Orienting Cognitions (TOCs)*

The Zigzag Form

1. **Write down in the top left-hand box of the zigzag form a belief that you want to strengthen.**

2. **In the next box down, write your doubts, reservations, or challenges about the healthy belief.**

3. **In the next box, dispute your attack and redefend the healthy belief.**

4. **Repeat Steps 2 and 3 until you exhaust all your attacks on the healthy belief.**

5. **Re-rate, from 0 to 100 per cent, how strongly you endorse the healthy belief after going through all your doubts.**

Refer to Chapter 17 for more information about the zigzag form.

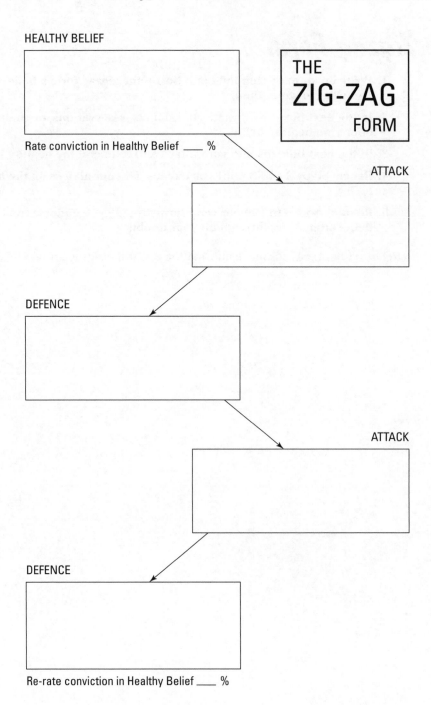

HEALTHY BELIEF

THE
ZIG-ZAG
FORM

Rate conviction in Healthy Belief _____ %

ATTACK

DEFENCE

ATTACK

DEFENCE

Re-rate conviction in Healthy Belief _____ %

The Vicious Flower

1. **In the Trigger box, write down the trigger that makes you feel anxious or upset.**

2. **In the central circle, write down the key thoughts and meanings you attach to the trigger.**

3. **In the flower petals, write down the emotions, behaviours, and sensations you experience when your uncomfortable feeling is triggered. In the top petal, write down what you tend to focus on.**

Chapter 7 has loads more about the vicious flower exercise, and a filled-in example.

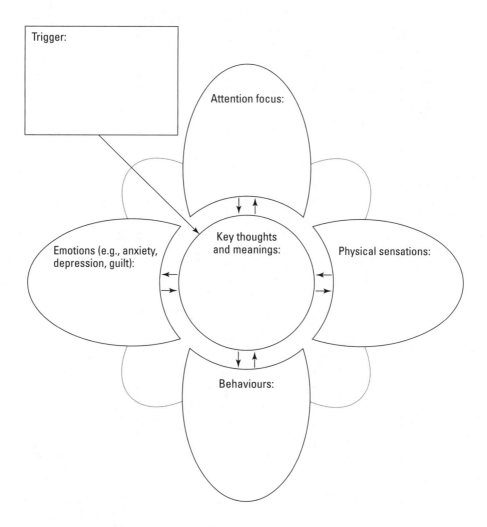

The Task Concentration Sheet

Head to Chapter 5 for more about the task-concentration exercise, and a filled-in example.

Situation	Attention	Excercise	Feeling	Results
Who were you with? Where were you? What were you doing?	Record your focus of attention. Note what you focused on most. 1. Self % 2. Task % 3. Environment and other people % (Total = 100%)	Use task concentration to direct your attention outward. Remember to focus on your task or environment. Note what you did.	Record how you felt.	Record anything you learned from the excercise. Note how the situation turned out, changes in your anxiety level, and your ability to complete the task.

The ABC Form 1

1. **In the 'Consequences' box, point 1, write down the emotion you're feeling.**

2. **In the 'Consequences' box, point 2, write down how you acted.**

3. **In the 'Activating Event' box, write down what triggered your feelings.**

4. **In the 'Beliefs' box, write down your thoughts, attitudes, and beliefs.**

5. **In the 'Thinking Error' box, consider what your thinking errors may be.**

Refer to Chapter 3 for more detailed instructions on filling out the first ABC form.

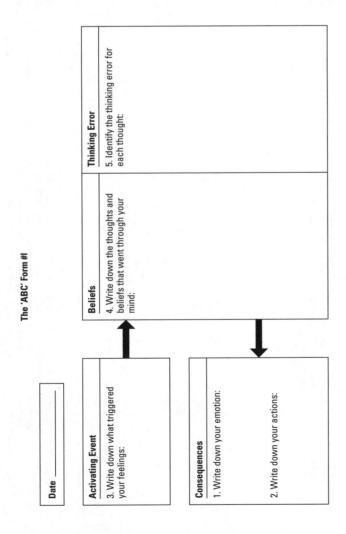

The 'ABC' Form #!

Date _____

Activating Event
3. Write down what triggered your feelings:

Beliefs
4. Write down the thoughts and beliefs that went through your mind:

Thinking Error
5. Identify the thinking error for each thought:

Consequences
1. Write down your emotion:

2. Write down your actions:

The ABC Form II

Follow the guidance at the bottom of the form and head to Chapter 3 for more detailed instructions on filling in the second ABC form.

Date _____

The 'ABC' Form #II

Activating Event (Trigger). 2. Briefly write down what triggered your emotions. (e.g. event, situation, sensation, memory, image)	Beliefs, thoughts, and attitudes about A. 3. Write down what went through your mind, or what A meant to you. B's can be about you, others, the world, the past, or the future.	Consequences of A+B on your emotions and behaviours. 1. Write down what emotion you felt and how you acted when you felt this emotion. Emotions e.g: Depression, guilt, hurt, anger, shame, jealousy, envy, anxiety. Rate intensity 0–100.	Dispute (question and examine) B and generate alternatives. The questions at the bottom of the form will help you with this. 4. Write an alternative for each B, using supporting arguments and evidence.	Effect of alternative thoughts and beliefs (D). 5. Write down how you feel and wish to act as consequence of your alternatives at D. Emotions Re-rate 0–100. List any healthy alternative emotion e.g. Sadness, regret, concern.
		Behaviour e.g. Avoidance, withdrawing, escape, using alcohol or drugs, seeking reassurance, procrastination		Alternative Behaviour or Experiment e.g. Facing situation, increased activity, assertion

Disputing (Questioning and Examining) and Generating Alternative Thoughts, Attitudes, and Beliefs: 1. Identify your 'thinking errors' at **B** (e.g. Mind Reading, Catastrophising, Labelling, Demands etc.). Write them next to the appropriate 'B'. 2. Examine whether the evidence at hand supports that your thought at **B** is 100% true. Consider whether someone whose opinions you respect would totally agree with your conclusions. 3. Evaluate the helpfulness of each **B**. Write down what you think might be a more helpful, balanced and flexible way of looking at **A**. Consider what you would advise a friend to think, what a role model of yours might think, or how you might look at **A** if you were feeling OK. 4. Add evidence and arguments that support your alternative thoughts, attitudes and beliefs. Write as if you were trying to persuade someone you cared about.

The Pricing up Addiction Form

Refer to Chapter 10 for the low-down on filling out your Pricing up Addiction form.

Costs to relationships	
Costs to work/career/study	
Costs to emotional and physical health	
Financial costs:	
Personal interest costs:	

The 'What does my addiction do for me?' Analysis Form

Head to Chapter 10 for instructions on how to use the 'What does my addiction do for me?' analysis form.

Benefits of using my drug of choice:	
Healthy alternatives to my drug of choice	

Index

• B •

• *T* •

Notes

Notes

FOR DUMMIES®

Making Everything Easier! ™

UK editions

BUSINESS

Marketing Kit For Dummies
978-0-470-74490-1

Business Plans Kit For Dummies
978-0-470-74381-2

Consulting For Dummies
978-0-470-71382-2

FINANCE

Investing For Dummies
978-0-470-99280-7

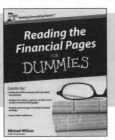

Reading the Financial Pages For Dummies
978-0-470-71432-4

Sorting Out Your Finances For Dummies
978-0-470-69515-9

HOBBIES

Growing Your Own Fruit & Veg For Dummies
978-0-470-69960-7

Researching Your Family History Online For Dummies
978-0-470-74535-9

Electronics For Dummies
978-0-470-68178-7

British Sign Language
For Dummies
978-0-470-69477-0

Business NLP For Dummies
978-0-470-69757-3

Competitive Strategy For Dummies
978-0-470-77930-9

Cricket For Dummies
978-0-470-03454-5

CVs For Dummies, 2nd Edition
978-0-470-74491-8

Divorce For Dummies, 2nd Edition
978-0-470-74128-3

eBay.co.uk Business All-in-One
For Dummies
978-0-470-72125-4

Emotional Freedom Technique For
Dummies
978-0-470-75876-2

English Grammar For Dummies
978-0-470-05752-0

Flirting For Dummies
978-0-470-74259-4

Golf For Dummies
978-0-470-01811-8

Green Living For Dummies
978-0-470-06038-4

Hypnotherapy For Dummies
978-0-470-01930-6

IBS For Dummies
978-0-470-51737-6

Lean Six Sigma For Dummies
978-0-470-75626-3

Medieval History For Dummies
978-0-470-74783-4

FOR DUMMIES®

A world of resources to help you grow

UK editions

SELF-HELP

978-0-470-74830-5

978-0-470-74764-3

978-0-470-68472-6

Origami Kit For Dummies
978-0-470-75857-1

Overcoming Depression For Dummies
978-0-470-69430-5

Positive Psychology For Dummies
978-0-470-72136-0

PRINCE2 For Dummies, 2009 Edition
978-0-470-71025-8

Psychometric Tests For Dummies
978-0-470-75366-8

Raising Happy Children
For Dummies
978-0-470-05978-4

STUDENTS

978-0-470-74747-6

978-0-470-74711-7

978-0-470-74290-7

Reading the Financial Pages
For Dummies
978-0-470-71432-4

Sage 50 Accounts For Dummies
978-0-470-71558-1

Self-Hypnosis For Dummies
978-0-470-66073-7

Starting a Business For Dummies,
2nd Edition
978-0-470-51806-9

Study Skills For Dummies
978-0-470-74047-7

Teaching English as a Foreign
Language For Dummies
978-0-470-74576-2

HISTORY

978-0-470-99468-9

978-0-470-51015-5

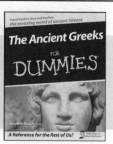

978-0-470-98787-2

Teaching Skills For Dummies
978-0-470-74084-2

Time Management For Dummies
978-0-470-77765-7

Work-Life Balance For Dummies
978-0-470-71380-8

**Available wherever books are sold. For more information or to order direct go to www.wiley.com
or call +44 (0) 1243 843291**

19546 (p2)

FOR DUMMIES®

The easy way to get more done and have more fun

FOR DUMMIES®

COMPUTER BASICS

978-0-470-57829-2

978-0-470-46542-4

978-0-470-49743-2

DIGITAL PHOTOGRAPHY

978-0-470-25074-7

978-0-470-46606-3

978-0-470-59591-6

MICROSOFT OFFICE 2010

978-0-470-48998-7

978-0-470-58302-9

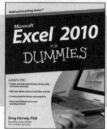
978-0-470-48953-6

Access 2007 For Dummies
978-0-470-04612-8

Adobe Creative Suite 5 Design Premium All-in-One For Dummies
978-0-470-60746-6

AutoCAD 2011 For Dummies
978-0-470-59539-8

C++ For Dummies, 6th Edition
978-0-470-31726-6

Computers For Seniors For Dummies, 2nd Edition
978-0-470-53483-0

Dreamweaver CS5 For Dummies
978-0-470-61076-3

Excel 2007 All-In-One Desk Reference For Dummies
978-0-470-03738-6

Green IT For Dummies
978-0-470-38688-0

Macs For Dummies, 10th Edition
978-0-470-27817-8

Mac OS X Snow Leopard For Dummies
978-0-470-43543-4

Networking All-in-One Desk Reference For Dummies, 3rd Edition
978-0-470-17915-4

Photoshop CS5 For Dummies
978-0-470-61078-7

Photoshop Elements 8 For Dummies
978-0-470-52967-6

Search Engine Optimization For Dummies, 3rd Edition
978-0-470-26270-2

The Internet For Dummies, 12th Edition
978-0-470-56095-2

Visual Studio 2008 All-In-One Desk Reference For Dummies
978-0-470-19108-8

Web Analytics For Dummies
978-0-470-09824-0